D0939368

LARGE
APPLIANCE
REPAIR
MANUAL

Popular Mechanics

LARGE APPLIANCE REPAIR MANUAL

HEARST BOOKS

**Library of Congress Cataloging in
Publication Data**

Popular mechanics home appliance
repair manual.

    Selections.

    Popular mechanics large appliance
repair manual.

    Excerpted from: Popular mechanics
home appliance repair manual.

    Includes index.

    1. Household appliances—
Maintenance and repair—
Amateurs' manuals. I. Popular
mechanics (New York, N.Y. :
1959) II. Title.
TX298.P6625   1982   643'.6   82-12132
ISBN 0-87851-244-1

Photography: Al Freni
Cover design: Lawrence Daniels & Friends

10 9 8 7 6 5 4 3 2 1

Printed in the United States of America

Contents

Introduction
How to get the most out of this book

However sophisticated an appliance might seem, its components are usually simply assembled and its operating principles easy to understand. If you know how it works and follow correct procedures, repairs are easy to make in the vast majority of appliance malfunctions. It is for the home owner who decides to do his or her own repairs—whether to save on repair costs or simply for the satisfaction of doing the job at home—that the *Large Appliance Repair Manual* has been conceived and edited.

The main portion of the book covers all the large appliances found in homes and apartments that ordinarily would require a service call when they break down. The separate articles, one for each appliance, are arranged alphabetically. Each article begins with a detailed exploded view showing how the parts of the appliance interconnect and operate, and, most important, where the likely sources of trouble lie. These "Troublespots," as we call them, are your visual troubleshooting guide. They tell you where to look in the repair instructions to find out how to deal with the problem. All the repair instructions that follow are illustrated. We photographed the most competent professionals in the business doing the jobs you will be able to do. Wherever a photograph can't show a procedure or component clearly, we have included a detailed drawing.

All appliances, especially large ones, benefit from periodic tune-ups and regular maintenance just as much as any automobile does. The information and step-by-step tune-up and maintenance procedures for large appliances are probably the most important parts of those entries. Even if you never make a large appliance repair yourself, you can save real dollars in repair costs, energy costs, and a long service life for your appliances by following the instructions given in this book.

All the procedures that you need to follow to fix mechanical and electrical problems that occur in large appliances are described and illustrated step-by-step in each article. If there are problems that you should leave to professionals to solve, this is pointed out. At the end of each article you will find a complete Troubleshooting Chart that summarizes all the information that has been given for the appliance. Each problem, the probable causes, and the appropriate actions are listed in concise tabular form.

Don't overlook the boxes of tips that accompany most articles. If you follow these Tips for Energy Efficiency and Tips for Operating Efficiency you'll not only save money in day-to-day operation but your appliance will have a longer useful life.

Read the Blue Pages, the section that begins on page 10. This section describes in simple language how electricity works in your home and what you need to know about it to work safely on electrical appliances. Also read Appliance Repair Basics, which starts on page 24. It gives you a lot of useful facts that apply to all appliances—how motors work, where to look for hidden screws, and the like. The Appendix, beginning on page 139, describes and shows the tools you need to make successful repairs.

Look for These Important Symbols

These little needle-nose pliers identify Bench Tips—shortcuts and tricks that professionals have developed by doing the same repair jobs again and again. The Bench Tips will save time and frustration.

CAUTION We repeat the general rules of appliance repair safety throughout the book. But we mark special cautions as reminders. Don't ignore them! Observing the cautions will make the job go safely and successfully.

Blue Pages

**Everything you need to know
about electricity**

Basic electricity

To locate trouble in an appliance and to correct the trouble in the most efficient way, it is helpful—not absolutely essential, but helpful—to know something about what electricity is and what some of the most common electrical terms mean. The words and pictures in this section provide a quick review of basic electricity. The electrical terms used in this book are defined in the Glossary found on page 12.

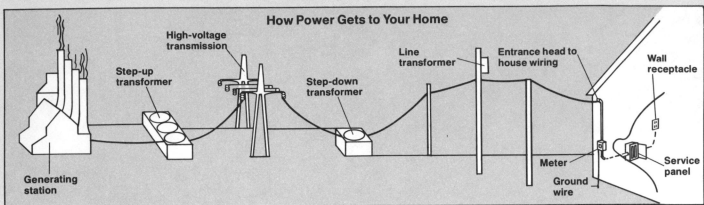

How Power Gets to Your Home

Generating stations operated by electric utility companies convert either fossil fuel (coal, oil), hydroelectric energy (flowing water), or atomic energy (from nuclear reactors) into electrical energy. This electrical energy is then transmitted by wires to factories, offices, schools, and homes, where it is used.

Unless the power lines in your neighborhood are underground, you have probably noticed that power lines to buildings lead from large canister-shaped devices on utility poles. These devices are called line transformers or pole transformers.

Electricity is transmitted over long distances most efficiently when the voltage is extremely high and the amperage low. The voltage in alternating-current systems is raised or lowered very efficiently by transformers. Applying power to step-up transformers automatically raises the voltage and reduces the amperage. Applying power to step-down transformers reverses the process.

Transformers allow utility companies to get the high voltage levels needed for low-loss cross-country transmission and to reduce voltage when power reaches the consumer.

Utility companies distribute power by raising the voltage to high levels (sometimes as much as 750,000 volts), and then sending it over the high-power lines often seen in rural areas. When these lines reach towns and cities, transformer action is again used to reduce the voltage. The reduction is accomplished in steps as power is distributed, so that the highest practical voltage level can be maintained until the power reaches the consumer. The final voltage reduction takes place on the line transformers mounted on utility poles. Power is carried from these transformers to buildings for use by the consumer.

All matter is composed of atoms. Atoms, in turn, are made up of particles called protons, neutrons, and electrons. One of these particles, the electron, is the source of electrical energy.

Most electrons are bound to a single atom, but some can move from one atom to another. The ones that can move are called free electrons. Copper, steel, and aluminum are called conductors because their atoms have many free electrons and so can conduct electricity efficiently. Wires made of these metals are ideal for transmitting electricity with little loss of power.

Test Your Knowledge of Basic Electricity

If you can score 100 on this quiz, you probably know enough to skip to the *Electrical testers* section of this introduction on page 14.

PART 1
Fill in the blanks in the following statements:

1. Electric current is the free flow of _____ along an electrical conductor.

2. The rate of electron (current) flow is measured in_____

3. Resistance to the free flow of current in an electrical circuit is measured in _____

4. The pressure to restore electron balance in a circuit from either a shortage or a surplus to neutral is measured in_____

5. The work performed by electrical energy is measured in_____

6. Which of the following are conductors rather than insulators: rubber, copper, plastic, steel, aluminum, paper, wood?_____

PART 2
Choose the correct word or phrase to complete each statement:

1. The voltage level(s) available in virtually every U.S. household is: (1) 60 and 120; (2) 100 and 150; (3) 200; (4) 120 and 240.

2. The formula for measuring work done by electrical energy is: (1) voltage equals amperage times wattage; (2) wattage equals voltage times amperage; (3) voltage equals wattage divided by amperage; (4) wattage equals voltage divided by amperage.

3. Wire is sometimes coiled around a metal core to: (1) produce heat; (2) increase resistance; (3) create a magnetic field; (4) regulate voltage.

PART 3
Match each wire type with its insulation color (NOTE: More than one insulation color may be used for each type of wire):

hot wire _____

neutral wire _____

grounding wire _____
(1) black; (2) green; (3) gray; (4) red; (5) no insulation; (6) white; (7) blue.

PART 4
The following statements are either true or false:

1. Direct current is required by most kinds of appliances._____

2. The grounding wire in an electrical circuit is the most dangerous as a cause of shock.

3. The neutral wire in an electrical circuit is the main power source_____

4. A high-resistance short circuit makes an appliance operate abnormally without blowing a fuse or tripping a circuit breaker_____

5. The neutral wire in an electrical circuit never causes shock. _____

6. An electrical circuit is a combination of source, conductor, load, and switching that enables electrical power to do work._____

Answers to this quiz appear on page 12.

Free Electrons Moving from Atom to Atom

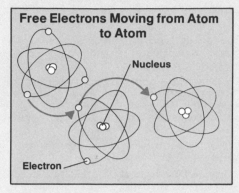

Other materials such as rubber, plastic, paper, and wood are composed of atoms that have almost no free electrons. These materials cannot conduct electricity efficiently, and so they are called insulators.

A wire made of copper or aluminum enclosed in some insulating material provides a safe and efficient way to move electrical energy. These insulated wires are used to carry electricity from the generating plant to the user.

Current Flow between Wires

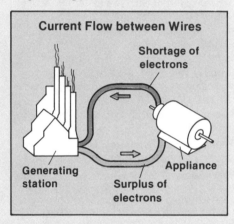

The action of an electrical generator causes all the free electrons in a conductor to move in the same direction. When this happens, a surplus of electrons is created in the atoms of one wire at the output of a generator and a shortage of electrons is created in the atoms of a second output wire from the generator.

When an electrical appliance is connected to the generator wires, electrons move along an electrical path through the appliance in order to restore the natural balance. As long as the generating station is in operation, the electron shortage and surplus in the two wires will be maintained and a force will exist between the two wires to cause an electron to move.

The term current flow describes this electron movement. The rate of the current flow (that is, the number of electrons that pass a point in one second) is measured in units called amperes, commonly shortened to amps.

The force that exists to restore the natural electron balance depends upon how great the difference is between the surplus and the shortage. The larger the difference, the greater the force. This force (or pressure) is called voltage, and the units in which it is measured are volts.

A point that has neither a surplus nor a shortage of electrons is electrically neutral. Electrically neutral points are called ground. Ground means simply the earth or a conductor connected to the earth. The connection can be made via a metal cold-water pipe in your home

(below) or a copper rod driven into the ground near where electrical power enters a house (see drawing, page 18).

The volume of matter represented by the earth is so large that a measurable surplus or shortage of electrons never exists in it. Therefore, earth, or ground, is always electrically neutral. Ground, as well as wires connected to ground, can accept electrons or give them up as necessary to cause electron flow (current flow) between ground and a point at which a shortage or surplus exists.

In home electrical systems, power is distributed to most appliances by two wires. One of the two wires always has either a surplus or a shortage of electrons. This wire is commonly called the hot wire and it almost always has black or red (sometimes blue) insulation. The other wire must always have white or gray insulation and it is called the neutral (or power ground) wire because at some point it is connected to ground. **CAUTION** Remember, electrons will flow from *any* ground point to the hot wire when a path exists. When the path is through a human body, shock occurs. To reduce the possibility of shock, some electrical circuits have a third wire called a grounding wire. When a failure occurs in electrical wiring, the grounding wire provides a lower-resistance path to ground than the human body. The grounding wire is usually bare (no insulation), but it may have green (occasionally green and yellow) insulation.

Basement Ground

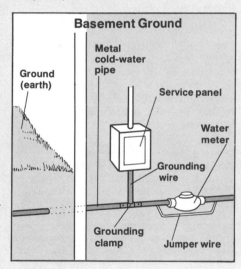

Both the neutral and the grounding wires are connected to ground, but each performs a different job in electrical wiring. The job of the grounding wire is to provide a path to ground for electrical energy when any failure occurs in the house wiring system or in an electrical appliance. Throughout this book the term grounding wire refers to these safety wires. The job of the white or gray neutral wire is to provide the normal path

---

BENCH TIP

The color of the wire tells you something about the wire in your home electrical system.

Black, red, or blue	hot wire
White or gray	neutral wire
Bare or green	grounding wire

---

for return current flow to the source when no wiring failure exists. Throughout this book the term hot wire refers to the wire with black, red, or blue insulation. This is the wire that causes current to flow between it and the neutral wire (or the grounding wire if a failure occurs).

Magnetic Field around a Wire

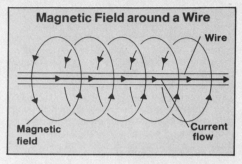

When electricity is generated, the electron imbalance that occurs represents stored energy. If electrons can move between the two points of surplus and shortage, some of the stored energy is released. All materials offer some opposition to this movement of electrons. This opposition is called electrical resistance, and it is measured in units called ohms. When resistance is low, current flow (electron flow) is heavy. When current flow is heavy, electrons tend to bump into each other. When this happens, some of the electron energy is converted to heat. It is this action that makes the wires in room heaters and surface units on electric ranges glow red when the units are turned on.

When current flows through a wire, another phenomenon occurs. A magnetic field is created around the wire.

Magnetic Field in a Motor Winding

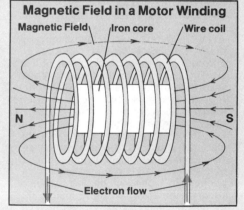

The strength of this field in a single wire is quite small. When many coils of wire are wound around an iron core, however, the magnetic field of each strand adds to the one next to it, and a strong magnetic field is created. It is the attraction and repulsion of the magnetic fields created in this way that makes an electric motor run.

Now, to review for a moment, electricity consists of voltage and current. Voltage can be thought of as pressure, the pressure that exists to restore the natural balance of electrons in atoms. Current can be thought of as the movement of electrons that occurs as a result of the voltage. Both voltage and current flow must be present for electricity to do work.

VOLTS X AMPERES = WATTS

The work done by the combination of voltage and current is found by multiplying the number of volts (pressure) present between two points (wires) by the number of amps of current that flow through the resistance along a path between the two points. The units in which the product of the multiplication is expressed are called watts. In other words, watts equals volts times amps.

Watts represent work performed by electrical energy. Most electrical appliances are rated according to wattage. Nameplates on toasters, vacuum cleaners, and ovens show power consumption in watts. Virtually all households have two voltage levels available: 120 and 240 volts. The nameplate also shows the voltage at which the appliance should be operated. Because wattage is the product of voltage times amperage (current), when you know the voltage you can find the current flow by dividing the wattage by the voltage. A toaster designed to plug into a 120-volt wall receptacle and rated at 1,320 watts has a current flow of 11 amperes (1,320 ÷ 120).

Note that the amount of power consumed by the toaster depends on how long it is used. To calculate power, time as well as voltage must be considered. A 100-watt lamp turned on for an hour uses the same amount of power as a 200-watt lamp turned on for half an hour.

About AC and DC

Electricity can be generated in two quite different forms. One is called alternating current (AC), the other, direct current (DC).

Alternating current is almost universally used for home electric appliances and is, therefore, the form of electricity this book is primarily concerned with. In an AC circuit, the amount of voltage present in the circuit is constantly changing from zero to a peak value and back to zero in one direction and then from zero to a peak value and back to zero in the other direction. The peak voltage is determined by the generating plant. Because voltage is the force, or pressure, that causes current to flow, the current also changes from zero to a peak value to zero and will reverse direction and repeat. The peak amount of current, however, is determined by the load resistance; it can vary as the load resistance varies. Each complete change from zero to maximum to zero in one direction and then zero to maximum to zero in the opposite direction is called 1 hertz (formerly "cycle per second"). The term hertz implies *per second*; therefore, 60 hertz means 60 cycles per second. You may see "cycles per second" marked on older appliances; the abbreviation is "cps."

Direct current in homes is found mostly in the form of electrical energy stored in batteries. The voltage and the direction of application are constant in a DC circuit. The amount of voltage is determined by the type and size of the battery. The direction of current flow is also constant and, as in AC circuits, the amount of current flow will vary if the load resistance varies. Batteries convert chemical energy to electrical energy. Batteries can be either wet as in a car battery or dry as in flashlight and transistor radio batteries. All wet batteries and some dry ones can be recharged from a DC rectifier plugged into an AC source. Unless recharged, the voltage from all batteries will gradually decrease.

Glossary

Alternating current (AC). The voltage and current in this form of electrical energy are constantly changing in amount and are periodically changing in direction of flow. This is the form of electrical power used in almost all home utility systems. (See box, below, left, for details.)

Ampere (amp), aperage. These terms refer to the amount of current flowing in a circuit as a result of the voltage applied and the resistance of the load (an appliance, a motor, or a lamp).

Branch circuit. A circuit wired from the service panel to a part of your home. Every branch circuit has its own circuit breaker or fuse to prevent too much current from flowing into the circuit.

Circuit. A combination of power source, conductors, switching, and load that allows electrical power to do work.

Circuit breaker. A switch that cuts off power to a circuit automatically when current flow is greater than the rating for the circuit breaker. Circuit breakers can also be operated manually so that power can be switched off, for example, for making repairs.

Conductor. Any material (usually metal) that offers low resistance to electrical current and can therefore be used to transmit it.

Direct current (DC). The form of electrical energy stored in batteries. The voltage in a DC circuit remains constant as long as the source (usually a battery) remains charged. (See box at left for details.)

Electron. One of the particles in an atom. Free electrons can move from atom to atom, and this produces an electrical current.

Fuse. A device that safely breaks the flow of current in a circuit when the amperage exceeds the rating of the fuse.

Ground. A path for current flow that leads outside the circuit. It can be provided intentionally as a safety feature of the circuit (see *Grounding wire*, below). A ground can also occur inadvertently if, owing to broken insulation, a bent heating element, or a faulty repair, a part of the circuit within the appliance touches a material—such as the housing of a toaster—that offers a path for some of the current flow. This is also known as a high-resistance short.

Grounding wire. A safety wire, usually bare but sometimes with green (and occasionally green and yellow) insulation, that provides a safe path to ground for hot-wire current in case of circuit failure.

Hertz (Hz). A new term for the older "cycles per second" ("cps"). The number of hertz in an AC power source is the number of times per second the electrical power goes through a complete change in amplitude and direction. Home power is 60 hertz. The term applies to AC only, not DC.

Hot wire. The electric wire that causes current to flow through any path to ground. Any electrical wire can give a shock, but a hot wire is the most dangerous. This wire usually has black or red (occasionally blue) insulation.

Kilowatt-hour (kwh). The unit of measurement for power consumed. One kilowatt-hour is the equivalent of 1,000 watts used for one hour. Electric bills are based on kilowatt-hours.

Load. Any device in an electrical circuit that changes electrical power into another form of energy: light, mechanical movement, heat, etc.

Neutral wire. The electric wire in your home with white or gray insulation. This wire provides the normal return path for current flow to the power source. It is sometimes called the power ground wire.

Ohm. The term for the unit of measure for resistance to the flow of electrical current.

Overload. The result of too many appliances connected to one circuit or of a circuit or appliance failure. Overload may merely result in minor overheating in wires; in more severe cases, the circuit breaker trips or the fuse blows.

Power (electrical). The combination of voltage and current that provides the electrical energy to perform work. The unit of measure for power is the watt (see below).

Resistance. The characteristic of some materials and devices whereby the material opposes current flow. The unit of measure of resistance is the ohm.

Service panel. A panel, containing either circuit breakers or fuses, that distributes power entering your home to the branch circuits.

Source. Any point of origin for power. The service panel or a wall receptacle in your home can be considered a source.

Switch. A device for interrupting and restoring current flow.

Transformer. Transformers are used in AC power systems to raise or lower the voltage.

Volt; voltage. The unit of force that causes current to flow between a hot wire and any point connected to ground is the volt. Most home electrical systems are supplied with either 120 or 240 volts.

Watt; wattage. The electrical power consumed by a load is measured in watts, which are found by multiplying voltage by amperage: i.e, if a 3-amp current is flowing in a 120-volt circuit, 360 watts are being consumed.

Answers to Basic Electricity Quiz on page 10

PART 1	PART 3
1. electrons	Hot wire—(1), (4), (7)
2. amps	Neutral wire—(3), (6)
3. ohms	Grounding wire—(2), (5)
4. volts	
5. watts	
6. copper, steel, aluminum	PART 4
	1. False
	2. False
PART 2	3. False
1. (4)	4. True
2. (2)	5. False
3. (3)	6. True

Electrical circuits

To get work done with electrical energy (volts and amperes), there must be a continuous path for electron flow between a wire having an electron shortage and a wire having an electron surplus. Electrons will move along this path and provide energy to generate heat or light and to make motors run. The path along which electrons flow is an electrical circuit. Electrical circuits have four parts: a source of power, wires to carry the power where it is needed, some way to control power (stop and start the flow), and an appliance or other device to use the power.

The real source of power is the utility company generator plant. However, for the purposes of appliance repair, the source is considered to be the wall receptacle into which the appliance is plugged.

Conductors. The wires or strips of metal that carry the electrical energy to the place at which work will be done are conductors. Conductors offer only slight resistance to current flow because the atoms in the metals they are made of have lots of free electrons. The external conductors for most appliances are in the cord and plug. Of course, appliances also have internal conductors.

Load. Any device (a lamp, a radio, a washing machine) that uses electrical energy to perform some work is a load. The load (unlike the con-

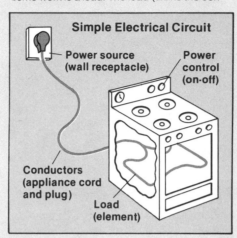

Simple Electrical Circuit

Power source
(wall receptacle)

Power control
(on-off)

Conductors
(appliance cord
and plug)

Load
(element)

ductors) offers considerable resistance to current flow. This high resistance makes it possible for the device to convert electrical energy to another form of energy: light, sound, or mechanical movement. The load resistance determines how much current flows in a circuit. If the resistance in the load increases, the current flowing in the circuit automatically decreases. The watt is a unit of power that indicates the rate at which the load is consuming power. To get the wattage, multiply the voltage applied to a circuit (which is usually constant) by the current in amperes.

Switch. The final necessary element in a circuit is a means of controlling the flow of energy. Control is provided by a switch, which can interrupt and restore current flow as desired by the user. Switches in home appliances control current flow by introducing a high resistance (air gap) in the circuit to stop current flow, and by removing resistance (closing the air gap) to start current flowing again. Some appliances (electric grills, for example) have no separate switch. The appliance is turned on and off by inserting and removing the plug.

Circuit Faults

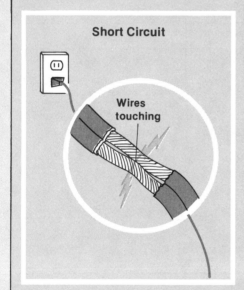

Short Circuit

Wires
touching

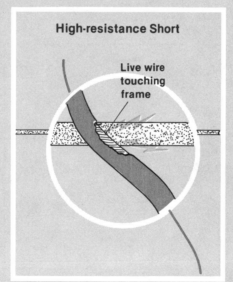

High-resistance Short

Live wire
touching
frame

Open Circuit

Broken wire

Now that you know what an electrical circuit is, let's find out about the two most common circuit faults: the short circuit and the open circuit.

A short circuit is a fault that exists when there is a path for current flow other than the normal path through an appliance. For example, a short circuit (above, left) could occur if, because of wear or broken insulation, the two conductors in the line cord touched. The resulting high current flow would cause the fuse to blow or the circuit breaker to trip, thus shutting off power to the appliance.

A high-resistance short is another type of short circuit. Typically, this fault occurs inside the appliance itself: through wear or

breakage, a part of the circuit touches a metal part (above, center), such as the metal housing or a motor part, forming a secondary path for current flow. This type of short is also called a ground, because current is diverted out of the circuit. This ground does not lead to earth, however, but to a metal part of your appliance.

The path may offer enough resistance so that current flow remains low: the fuse will not blow; the circuit breaker will not trip to OFF. The appliance, however, will not operate normally because the secondary path diverts current from the appliance load. If the short is to the housing of the appliance, you may get a shock when you touch it. To test whether a high-resistance short has occurred, see *Testing for ground,* page 16. You

should test an appliance for ground after every repair, and it is a good idea to test any new appliance for ground before plugging it in.

An open circuit is simply a break in the continuous path necessary for current flow (above, right). The effect is usually the same as turning off a switch or pulling a plug. The difference, of course, is that the appliance cannot be turned on again. In an appliance containing both motors and heating elements, breaks may cause only part of the appliance to stop working. Motors contain coils of wire. If a break occurs in these coils, the motor will not run, but heating elements and indicator lights will still function normally.

Electrical testers

Open circuits, short circuits, and high-resistance shorts (grounds) in electrical appliances are generally not visible from outside the unit. Testers must be used to find the source of the trouble. Before using any tester, disconnect the appliance or the part being checked from the supply of electricity. It is not enough to turn the appliance off; the cord must be pulled from the receptacle also.

Continuity refers to the continuous path through which electricity flows without being interrupted. Continuity is mentioned often in this book. When there is an interruption in electron flow, electricity cannot reach the point it is supposed to reach, and the appliance will not work. The job of the home appliance repairman, therefore, is to find the point of interrruption and fix it. The simplest instrument for making continuity tests is called a continuity tester.

Continuity tester

The continuity tester can be a penlike or flashlight-type device. The first has a needle probe at one end and a flexible test lead with an alligator clip at the other; the flashlight device has two alligator clips. The tester generally contains one or two batteries and a low-voltage lamp. (Some testers can be plugged into a wall receptacle for power.) When current flows from the alligator clip to the tip of the probe, the lamp lights. The continuity tester contains its own source of power and is *always* used with the appliance's power turned off at the fuse box or circuit breaker. It is an excellent device for checking repairs before applying power. It is also used to test for ground. You can also test the tester itself; see *Bench Tip* below.

Voltage tester

The voltage tester consists of a plastic holder containing a neon lamp and two probes (test leads) attached to the holder. The neon lamp lights if the test leads touch live power lines or anything connected to those lines. When no voltage is present, the lamp does not light. Since the lamp will also not light when the tester is defective, it is important to test the tester before using it (see *Bench Tip*, below). This tester is useful when you are repairing both small and large appliances; make sure yours can be used to test both 120- and 240-volt lines.

The continuity tester and the voltage tester are "yes-or-no" testers. If the continuity tester lights when the leads are touched to each end of a circuit, there is a low-resistance path for current flow between the points where the test was made. If the tester does not light, there is either a break in the current-flow path or there is a high-resistance path that limits current flow to an amount so small the tester lamp does not light. Also, the voltage tester tells only whether voltage is or is not present at the points tested.

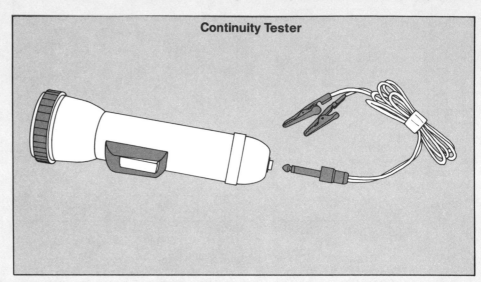

Continuity Tester

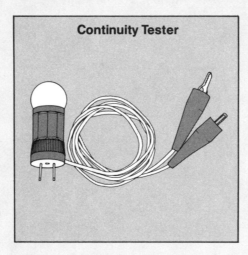

Continuity Tester

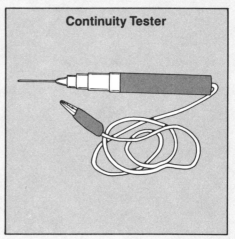

Continuity Tester

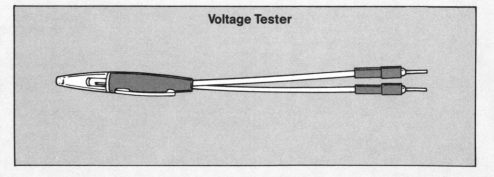

Voltage Tester

 BENCH TIP

Testing the Tester

The continuity tester can easily be checked by touching the tips of the alligator clips or the probes together. If the light goes on, the battery, the bulb, and the tester are all OK. If the light doesn't go on, try changing the bulb. If the light still doesn't go on, replace the battery. If the light still doesn't go on, the wiring in the tester is defective and you should buy a new one. Always test the tester!

The voltage tester can be tested by plugging it into a live receptacle. Touch one probe to the screw on the outside of the cover plate (or the ground slot in a three-slot outlet) and the other to each slot. The bulb should light in one of the two slots.

The multitester or VOM

For more efficient troubleshooting, it is often desirable to know *how much* resistance there is in a current path, or *how much* voltage is present at some point in an appliance, or *how much* current is flowing between two points. For this type of measurement, the best instrument is a multitester called a VOM, or volt-ohm meter. A VOM combines a number of functions in one instrument, usually including an AC/DC voltmeter, ammeter, and ohmmeter. The instruction booklet accompanying a new VOM explains exactly how to use the tester for the various functions it performs. VOM controls are described below.

Volt-ohm Meter (VOM)

Dial and pointer. Test results are shown by needle movement across a dial. The dial contains several scales to show results of resistance tests, voltage tests, and current tests. Note that the resistance scale on most multitesters is the back-off type: that is, the 0 on the resistance scale is opposite the 0 on the voltage and current scales.

Pointer adjustment. A slotted-screw adjustment at the center of the dial allows the meter needle to be set exactly to 0 volts, an adjustment for voltage readings only. Remove the test leads when making this adjustment.

Ohms adjustment. A separate adjustment—usually a small knob—is used to zero the resistance reading. Insert the test leads in the jacks. Set the selector switch to an OHMS position, and touch the tips of the test probes firmly together. Adjust the knob until the meter reads 0 ohms. VOMs contain one or more penlight (type AA) batteries that supply the power for resistance measurement. If the meter cannot be set to 0, the batteries should be replaced. NOTE: Adjust your meter to 0 every time you change the RX setting.

Test lead and jack. Test leads and test jacks are color-coded. The black lead is inserted in the black jack and the red lead in the red jack. Some meters have more than one set of test jacks. Different jacks may be used for different types of measurement.

Selector switch. The switch sets the meter to measure either voltage, resistance (ohms), or current (amps). Note that there is more than one switch position (for different ranges of magnitude) for each type of measurement. NOTE: The number of switch positions may vary from VOM to VOM.

For voltage and current measurement, the switch position indicates the amount of voltage or current that causes full-scale deflection in that range. Readings are taken on the scale that applies to the switch setting of the meter needle chosen. To avoid damage to the meter when you are not sure how much voltage is present at a test point, set the selector to the highest voltage available, such as 1,000 volts AC. If only slight movement of the needle occurs, move the switch to the next lower position, such as 250 volts AC. For greatest accuracy, use the meter scale that gives you a reading somewhere near the middle of the scale.

At the settings for resistance (ohm) measurement, numbers must be multiplied by the reading in order to get the correct resistance. The same scale is used for all readings, but the number on the scale is multiplied by the number shown at the switch position. "RX1" means the scale is read directly. "RX10" means scale numbers must be multiplied by 10 to obtain the value of resistance being measured. "RX100" means multiply by 100.

Test probes. The bare metal needles at the ends of the test probes must be touched to the points at which readings are to be taken. To avoid shock when testing a live circuit, it is best to use alligator clips, which are available as accessories to VOMs. The procedure for testing is as follows: disconnect the appliance (pull out the plug) and attach the alligator clips to the test point in the appliance. When the test probes are in place, plug in and turn on the appliance and note the meter reading without touching the appliance. After the test, remove the wall plug and then disconnect the alligator clips.

Jack

Test lead

How to use a VOM

A VOM is an extremely versatile and useful instrument that can do many jobs. It can, for example, measure current (in milliamps) drawn by a small appliance from a power line, measure the voltage used by an appliance, and check the value of a resistor.

How you check continuity with a VOM depends on what you are testing. If the component you are testing on an appliance does not have resistance (load) built into it—for example, a line cord or a switch—continuity is checked with a VOM (set at RX1) the same as with a continuity tester. If the needle moves to the right, it indicates continuity.

If, however, you are testing a component that has resistance (load) built into it—for example, a circuit containing a heating element or a motor—a simple yes-or-no test for continuity does not tell you enough. You need to know whether the component is offering the right *amount* of resistance. For this you use the ohmmeter function on the VOM (set at RX1 or higher), which indicates the amount of resistance in the component. If the amount meets the manufacturer's specifications, the circuit is in proper working condition. If the resistance is too high or too low, the component is damaged and should be repaired or replaced.

Testing a switch

To test switch continuity, turn the appliance off and disconnect the switch leads. Set the VOM at RX1 and touch the probes to the switch terminals. The meter should show continuity at all settings except off.

Testing a heating element

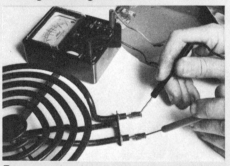

To measure heating element resistance, turn the appliance off and disconnect the element leads. Set the VOM meter at RX1 or higher and touch the probes to the element terminals. Read the resistance on the meter's ohmmeter scale.

Testing for Ground

When you have finished reassembling any appliance, before you plug it in test it for ground to make sure there is no short within it. (It is also a good idea to test a new appliance to be sure it's not a lemon!) The test is simple but necessary. It can be made with a continuity tester or a VOM.

If you are using a continuity tester, clip one lead to one of the prongs on the cord plug. Turn the switch to ON. Touch the other lead to various metal parts on the outside of the appliance, including screws and metal trim. If the tester shows continuity at any point, you have a short (ground). Disassemble the appliance and fix the unwanted contact. Then reassemble it and test again for ground.

If you are using a VOM, set it to RX10 or RX1K and follow the same procedure as for

the continuity tester. If you have any reading at all on your multitester, however slight, take the appliance apart and find the short. Reassemble it and repeat the test.

Most electrical repairs are made to restore continuity to an electrical circuit. A continuity test helps locate the break in the circuit, and enables you to test the success of your repair job—without plugging in your appliance.

To check continuity, let's use the example of a clothes drier. The illustration at right is a schematic of a clothes drier. The dashed line encloses items inside the drier, the rest of the drawing is the cord and plug.

The test. Any or all segments of an electrical circuit in an appliance can be tested for continuity. Start by attaching the VOM to the prongs of the plugs (points A and B). Turn the appliance switch to ON (unit is unplugged). If the VOM records a reading, there probably is continuity through the whole appliance—"probably," because a short circuit in the line cord can cause the VOM to show continuity. To test the cord, turn the appliance to OFF. If the meter indicates a resistance, the line cord may be shorted. The switch may also be defective. Disconnect a switch lead and test again. If the meter stays where it is, then the line cord is OK.

You can find the point of trouble by probing each segment. For example, place the leads of the VOM across the switch (points C and D). Flip on the switch but do not plug in

This symbol represents the drier on/off switch.

This symbol represents the thermostat that senses the temperature in the appliance and turns the heating coils on and off automatically to maintain an even temperature. (Heat controls are described in more detail on page 26.)

This is the symbol for electrical resistance. As used, it represents the heating coils, the wires that glow red when the appliance is turned on. Whenever this symbol is used, it identifies concentrated, or "lumped," resistance, that is, any location having more resistance than straight (not coiled) wire.

Clothes drier schematic

C   D   E   F

the drier. If the switch is off, electricity cannot flow and no continuity should show. With the switch on, there should be a reading on the meter. If there is not, the switch is defective. Replace it.

Now skip to points D and E, across the thermostat. The thermostat points have to be closed, too. Now skip to points E and F. There should be some resistance.

Lack of continuity indicates a defective thermostat. All segments in an electrical circuit in an appliance can be tested this way to locate breaks in continuity. In this book, you

will often be directed to make a continuity test.

Important steps to keep in mind

1. Always, always, unplug an appliance from the wall receptacle before making a continuity test. The purpose of the continuity test is to locate the interruption in the circuit, the path along which electrons flow. To do this, an independent source of electricity (the continuity tester) must be used.

2. The appliance switch must be turned on when testing *most* segments of a circuit.

Two Common Continuity Tests

Testing a cord for continuity

1. Detach one cord lead.

2. Place one tester probe on one prong of the plug.

3. Place the other probe first on one cord lead, then the other. The tester should show continuity on one side only. Continuity on both sides means you have a short circuit in the cord. No continuity means you have an open circuit.

4. Bend the cord back and forth while testing it. If the tester shows intermittent continuity, the cord is defective.

5. Attach one tester probe to the other prong of the plug and repeat the test.

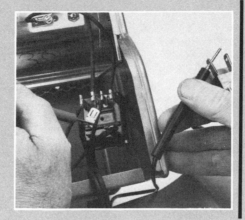

Testing a simple on/off switch for continuity

1. Remove one lead from the switch terminal.

2. Turn the switch to the ON position.

3. Place one tester probe on each terminal. There should be continuity. In the OFF position, there should be no continuity.

Important safety precautions

Remember, you are dealing with electric appliances, and electricity can kill. Read and remember these few precautions. The first is the most important.

1. Never work on an appliance that is plugged in.

2. Have someone around who knows where the service panel is and how to trip the circuit breaker or pull the main fuse block, so that if you make an error, they can cut the power off.

3. Never touch a bare wire without double-checking that the appliance is unplugged. Develop the habit of taping the cord to something so that you see the plug while you work on the unit. The fact that the appliance switch is off (open) does not mean that the appliance is safe. Electricity may find a path to a certain point and that might be the point where you are working.

4. There are times in the course of repairing an appliance when you have to put the plug into the wall and turn on the appliance— when you want to check for voltage, for example. To do this test correctly, follow these steps:

A. Set your VOM for the test you intend to make.

B. Unplug the appliance.

C. Connect the alligator clip lead of the VOM to one of the points where the test is to be made.

D. Now fasten the other alligator clip to the other test point. Keep your free hand away from the appliance.

E. Plug in the appliance and turn the switch to ON.

5. If you must replace a faulty cord, make certain the new cord has conductors of the same gauge as the original. If you are not sure of the gauge, take the old cord with you to the dealer. Undersized cords can cause fire.

6. After you have repaired an appliance, make sure there is no short within it. A short happens when a loose wire comes into contact with part of the housing, deflecting electricity out of the circuit and into the housing or metal parts when the appliance is plugged in and turned on. The user can get a severe shock from touching the housing (see *Testing for ground,* opposite).

7. *Always* check the voltage tester before using it (see page 14).

A word about shock

Electric shock occurs when the human body provides a path along which electric current can flow. When two or more paths are available for the flow of electrical energy, most of the flow will occur along the path that offers the least resistance. The body has many low-resistance paths. If it accidentally becomes part of an electrical circuit, it experiences the heaviest flow of electrical energy—an electric shock.

The way to avoid shock, then, is to avoid contact with the flow of electrical energy: always unplug an appliance before working on it. After you have made your repair, always test for ground before plugging the appliance in again.

The standard means of preventing the possibility of shock are insulating and grounding. By means of insulation, electrical energy is contained in wires, lamps, electrical outlets, and appliances. The energy carrier is enclosed in some material that offers a high resistance to current flow. The rubber or plastic covering on electric wires provides this insulation. Grounding means providing a better path (or lower resistance) to ground for electric energy than the human body. (For a discussion of electrical grounding, see page 11.)

If shock occurs, the victim may not be able to release his or her grip on the hot lead. Turn off the main power immediately if it can be done. If it can't, use a nonconductor such as dry wood or a heavy coat to break the victim's grip on the hot lead; do not touch the victim yourself, or the current will flow through your body too.

When you have broken the victim's grip, call a physician or rescue squad. Keep the victim warm and give artificial respiration by any approved method until help arrives.

Initials for safety

Any discussion of electrical safety would be incomplete without mentioning the Underwriters' Laboratories and the National Electrical Code.

Underwriters' Laboratories (UL) is the most widely used electrical testing laboratory in the United States. Manufacturers submit products for safety tests, and UL issues a report on its findings. Any shortcomings that are uncovered must be corrected by the manufacturer and new samples submitted for testing. Products that perform satisfactorily are listed in UL product directories. Manufacturers whose products are listed in the UL directory are permitted to display the UL symbol on their product.

The UL symbol is your assurance that an appliance meets minimum safety standards. Appliances in a wide range of prices have the UL symbol. Underwriters' Laboratories makes no attempt to judge overall quality, durability, or convenience and is concerned solely with electrical safety standards.

The National Electrical Code (NEC). In 1895, the first nationally recommended electrical code was published. In the years since, this code has developed and changed as technical knowledge and the uses of electricity have increased. It is now called the National Electrical Code (NEC) and is printed and distributed by the National Fire Protection Association; it is everywhere accepted as the basis for safe electrical wiring. The NEC is an advisory document only, but it is meant to be used by lawmakers and regulatory agencies as a basis for local electrical standards and building codes. The NEC becomes law only when it becomes a part of local building codes. Most local codes do, however, refer to the NEC. Whenever applicable, troubleshooting and replacement procedures in this book are in accordance with the NEC.

Power to your appliances

In most houses and apartments, electrical power enters the building on three lines. Two of these are called hot wires because current flows from them to any grounded point. Each carries approximately 120 volts. The third wire is connected to ground and is known as the neutral (or power ground) line. This combination of wires provides two voltage levels for appliances in your home: 120 and 240 volts.

Power enters some small houses and apartments on only two wires, providing only 120 volts. This greatly restricts the use of appliances because of the limited current safely available.

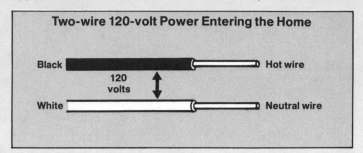

Three-wire 240-volt Power Entering the Home

Red — Hot wire
240 volts — 120 volts
White — Neutral wire
120 volts
Black — Hot wire

Two-wire 120-volt Power Entering the Home

Black — Hot wire
120 volts
White — Neutral wire

Electric service to your home

Various devices are used to secure power lines to buildings. The lines must be able to withstand varying weather conditions such as heavy winds or ice. In many cases, the neutral wire doubles as a line support. The wire consists of braided aluminum strands, making it thicker and stronger than the two hot wires. The three wires are then twisted or enclosed in an outer sheath so that the anchoring of the neutral wire to the house provides support for the other two lines. The incoming lines are heavily insulated and sometimes enclosed in a metal conduit, and are then routed to the meter box. Meter boxes are usually mounted on the outside wall of a house, although in some apartment buildings and older houses meters are in the basement.

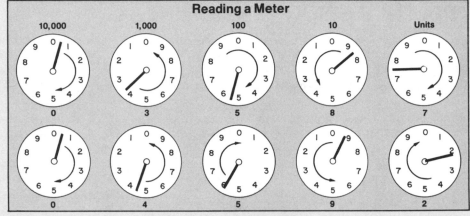

Reading a Meter

10,000 — 0
1,000 — 3
100 — 5
10 — 8
Units — 7

0 — 0
4 — 4
5 — 5
9 — 9
2 — 2

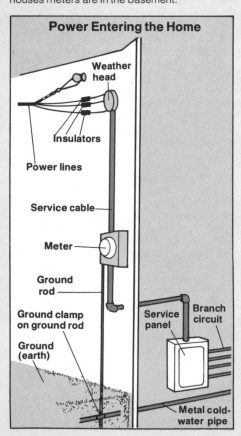

Power Entering the Home

Weather head
Insulators
Power lines
Service cable
Meter
Ground rod
Ground clamp on ground rod
Ground (earth)
Service panel
Branch circuit
Metal cold-water pipe

How to read your meter

Utility company bills show the meter readings on which billing is based. If you know how to read your meter, you can check the bill to make certain the reading was accurate.

Meters record power used in units called kilowatt-hours (kwh). Watts are units of power equal to the voltage times the current. A kilowatt-hour represents the use of 1,000 watts for one hour (*kilo* is Greek for 1,000). For example, a washing machine and a refrigerator both running continuously for one hour would consume about one kilowatt of electricity, or 1,000 watts.

The reading on your meter is determined by the positions of pointers on either four or five dials. (While all meters are not the same, most work this way.) Each dial has markings from 0 to 9. The markings on the dials from right to left represent units, tens, hundreds, and so on. The pointer always moves from 0 to 1 to 2 to 3, etc., and back to 0. The pointers on alternate dials move in opposite directions, that is, the numbering of the 10,000-unit dial increases in a clockwise direction, the 1,000-unit dial counterclockwise. The direction of dial rotation is indicated by the way the dials are numbered. Whenever electricity is being used in your home, all the dials move. Each dial moves ten times faster than the dial to its right. Unless power consumption is unusually heavy, movement will be noticeable only on the right-hand dial. To read the meter, start with the dial on the right and note the number the pointer has just passed according to each dial's direction of rotation.

For example, here is a reading of 03587, or 3587 kwh. Meter dials are not precisely marked. The pointer on a dial that may appear to be exactly on a number may actually be slightly above or below it. To decide when a number has been reached or passed, note the pointer on the next dial to the right. If it has not reached 0, the dial you are reading has not reached the nearest number. If the pointer to the right has passed 0, use the next higher number for the dial you are reading.

In the illustration below, the bottom middle dial appears to be on 6, but because the next dial to the right is below 0, the correct reading for the middle dial is actually 5. The full reading is 04592, or 4592 kwh.

Three lines carry power to your home or apartment, going through the meter and then into a service panel that divides the incoming power into circuits. The service panel also contains circuit breakers or fuses to provide protection against overload. The circuit breakers or fuses automatically shut off the power when current flow exceeds a safe level.

All service panels must contain a quick means of shutting off power. Some circuit breaker panels have two main line breakers to produce complete shutoff. Fuse panels often contain a main pullout fuse block that cuts off all incoming power. It is wise to familiarize yourself with the main shutoff on your service panel (the main shutoff may be located outside the house directly under the meter), because in an emergency it is the quickest means of turning off all power.

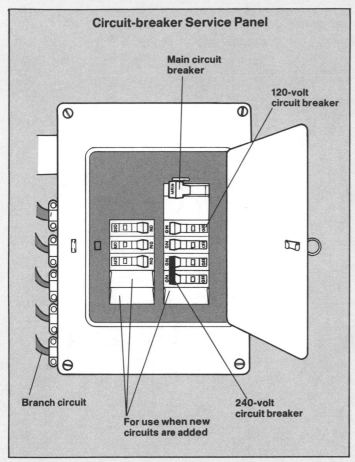

Circuit-breaker Service Panel

Main circuit breaker

120-volt circuit breaker

Branch circuit

For use when new circuits are added

240-volt circuit breaker

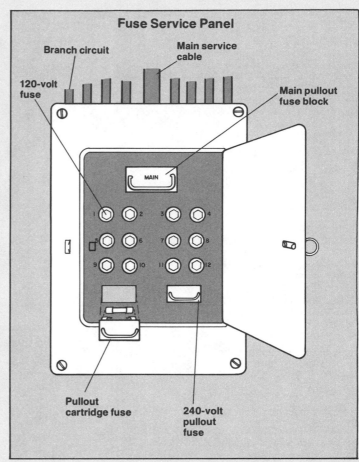

Fuse Service Panel

Branch circuit

Main service cable

120-volt fuse

Main pullout fuse block

MAIN

Pullout cartridge fuse

240-volt pullout fuse

Household circuits

The service panel is the point at which incoming power is divided into individual circuits. Each circuit is protected by its own circuit breaker or fuse. Modern service installations have any-where from twelve to thirty-two circuits. Four types of individual circuits are used in home power systems:

General-purpose circuits. These 120-volt two- or three-wire (one hot, one neutral, and sometimes one ground) circuits carry power to wall receptacles for general lighting and small appliances. They are usually protected by a 15-amp circuit breaker or fuse.

Appliance circuits. Kitchen and laundry areas, which have greater power needs than other living areas, also have 120-volt two- or three-wire circuits; 20 amps are provided to handle appliance loads.

Individual circuits. Single large appliances such as furnaces and washing machines have individual circuits with a single outlet or recep-tacle. The 120-volt two- or three-wire circuits are usually protected for a 15- or 20-amp load.

Heavy-duty circuits. Large appliances such as central air conditioners, ranges, and clothes driers are more efficiently operated at 240 volts than at 120. A 240-volt circuit may require three wires: two hot and one ground wire. Occasion-ally a 240-volt circuit has a fourth wire (neutral); these circuits are protected by two circuit breakers or fuses joined together by a common connector.

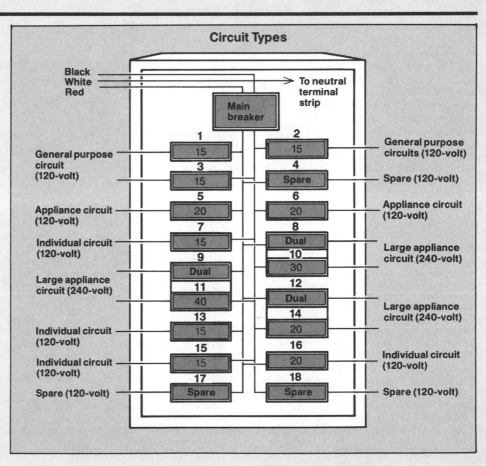

Circuit Types

Black
White
Red

To neutral terminal strip

Main breaker

General purpose circuit (120-volt) — 1 — 15

General purpose circuits (120-volt) — 2 — 15

General purpose circuit (120-volt) — 3 — 15

Spare (120-volt) — 4 — Spare

Appliance circuit (120-volt) — 5 — 20

Appliance circuit (120-volt) — 6 — 20

Individual circuit (120-volt) — 7 — 15

Large appliance circuit (240-volt) — 8 — Dual — 10 — 30

Large appliance circuit (240-volt) — 9 — Dual

Individual circuit (120-volt) — 11 — 40

Large appliance circuit (240-volt) — 12 — Dual

Individual circuit (120-volt) — 13 — 15

Individual circuit (120-volt) — 14 — 20

Individual circuit (120-volt) — 15 — 15

Individual circuit (120-volt) — 16 — 20

Spare (120-volt) — 17 — Spare

Spare (120-volt) — 18 — Spare

Circuit breakers

Circuit breakers are toggle or push-button switches that are automatically tripped by an overload but that can also be operated manually. They are available in ratings from 15 to 150 amps, with the rating marked on each circuit breaker. If the current exceeds the rating, the circuit breaker automatically switches to the OFF or TRIP position before any damage can occur. You can also turn off any circuit breaker by hand, to turn off all the power in a particular circuit.

Although circuit breakers are reliable devices and have a long life span, they can become defective. Because replacing them can be hazardous, it is best to have a licensed electrician do the job.

Toggle-switch circuit breakers have either two or three positions. Whether the circuit breaker is at ON or OFF is shown by the position of the toggle: up for ON and down for OFF. Three-position toggles have a center position marked TRIP. For resetting, toggle types must be switched back to the ON position, and three-position types must be moved from the center TRIP position to the OFF position, then back to ON.

Push-button circuit breakers have an on/off indicator. To reset one, simply depress and release the push button and the indicator will change from OFF to ON.

Fuses

All fuses contain a metal strip, enclosed in an insulated housing, that melts when more than a specified amount of current flows through it. The kind of metal and its thickness determine how much current the fuse can carry. When a fuse is removed, all power to the circuit it protects is cut off. **CAUTION** A fuse should *never* be replaced with one rated for higher amperage.

Ordinary plug fuses are screwed into the fuse panel by hand. The metal strip that protects the circuit is visible through a plastic window.

Time-delay fuses look like ordinary plug fuses, but they can carry more than their rated current for a short period. They are useful in circuits powering motor-driven appliances, in which the high current needed only briefly to start the motor would blow other types of fuses.

S-type fuses (also called nontamperable fuses) are time-delay fuses with an added feature — a special separate base that is inserted into the fuse panel socket. The base prevents higher-rated fuses from being screwed into lower-rated sockets. A 20-amp fuse, for example, cannot be screwed into a 15-amp socket.

When a short circuit blows a fuse, the sudden surge of current may cloud the plastic window. When a blown fuse has a clear window, it usually means that current greater than the fuse rating continued to flow long enough to heat the metal strip slowly and eventually to melt it.

Cartridge fuses are used mostly in high-amperage circuits. There are two types: ferrule cartridges, for currents using 10 to 60 amps, have rounded ends that make electrical contact; knife-blade cartridges, for currents above 60 amps, have flat ends to make better electrical contact.

Both types of cartridge fuses make an electri-cal connection by snapping into spring clips. Because the spring clips are live and exposed, a special tool called a fuse puller must always be used to remove cartridge fuses.

It is impossible to tell from its appearance whether or not a cartridge fuse has blown. A continuity tester must be used. Connect one lead from the tester to each end of the fuse. If the test lamp lights, the fuse is good; if it does not, the fuse is blown.

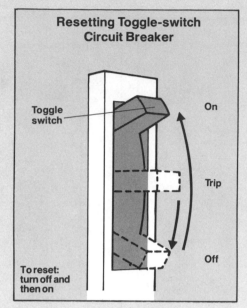

Resetting Toggle-switch Circuit Breaker

Toggle switch · On · Trip · Off

To reset: turn off and then on

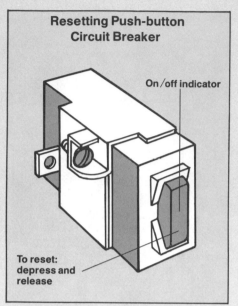

Resetting Push-button Circuit Breaker

On/off indicator

To reset: depress and release

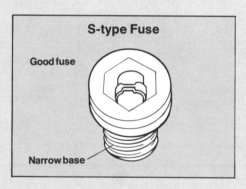

S-type Fuse

Good fuse

Narrow base

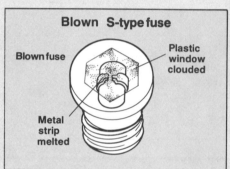

Blown S-type fuse

Blown fuse · Plastic window clouded · Metal strip melted

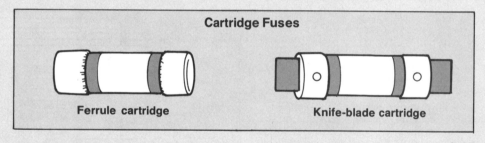

Cartridge Fuses

Ferrule cartridge · Knife-blade cartridge

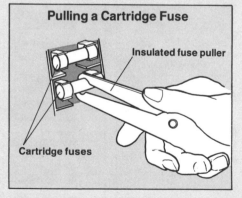

Pulling a Cartridge Fuse

Insulated fuse puller

Cartridge fuses

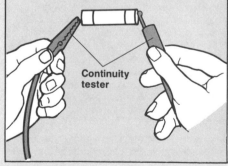

Testing a Cartridge Fuse

Continuity tester

Color coding

Virtually all 120- and 240-volt household circuits are wired in accordance with an industrywide color code, partly mandated by the National Electrical Code and also resulting from industry standardization and long–standing trade practices. The NEC requires that all neutral wires be either white or gray. Grounding wires are usually bare, but they may have green or green and yellow insulation. Grounding wires provide a safe path to ground for electrical power when trouble occurs in the electrical system. They do not *normally* carry current, but if there is a faulty wire in the appliance or in the wall receptacle, leaking current will be carried to ground by this wire.

The following color codes are used for various conductors:

Two-wire 120-volt circuits: black or red (occasionally blue) for hot wire; white or gray for neutral wire.

Three-wire 120-volt circuits: black or red (occasionally blue) for hot wire; white or gray for neutral wire; bare or green (occasionally green and yellow) for grounding wire.

Three-wire 240-volt circuits: black and/or red (occasionally blue) for hot wires; bare or green for grounding wire.

Four-wire 240-volt circuits: black and/or red (occasionally blue) for hot wires; white or gray for neutral wire; bare or green (occasionally green and yellow) for grounding wire.

The terminals on receptacles, switches and most appliances that are directly connected to power lines or ground wires are also color-coded. On a receptacle (right), the hot wires are always connected to the brass or brown terminals. These terminals lead to the narrow plug slots. The neutral wires are connected to the silver or white terminals, which lead to the wide plug slots. Terminals for the grounding wire are colored green.

The NEC requires that the white-insulated (neutral) wire be continuous throughout the electrical system. Whenever you remove a receptacle or switch that is connected to two white wires, you must connect the ends of the white wires with a wire nut. Switches work by interrupting the electrial circuits, and must, therefore, always be connected to the black or red (hot) wires, *with this exception:*

The cabling for residential wiring contains wire conductors with color-coded insulation. Two-wire cable has one black and one white wire. The NEC permits this cabling to be used in switch loop circuits like the one shown at bottom right. This is the only situation in which black and white wires may be joined. Thus, if you find a white-insulated wire connected to a brass switch terminal, do not assume it is a neutral wire.

CAUTION In a switch loop, the white wire may be hot. Always test before you touch. See *Testing and replacing a switch,* page 23. If you install or repair a switch loop, wrap a piece of black tape around the white wire to show that it is hot when the switch is on.

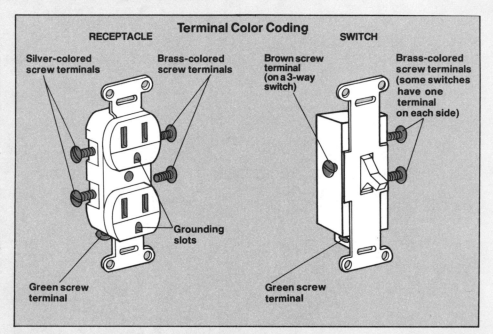

Terminal Color Coding

RECEPTACLE — Silver-colored screw terminals — Brass-colored screw terminals — Grounding slots — Green screw terminal

SWITCH — Brown screw terminal (on a 3-way switch) — Brass-colored screw terminals (some switches have one terminal on each side) — Green screw terminal

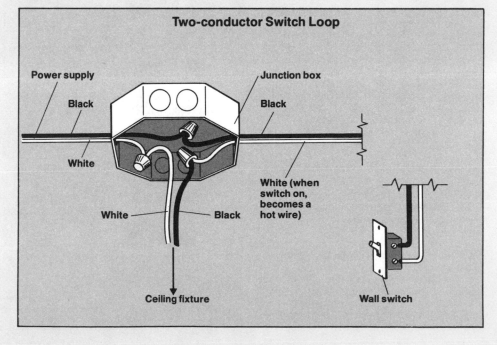

Two-conductor Switch Loop

Power supply — Black — White — White — Black — Ceiling fixture — Junction box — Black — White (when switch on, becomes a hot wire) — Wall switch

Checking the wall receptacle and switch

Appliance troubles often turn out to be caused by defective switches or wall outlets rather than by a defect in the appliance. When an appliance does not work or runs intermittently, and when inspection of its cord and plug shows no faults, check the wall receptacle or outlet. If the receptacle is controlled by a switch, the switch should also be checked. **CAUTION** Do not try to check or work on 240-volt switches or receptacles yourself. Have a licensed electrician do it. It is also wise to leave to an electrician any work on circuits other than switches and receptacles.

The quickest and easiest way to check the receptacle is to manipulate the plug in the receptacle. (If the faceplate of the receptacle is loose, tighten it before you make these tests.) Move the plug from side to side and up and down while pressing it into the receptacle. (You might also sepa-

rate the prongs of the plug slightly to ensure better contact.) If the appliance runs at all when this is done, the receptacle was not making good electrical contact with the prongs on the plug, and it should be replaced. **CAUTION** Always make the replacement with a receptacle rated for the same amperage.

As an additional check, plug a lamp into the receptacle and then turn it on. If the lamp does not light, the receptacle is electrically dead. If the receptacle is controlled by a switch, turn the switch on and off slowly several times. (If the faceplate on the switch is loose, tighten it first.) If the lamp lights, the switch works only intermittently and should be replaced. **CAUTION** Always make the replacement with a switch rated for the same amperage.

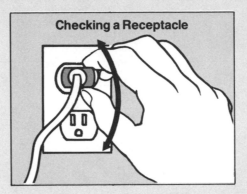

Checking a Receptacle

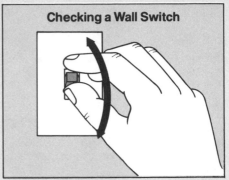

Checking a Wall Switch

Testing and replacing a receptacle

Removing a receptacle. Turn off power to the switch at the service panel. Remove the faceplate. If in doubt as to which circuit breaker or fuse controls the switch, use a flashlight and turn off the main power. Remove the mounting screws at the top and bottom, and pull the receptacle out of the outlet box. Loosen the screw terminals to remove the connecting wires. If the receptacle has push-in connections, insert a small screwdriver in the slot next to the hole where the conductor enters the receptacle. Push in on the screwdriver while pulling out the conductor.

Testing a receptacle. After the receptacle has been removed from its wall box, you should check it with a VOM. With the tester set on RX1, attach one probe to the brass-colored terminal. Touch the other probe to the metal frame of the receptacle. Then touch the probe to the silver-colored terminals. Then touch the probe to the ground terminal (green). All of these tests should show no continuity. If you get a continuity reading at any point, the receptacle is defective.

After completing this series of tests, put one probe of the VOM into one of the plug slots on the receptacle. Put the other probe on the terminal on the same side. The VOM should indicate continuity. Do the same on the other side of the receptacle. If either side shows no continuity, the receptacle is defective.

Installing a new receptacle. If the old receptacle has a green terminal, connect the existing bare or green-insulated wire to the green terminal on the new receptacle. If it does not have a green terminal, a grounding jumper must be added (see opposite page). Connect the black or red wire or wires to the brass-colored terminals and the white or gray wire or wires to the silver-colored terminals. Remount the receptacle in the outlet box and replace the faceplate.

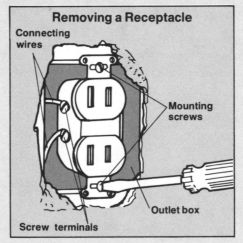

Removing a Receptacle

Connecting wires

Mounting screws

Outlet box

Screw terminals

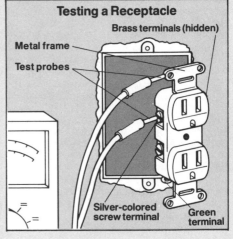

Testing a Receptacle

Brass terminals (hidden)

Metal frame

Test probes

Silver-colored screw terminal

Green terminal

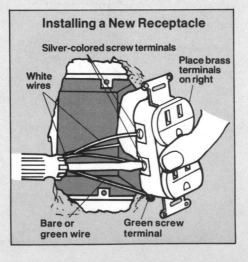

Installing a New Receptacle

Silver-colored screw terminals

White wires

Place brass terminals on right

Bare or green wire

Green screw terminal

Testing and replacing a switch

Removing a switch. Turn off power to the switch at the service panel. Remove the faceplate. If in doubt as to which circuit breaker or fuse controls the switch, use a flashlight and turn off the main power. Remove the mounting screws at the top and bottom of the switch, and pull the switch out of the outlet box. Loosen the brass-colored screw terminals and remove the wire connections. Some switches have push-in connections that you can remove by inserting a small screwdriver in the slot next to the hole where the conductor enters the switch. Push in on the screwdriver as you pull the conductor out. In most cases, both hot wires to the switch will have black or red insulation. CAUTION If you are replacing a loop switch, one of the hot wires may have *white* insulation (see *Color coding,* page 21).

Testing a switch. After the switch has been removed, check it with a continuity tester. Connect the alligator clip to one of the brass-colored terminals and touch the probe to the other. Turn the switch on and off several times, jiggling the toggle. The tester light will respond clearly without flickering to ON and OFF if the switch is good. Now, connect the alligator clip to the switch's mounting bracket or, if there is one, to the green grounding terminal.

Touch the probe first to one then to the other brass-colored terminal, and turn the switch off and on several times. A good switch will not cause the tester to light at all during testing.

Installing a new switch. Newer switches have, in addition to the two brass-colored terminals, a green grounding terminal required by the electrical code for new installations. If the switch being replaced has a green terminal, it is simple enough to connect the bare or the green-insulated wire to the green terminal on the new switch. If the old switch has no green terminal, a jumper must be added (see below). Next, connect the black and red wires (as already noted, one hot wire may be white) to the brass-colored terminals on the switch, and remount the switch in the outlet box. Replace the cover plate, then turn on the power and see if the switch works properly.

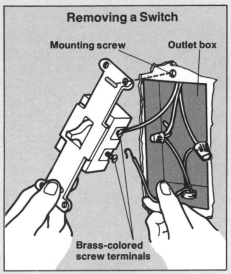

Removing a Switch

Mounting screw

Outlet box

Brass-colored screw terminals

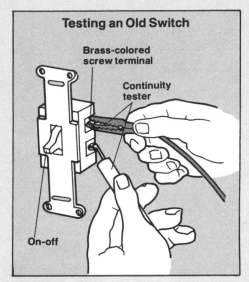

Testing an Old Switch

Brass-colored screw terminal

Continuity tester

On-off

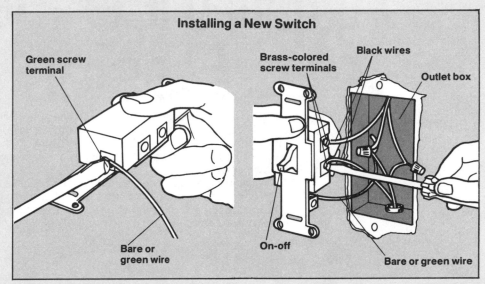

Installing a New Switch

Green screw terminal

Brass-colored screw terminals

Black wires

Outlet box

Bare or green wire

On-off

Bare or green wire

Adding a grounding jumper to a switch or receptacle

If the switch or receptacle you removed does not have a green grounding screw, you will have to add a grounding jumper when you install the new part. The procedure varies according to the type of power cables in the outlet box.

If the cables are the steel-armored (BX) type, connect a jumper of bare or green-insulated wire from a grounding screw in the outlet box to the green screw on the switch or receptacle.

If nonmetallic, plastic-sheathed (Romax) cables are used, the bare grounding wires from all cables entering the box should be joined with one end of a jumper wire by means of a solderless connector (wire nut). The other end of the jumper should be connected to the grounding screw in the box. A second jumper must now be added. Connect one end to the green screw on the switch or receptacle. Remove the wire nut and join the other end of the new jumper to the other grounding wires. Replace the wire nut.

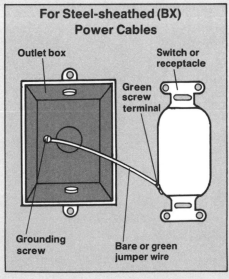

For Steel-sheathed (BX) Power Cables

Outlet box

Switch or receptacle

Green screw terminal

Grounding screw

Bare or green jumper wire

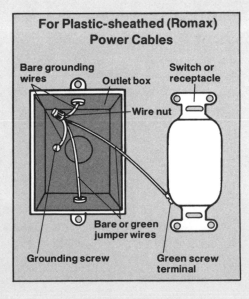

For Plastic-sheathed (Romax) Power Cables

Bare grounding wires

Outlet box

Switch or receptacle

Wire nut

Bare or green jumper wires

Grounding screw

Green screw terminal

Appliance Repair Basics

Virtually all appliances produce heat or mechanical motion or both. The means of producing and controlling heat is similar in all heat-producing appliances. The production of heat and the types of motors used to do the work in appliances are described in the next few pages.

Disassembling an appliance is often difficult because some manufacturers conceal the bolts and screws that hold the appliance together. You will find some tips in this section on how to find concealed parts.

How appliances produce heat

As the Blue Pages explained, what is commonly called current flow is, in fact, the movement of electrons in materials, usually metallic, that are called conductors. No matter how efficient the material may be in conducting current, there is always some opposition to electron movement; this opposition is called electrical resistance. When electron flow is impeded by resistance, some of the electrons' energy is converted to heat. This principle is basic to the design of heating elements in appliances.

How does the heating element get hot? The element is made of a special alloy wire (usually a nickel-chromium alloy called nichrome) that has electrical resistance and is also heat-resistant. Both characteristics are necessary for the heating element to do its job.

The special-alloy wire, generally called resistance wire, has a high melting point, which enables it to withstand the great heat the wire itself produces. The amount of heat depends on how many watts the element consumes. It can be as few as 500 watts or as many as 5,000. In other words, elements differ from one type and size of appliance to another. Those having higher wattage capacity draw more electricity and create more heat than those with low capacity.

To say that a heating element has resistance means that it allows only a certain amount of current to flow through it at one time. Resistance depends on such factors as the type of wire the element is made of, the gauge (size) of the wire, and the number of coils into which the wire is fashioned.

To determine how many watts (and, consequently, how much heat) a heating element can generate, always start with a constant figure. The amount of available voltage (or electrical pressure) at the receptacle is a known factor. In most U.S. homes, for example, the voltage available is 120 and 240.

As stated above, the amount of current that actually flows through a circuit depends on the size and makeup of the wire (that is, on the wire's resistance). The relationship between the current and the wire's resistance is the determining factor in heat output. The heat output in watts is the product of the voltage times the current.

WATTS = VOLTS X AMPS

A heating element that allows 10 amps of current to flow has a wattage of 120 X 10, or 1,200 watts. If another element allows 25 amps to flow, its heat output is 3,000 watts.

Heating coils and elements in large appliances cannot be repaired. If a VOM resistance test shows high or infinite resistance or if the continuity tester does not show continuity, the complete heating element should be replaced.

Replacement heating elements can be purchased from the manufacturer, appliance parts dealers, or hardware or electrical supply stores. Take the old element with you, since it is important to buy one of the same size and gauge. When ordering by mail, be sure to include the appliance model number, serial number, and if possible the element part number.

For information on removal and replacement of heating elements, see the instructions in the articles on specific appliances.

Electric range surface element heats cooking utensils by contact. It is held in place in the electrical terminal block by springs or by screws.

Electric water heater element is mounted on the tank wall and extends into the tank. It heats the water by direct contact.

Dishwasher heating element is mounted on the bottom of the tub. It keeps water hot during washing cycles and after the tub is drained heats the air to dry the dishes.

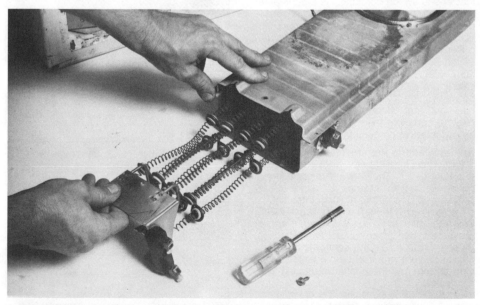

Electric clothes drier coil is mounted inside the heating duct. Air heated by the coil is blown into the drum by a fan.

Controlling heat levels

The heating elements of large appliances can be turned on and off. When an element is on, the heat output is fixed, determined by the size of the element and the material it is made of. How, then, are various levels of heat produced? Two methods are commonly used.

One method simply switches the heating element on and off periodically to produce an average heat output. If the on time is long and the off time brief, average heat output is high. When the reverse is true, average heat output is low. After the unit has been turned on, heat is controlled automatically by means of either a fixed-heat or an adjustable-temperature thermostat.

The second method of heat control involves a tapped heating element. One connection to the element is made through a switch having several positions such as HIGH, MEDIUM, and LOW. Each switch position applies power to a different point on the heating element to produce a different level of heat. Appliances with this type of control may also have an automatic safety switch to prevent overheating.

Thermostats

Bimetallic units. The basic way of controlling heat in a thermostat is by means of a bimetallic unit consisting of two different metals fused together. Both expand when heated, but one expands faster than the other, causing the bimetallic unit to warp or bend. This in turn opens and closes electrical contacts.

Fixed-heat thermostats. These controls have a factory-set temperature. The heat control is a circular bimetallic unit. When a certain temperature is reached, the bimetallic disc expands and snaps up, pushing a plunger that opens switch contacts. As the temperature drops, the disc contracts and snaps down, closing the contacts. The correct temperature is maintained by this on-off action.

Repair work is limited to cleaning the switch contacts, if they are accessible. Clean the contacts by pressing them together after inserting a piece of soft cloth or a dollar bill between them. Gently slide the cloth or bill back and forth. If the contacts are inaccessible, the complete thermostat assembly must be replaced when something goes wrong.

Adjustable-heat thermostats. These units are used on appliances that operate at various heat levels. They have a temperature-control knob that activates a plunger to apply pressure to one of two electrical contact arms, changing the spacing between them. When the bimetallic unit is heated, it applies pressure to the other contact arm. The less pressure applied by the control knob, the more pressure required by the bimetallic strip to separate the contact arms and switch off current.

Some repair is possible. The control-knob unit is usually accessible with some disassembly. Contacts can be cleaned, as described under fixed-heat thermostats. The

most common problem is uneven operation caused by bits of dirt that become lodged between the contact arms and the knob or plunger. Simply brush or scrape out the dirt and rub the contact points lightly with cloth or paper.

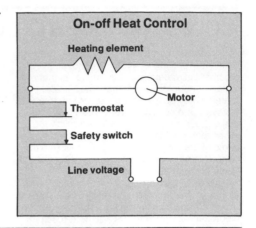

On-off Heat Control

Heating element · Motor · Thermostat · Safety switch · Line voltage

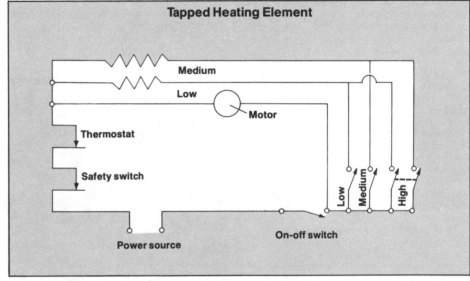

Tapped Heating Element

Medium · Low · Motor · Thermostat · Safety switch · Low · Medium · High · Power source · On-off switch

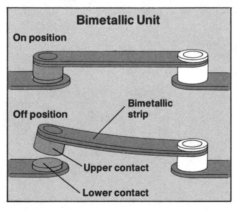

Bimetallic Unit

On position · Off position · Bimetallic strip · Upper contact · Lower contact

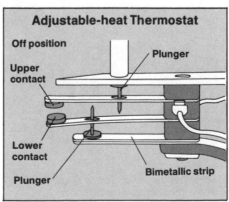

Adjustable-heat Thermostat

Off position · Plunger · Upper contact · Lower contact · Plunger · Bimetallic strip

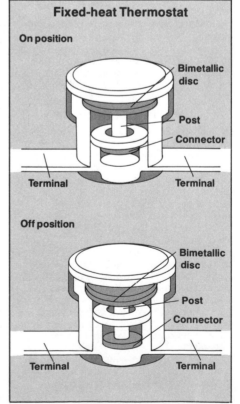

Fixed-heat Thermostat

On position · Bimetallic disc · Post · Connector · Terminal · Terminal · Off position · Bimetallic disc · Post · Connector · Terminal · Terminal

How motors work

A simple experiment with small permanent magnets shows that opposite poles attract and like poles repel. A magnetic field around each pole exerts force that causes attraction or repulsion.

When current flows through a wire, a circular magnetic field is created around that wire. The strength of the field can be increased by bundling many wires together. The direction of force of the magnetic field depends on the direction of current flow. If the wires are formed into a coil, the magnetic fields create north and south poles similar to a bar magnet. If some coils of wire are wound on a stationary frame, sometimes called a stator, and others are wound on a frame that is free to rotate, also known as a rotor, the magnetic fields can be so arranged that the attraction and repulsion forces will cause the free frame to rotate. This is the principle on which all electric motors operate.

Universal motors

The most widely used motor in appliances is the universal motor. It is called universal not because of its wide use, but because it can run on either AC or DC.

This motor has two important characteristics. First, it provides extremely high starting torque (a force that produces rotation) for its size and weight, and it can attain high speed quickly under a fairly heavy load. Second, it can operate over a wide range of speeds in both small and large appliances. A universal motor may be used in such appliances as oil burners and washing machines.

The rotor of a universal motor is made up of an armature, which is the iron core with coils of wire wrapped around it, and the commutator. The commutator and armature together constitute a single assembly.

The commutator, which is positioned at one end of the armature, consists of a series of copper bars laid out in circular fashion. The commutator is basically a switching mechanism.

Passing right through the middle of the armature and commutator is a shaft that protrudes from both ends. How far the shaft extends from each end varies from appliance to appliance.

One end of the shaft is normally attached to a bearing assembly, enabling the rotor to rotate. In some cases, the shaft has a small fan that cools the interior of the appliance. The other end of the shaft is attached to the appliance's working device. Or the working end of the shaft may be attached to a gear train, which in turn is attached to a working element. This is the case with washing machines.

The stator is the part of the motor in which the rotor is positioned. It is a frame (usually iron) containing coils of wire called field coils. Keep in mind that the rotor is positioned in this way so its movement cannot be impeded.

Essentially, this is what happens: electricity enters one of the field coils through the appliance cord, which is plugged into a wall receptacle. Current passes from the field coil into one of two carbon segments, called brushes, which are positioned directly opposite each other on the commutator. The brushes are held in contact with the commutator by springs.

Current flows through the brush to the one commutator bar the brush is touching, through the armature coil to which the armature is connected, out through another commutator bar that is in contact with the other brush, into another field coil, and back to its source. This means that the brushes and commutator bars act as an automatic switching device that connects and disconnects each coil at exactly the right moment as the armature revolves.

All components of a universal motor are wired together in tandem, and current at every point is the same. This is called a series circuit.

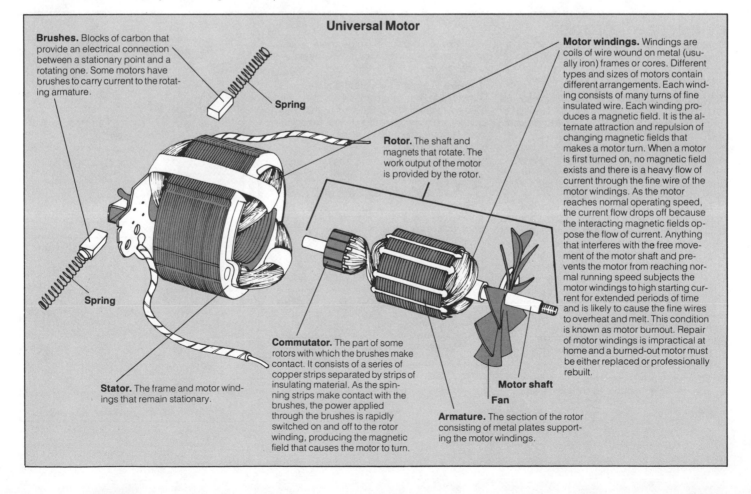

Universal Motor

Brushes. Blocks of carbon that provide an electrical connection between a stationary point and a rotating one. Some motors have brushes to carry current to the rotating armature.

Spring

Spring

Stator. The frame and motor windings that remain stationary.

Rotor. The shaft and magnets that rotate. The work output of the motor is provided by the rotor.

Commutator. The part of some rotors with which the brushes make contact. It consists of a series of copper strips separated by strips of insulating material. As the spinning strips make contact with the brushes, the power applied through the brushes is rapidly switched on and off to the rotor winding, producing the magnetic field that causes the motor to turn.

Motor shaft

Fan

Armature. The section of the rotor consisting of metal plates supporting the motor windings.

Motor windings. Windings are coils of wire wound on metal (usually iron) frames or cores. Different types and sizes of motors contain different arrangements. Each winding consists of many turns of fine insulated wire. Each winding produces a magnetic field. It is the alternate attraction and repulsion of changing magnetic fields that makes a motor turn. When a motor is first turned on, no magnetic field exists and there is a heavy flow of current through the fine wire of the motor windings. As the motor reaches normal operating speed, the current flow drops off because the interacting magnetic fields oppose the flow of current. Anything that interferes with the free movement of the motor shaft and prevents the motor from reaching normal running speed subjects the motor windings to high starting current for extended periods of time and is likely to cause the fine wires to overheat and melt. This condition is known as motor burnout. Repair of motor windings is impractical at home and a burned-out motor must be either replaced or professionally rebuilt.

Shaded-pole motors

One motor used in smaller appliances is known as the shaded-pole motor. It is small (1/100 to 1/20 horsepower) and produces low starting torque. Typically, it is used in such appliances as electric fans and humidifiers. Shaded-pole motors operate on AC only.

A shaded-pole motor has no commutator on its rotor and no brushes. Its winding consists of solid copper rings, called shades, on each pole tip. The rings set up a magnetic field that alternately aids and opposes the main field coil. The effect is a field that produces a turning force and starts the rotor spinning.

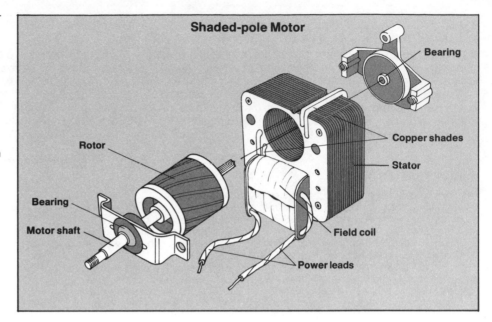

Shaded-pole Motor

Rotor · Bearing · Copper shades · Stator · Bearing · Motor shaft · Field coil · Power leads

Motor speed controls

Controlling motor speed is often desirable. Universal motors are especially well suited to this purpose, because speed can be controlled by any one of three devices.

Tapped-field speed controls. When a control has stepped settings such as HIGH, MEDIUM, and LOW, it is likely that a tapped field is used. With a tapped-field speed control, the point at which power is applied to the motor winding can be varied. When only part of the winding is energized, the magnetic field is smaller and the motor speed is reduced. Motor torque remains fairly constant at each tapped setting.

Tapped-field speed controls are relatively trouble-free. If a motor operates at some speeds but not at others, the speed selector switch may be defective and not making contact at those settings. If the motor operates at only one speed, the selector switch is again the likely source of trouble. Switches are usually not repairable.

To replace a switch, make a sketch of the connections to the old switch before you remove it. Note the colors of the wires and terminals they are connected to, or label the wires with masking tape, so when the new switch is installed, the motor will operate in accordance with the marked speed settings.

Solid-state speed controls. These controls are electronic and employ a device called a silicon-controlled rectifier (SCR). The current flow through the rectifier can be controlled by varying a small control voltage, thereby allowing motor speed to be continuously variable over a wide range.

Diodes. A simpler form of solid-state device employs a diode to provide two motor speeds. Current to the motor is switched so that it is connected either directly to the motor or indirectly through the diode. The diode effectively cuts current in half.

The Solid State of the Art

It is characteristic of solid-state devices that when they fail they fail completely. They rarely deteriorate gradually or fail partially. Another characteristic is high reliability, so check other features carefully before deciding that the speed control is at fault.

When solid-state speed controls fail, the complete unit must be replaced.

When a diode-rectifier speed control is defective, the appliance should operate normally at the high setting, but will either not operate at all on a lower setting or will continue to operate at high speed.

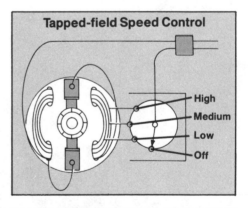

Tapped-field Speed Control

High · Medium · Low · Off

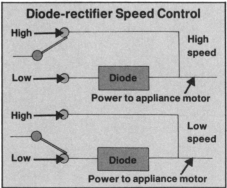

Diode-rectifier Speed Control

High · Low · Diode · High speed · Power to appliance motor

High · Low · Diode · Low speed · Power to appliance motor

Preventing motor breakdowns

Defects in the brushes and commutator of a universal motor can cause the motor to run sluggishly and lose power. Servicing these parts takes a few moments but can restore a motor to almost new.

If a motor is sluggish, check the brush contact by running the appliance in a dimly lighted area. Sparking will be visible through the ventilation openings in the appliance. Small bluish sparks where commutator and brush meet are normal. Light, bright sparks or bright and dim sparks indicate poor brush contact or worn brushes. Disassemble the motor and inspect the brushes and commutator. A good rule of thumb is that brushes should be longer than they are wide. If they aren't, they should be replaced. Check the brush holder and spring to be sure the spring supplies enough pressure to hold the brush firmly against the commutator. If spring tension appears weak, replace both springs.

If brushes are replaced, they may need shaping to fit the curvature of the commutator. You can shape brushes to make good contact in two easy steps. First, wrap a piece of fine-grit sandpaper (rough side out) around the commutator. (Be sure to use sandpaper, not emery cloth, because in emery cloth the abrasive material is a conductor. A short could result, causing the segments of the commutator to arc together.) Then insert the brushes in the holder so they press against the sandpaper. Rotate the commutator back and forth by hand until the brush ends are shaped to fit.

If the copper surfaces are rough, polish them by holding very fine sandpaper against the commutator while turning it. To keep the sandpaper flat against the commutator surface, wrap the sandpaper around a flat stick or use the stick to press it against the commutator.

Excessive brush wear or chipping may be caused by a worn commutator. The commutator consists of copper bars separated by mica insulators, and if the mica projects above the surface of the copper bars, it should be carefully scraped until it is a bit lower than the copper surface.

Bearings and gears. Because heat can be destructive to any motor, some appliances have fan blades attached to one end of the motor shaft to force cooling air through the housing. Make sure ventilation openings are not blocked.

Most appliances are not intended for continuous use. Motor bearings can overheat and bind or seize up, causing severe motor damage. Units should be turned off and allowed to cool if the housing gets too hot. When a motor becomes hot even though properly ventilated, it may be overloaded by excessive friction in the bearings or gears.

Lubrication. Motor bearings reduce friction between fixed and moving parts. If bearings become excessively worn or misaligned, the appliance may perform poorly or the motor may burn out. Excessive wear and misalignment are often caused by insufficient lubrication. The problem is avoided on many small motors because of permanently lubricated bearings that are sealed and sufficiently lubricated to last for the life of the motor; no attempt should be made to add more lubricant. In larger motors (⅛ horsepower and up) bearings generally need periodic lubrication.

Both ends of the motor housing should be checked for lubrication points. Look for small holes marked OIL or small metal cups with spring-loaded tops. The type of oil required and the frequency of lubrication are often marked on the motor or elsewhere, or it may be in the appliance manual. If no guide is available, use a light general-purpose oil (SAE 10), adding only a few drops every three or four months. Oil should be used sparingly and only in the bearings.

Oil cups often contain felt wicks to absorb the oil and allow it to flow slowly to the bearings. If these wicks become clogged with dirt, oil will not reach the bearings. To clean a wick, pull it out of the cup with tweezers and dip it in a dry-cleaning solvent. When it is dry, oil it until the wick is saturated, and replace it.

Gears, made of either metal or plastic, convert motion from the motor to the part being driven. Metal gears require heavy lubrication; plastic ones need little or none. If the motor hums but the appliance runs slowly, noisily, or not at all, the gears may be at fault. Gears can jam if they suffer mechanical damage when an appliance is dropped or the motor is severely overloaded. You can repair jammed gears by freeing them; broken or worn gears must be replaced. To free jammed gears, separate them with a wooden or plastic stick. Rotate the gears by hand to check for free movement. If they do not move freely, the gears or the appliance must be replaced. **CAUTION** Gears are sharp, and it is easy to cut yourself.

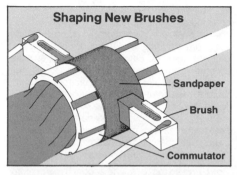

Shaping New Brushes

Sandpaper

Brush

Commutator

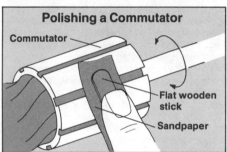

Polishing a Commutator

Commutator

Flat wooden stick

Sandpaper

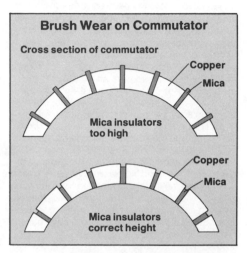

Brush Wear on Commutator

Cross section of commutator

Copper

Mica

Mica insulators too high

Copper

Mica

Mica insulators correct height

Lubrication of electrical motors extends their life and helps them run more efficiently. The fan motor on the dehumidifier shown above has one small oil port above the shaft, opposite the fan. Be sure the port is clean before adding a few drops of light lubricating oil. If a motor runs constantly, lubricate it three times a year. If it runs seasonally, lubricate at the beginning and the middle of the season.

Motors in large appliances

The basic operating principle behind all electric motors is the same. The forces of attraction and repulsion between a fixed magnetic field and one that can rotate cause the motors to run. The main difference between the sizes of appliance motors is a result of design changes necessitated by the heavier work load carried by larger appliances.

Large-sized universal motors are used in certain large appliances, such as oil burners. In most large appliances, however, one of two types of induction motor is used. Induction motors are well suited to heavy work and are simpler than universal motors: they have no armature, brushes, or commutator. They operate on AC only.

The rotors of induction motors are solid cores that become magnetized by a magnetic field. The stator windings are made up of a number of coils distributed around the stator in such a way that, when energized from an AC source, the magnetic fields of the coils constantly change.

If these magnetic fields were visible, the strength and direction of the magnetic force would appear to move around the stator. In effect, although the stator remains fixed, its magnetic field rotates. The force of this rotating field is transferred to the rotor. This process of transfer of magnetic fields is known as induction.

If the magnetic field induced in the rotor is not aligned with the stator's magnetic field, the rotor will turn as it tries to "catch up" with the stator field. Since the rotor must move its own mass as well as the load it is driving, it cannot catch up, and so the motor runs.

Designers of induction motors must overcome one inherent problem that occurs when the motor is turned on. The rotor is stationary and the magnetic field induced in it is aligned with the stator field; effectively, the rotor remains stationary. Special circuits are therefore added to create an initial magnetic displacement between rotor and stator.

Centrifugal switch. The special circuits that are added are needed only when the motor is started; if they were to remain connected, they would reduce the efficiency of the motor. Induction motors, therefore, have centrifugal switches that cut out the starting circuit when the motor reaches running speed.

Capacitor motors. Two types of starting circuits are used in the induction motors in large appliances, and they give their names to those motors. The motor used most widely in appliances with heavy starting loads, such as washing machines, is a capacitor, or capacitor-start, motor. A large capacitor, easily recognized by the capacitor box mounted on the main motor housing, supplies the initial field displacement that gets the motor going. Capacitor-start motors are highly efficient and draw relatively low starting current. They are available with ratings up to 7½ horsepower.

Capacitors act as temporary storage places for electrical energy. When power is applied to the leads of a capacitor, the capacitor is charged in much the way that a battery is charged. When power is removed and the leads are shorted or reversed, the capacitor discharges. In an AC circuit, this charging and discharging causes a time shift in the buildup of the resulting magnetic field. In capacitor-start motors, the centrifugal switch connects a capacitor across a part of the stator during start-up. The capacitor shifts part of the stator field to get the rotor moving. The centrifugal switch disconnects the capacitor when the motor reaches normal running speed.

Split-phase motors. The second type of motor used in large appliances is a split-phase motor. One winding on a split-phase motor has three electrical connections rather than the customary two. The third tap provides the field displacement necessary to start the motor.

When the motor reaches normal speed, the centrifugal switch opens the connection to the tap. These motors cannot be used to start heavy loads, and they also draw high starting current. They are available with ratings only up to ⅓ horsepower. Split-phase motors look like capacitor-start motors, without the capacitor housing.

Starting circuitry

The problems peculiar to large-appliance motors are those associated with the starting circuitry. Centrifugal switches have a disc that moves back and forth on the motor shaft, on which it is mounted. When the motor is turned off, a spring positions the disc so that it holds a pair of electrical contacts closed. As the motor begins to turn and speed up, a pair of weights moves outward by means of centrifugal force. The weights overcome the spring force and move the disc away from the electrical contacts, allowing them to open.

If switch contacts are clogged or dirty, the switch mechanism will stick and the motor will not start. To clean them, remove one end of the motor housing and run a fine-toothed file between switch contacts to clean them. (This is a temporary repair only. Replace the switch plate as early as possible.) Clean mechanical parts of the switch with a small brush dipped in any household solvent. Dab light oil on sliding surfaces and the pivot point, never on electrical contact points. Hand-operate parts to ensure free movement. Badly bent, pitted contact points or broken switch parts must be replaced.

To check the capacitor on capacitor-start motors, always discharge the capacitor first (see page 42). Then remove the electrical connections, usually push-on types that you can pull off by gripping the end of the connector with pliers.

You will need a VOM to check the capacitor. Set the selector switch to the RX100 resistance scale. Touch the test leads to the capacitor terminals. The needle should swing toward 0 ohms and then gradually drift back to the high-resistance end of the scale. If the needle stays at or near 0, the capacitor is shorted. If the needle stops at the high-resistance reading, the capacitor is open. In either case, the only remedy is to replace the capacitor.

Getting Inside

It's easier than it looks to get inside a large appliance. In general, large appliances consist of metal panels enclosing a frame on which the main parts are mounted. You must remove the front, top, or rear panels (and sometimes side panels, when they are removable) to expose key parts. Rear panels are usually secured with accessible sheet-metal screws. Front and side panels are somewhat more complicated to take off: remove the screws or snap-out spring clips at the bottom edge. Pulling the panel out 2 or 3 inches and pushing it up will free it at the top. Try removing the front panel first to expose the side panel mounting screws. Appliance tops are often secured by hidden spring clips. To release them, slip a putty knife under the edge of the top panel. Push in on the putty knife and pull up on the panel to release it. These clips are usually located about 2 inches from each end.

Induction Motor with Capacitor Start

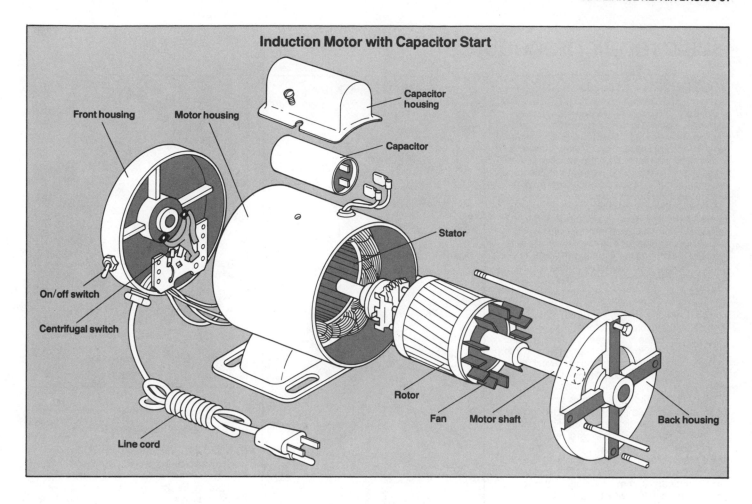

Capacitor housing

Capacitor

Front housing

Motor housing

Stator

On/off switch

Centrifugal switch

Rotor

Fan

Motor shaft

Back housing

Line cord

How to Test a Universal Motor

If the motor in an appliance doesn't run at all, check the appliance circuitry for loose connections and test the line cord, switch, and diode and fuse (if the appliance has them) for continuity. If these tests do not reveal the fault, the problem is most likely in the motor.

On universal motors with brushes, you can make a quick test without disassembling the motor to find the defective component.

To make the quick motor test, simply disconnect one or both of the power leads to the motor and attach VOM probes to the power lead terminals. Set the VOM on either the RX1 or RX10 scale (whichever brings the needle to the middle part of the dial). If the VOM doesn't register at all, the motor has failed the continuity test and its components must be tested individually. If the motor has continuity, turn the rotor slowly by hand and watch the needle on the VOM; it should continue to register roughly in the middle of the scale. If the needle dips suddenly, there is an open winding in the rotor, and the rotor must be

replaced. If the needle remains steady (an indication that the motor is OK) but the motor still does not work at all, have the field coil tested at a repair shop. As a last step, remove one VOM probe from the power lead terminals and touch it to the motor shaft. The VOM should show no continuity. If it shows continuity, the motor is grounded and should be serviced at a repair shop or replaced.

If the motor fails the continuity test, disassemble it and examine the brushes for wear (see page 29). If they are OK, test the rotor for continuity by placing one VOM probe on the first copper band and the other probe on each of the other copper bands successively. The VOM should show continuity for each band. If any band fails the test, replace the rotor. If the rotor is OK, make a simple continuity test on the field coil. If the VOM shows no continuity in the field coil, replace the coil. If the coil does have continuity and you have eliminated every other possible source of trouble, have the coil

professionally tested to be sure that none of the windings is defective (something that a continuity test can't show).

In most cases, universal motors can be rebuilt at local shops. Before deciding to have a motor rebuilt, consider the cost of the repair against the cost of replacement, which in some cases may be less.

Basic repair procedures

Testing the cord and plug

Often appliance troubles can be traced to a faulty cord and plug assembly. Inspection is sometimes all that is needed to discover the source of the trouble—whether it is a cracked plug, a loose prong, or a broken wire. In some cases, however, a test must be made to find out whether the cord and plug are at fault. Electrical testers and the tests you can make wth them are discussed in the Blue Pages.

Either a VOM (on resistance range RX1) or a continuity tester can be used. Make certain the appliance is not plugged into the outlet when you are performing these tests. Attach the test leads to the prongs of the plug with alligator clips. If the cord is detachable (with a female receptacle connecting to the appliance), disconnect the cord from the appliance. Make a jumper by stripping both ends of a short length of wire. Insert the stripped ends into the openings of the female receptacle. If the power cord is connected to the appliance internally, turn the appliance switch to OFF and open the unit. Jump the male plug end and, leaving the switch at OFF, measure across both leads of the incoming line cord.

The VOM should read 0 ohms or the continuity tester should light. Twist and bend the cord. If the needle flickers or the light goes out, there is a break in the cord or a loose connection in one of the plugs. With the tester still connected, remove the jumper at the other end, or turn the appliance off. The meter should indicate 0 ohms resistance: the test light on the continuity tester should not light. Again, bend and twist the cord. If the needle moves or the lamp lights, there is a short in the cord or in the plug.

If a cord and plug assembly is defective, you can replace it with a new one; if the trouble can be traced to a plug, the plug can be replaced. **CAUTION** Always replace cords and plugs with ones having the same specifications. A lamp cord used on an air conditioner, for example, creates a fire hazard.

Replacing a plug

When a plug for a wall outlet is replaced, the connections should be made with a strain-relief knot known as an Underwriters' knot. After looping the leads as shown, pull the knot tight and draw it back into the plug. Make a loop in the bare conductor and route the leads in opposite directions around the prongs.

Put the loop under the screw terminals so that the direction of tightening will be toward the open part of the loop. Do not overlap the wire. No strands of wire should stick out from under the screw head.

The female receptacle on a fully detachable cord and plug for a small appliance can be disassembled and replaced as shown. These plugs are becoming less common: most appliances now come with a built-in cord. If the cord and plug are connected internally to the appliance, refer to the entry on the specific appliance for replacement information.

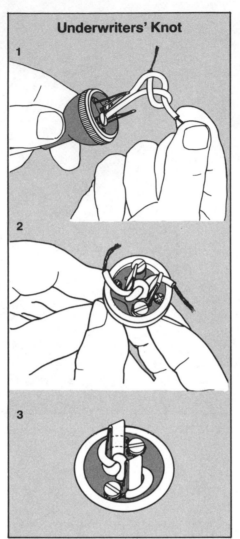

Underwriters' Knot

1

2

3

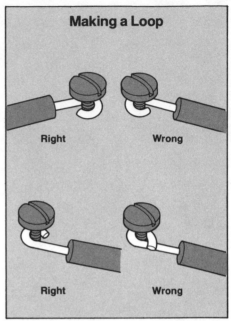

Making a Loop

Right   Wrong

Right   Wrong

Don't Overlook the Receptacle

When appliances work intermittently or the plug must be manipulated in the receptacle to make the appliance operate, it is natural to suspect the cord and plug. Keep in mind, however, that this type of problem can also be caused by a defective wall receptacle. In a receptacle controlled by a wall switch, a defective switch can cause the same problem. Replacement of wall receptacles and switches is described on pages 22 and 23.

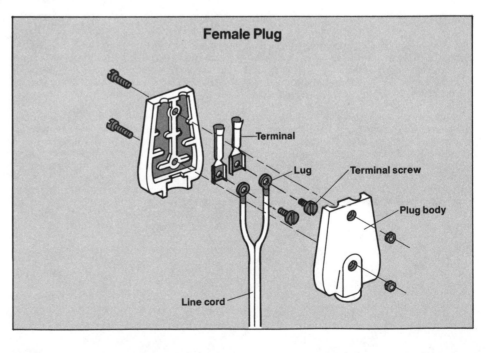

Female Plug

Terminal

Lug

Terminal screw

Plug body

Line cord

Splicing wires

Occasionally it may be necessary to splice wires when repairing appliances. The proper way to make safe, secure splices is to make a mechanical and electrical joint that is strong enough not to pull apart and tight enough to offer no electrical resistance. This is tricky; a continuous run of new wire is always better than any splice.

If you must make a splice, there are various types to choose from. All splices should be soldered and then taped. Splicing, taping and soldering are described below and on page 34.

The Western Union splice has long been used for maximum strength, particularly in dual-conductor cords and cables. To make this splice, begin by cutting one conductor about 2 inches shorter than the other so the completed splices will not be directly opposite each other. Offsetting the splices serves two functions: it

keeps them apart from each other, thus preventing a short circuit if the insulating tape tears or works loose, and it also minimizes the unsightly bulge that appears when two splices fall beside each other and each is wrapped with tape.

Strip each conductor or wire of insulation and scrape it clean of dirt and oxidation. Then wrap the bared ends around each other as shown. With light-gauge stranded wire, twist the ends tightly enough with your fingertips; for solid heavy wire, you will need pliers in order to make a tight twist. Solder and then tape the splice.

The pigtail splice makes a good electrical connection and is mechanically strong, but the finished splice is bulky. Strip off at least 1½ inches of insulation from the end of each wire. Twist the wires together tightly, starting at or near the first bit of exposed wire. Trim off sharp points

protruding from the end of the twist. Solder the twisted wires at the point where the twist began. Bend the pigtail parallel to one of the conductors and tape the bare splice from the end of the insulation on one side to the beginning of the insulation on the other.

The twist splice makes a good electrical connection, but it is not particularly strong. For light wire, cross about 2 inches of each end of prepared wire. Bend the ends of the wires over each other at right angles and twist them around each other. For heavy-gauge wire, two pairs of pliers are needed to make sure the connection is tight. Use one pair to hold the wires at the beginning of the twist, and the other to twist the wires. Use wire cutters to trim off the excess wire so no sharp ends can penetrate the tape. Solder the wires at the twist and tape them.

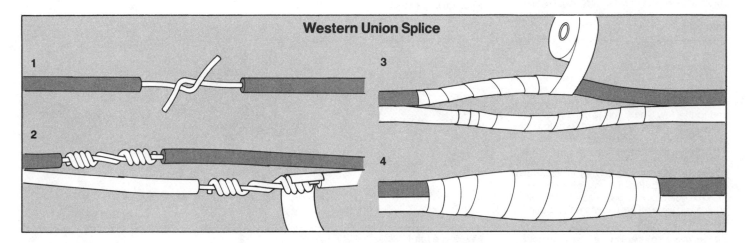

Western Union Splice

1
2
3
4

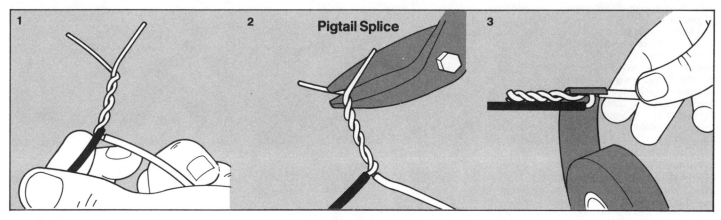

1 2 **Pigtail Splice** 3

1 Twist splice

2

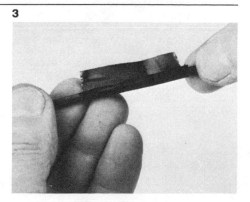

3

Soldering

To assure a permanent electrical connection always solder splices. A soldering gun with high and low heat settings is the most versatile soldering tool. Low heat (25 to 50 watts) is best for most appliances. Higher heat levels may damage internal parts, but higher levels can be used on splices not close to internal parts. A low-wattage soldering pencil and a high-wattage soldering iron can be used in place of the dual-heat gun.

Always use solder that is clearly marked as suitable for electrical work: 60/40 rosin-core solder is best. The numbers 60/40 refer to the percentage of tin and lead in the solder. A material called flux, which helps solder to spread and penetrate, must be used on solder joints. Flux also cleans the conductors and prevents tarnish from developing. The rosin in rosin-core solder automatically provides flux. **CAUTION** Never use acid-core solder or acid-core paste, which corrode electrical connections.

Tinning. Before a soldering iron or gun is used, its tip should be coated with a thin, even layer of solder, a process called tinning. First, clean the tip of the iron by sanding or filing it to bare metal. Next, snap off a short length of solder at the end of the spool by bending the short length back and forth a few times. This is done to expose the rosin flux so it will melt onto the tip before the solder does. If you are using a dual-heat soldering gun, set it for low heat. If you are tinning a high-heat iron, hold the solder against the tip before the iron reaches full heat. This will allow the flux to flow before the iron is hot enough to melt the solder. Coat the tip completely with solder and wipe off the excess with a clean cloth or some steel wool.

Soldering a splice. Tin the iron, then hold the wires to be soldered tightly against the iron's tip. Unwind a few inches of solder from the spool and hold the end of the solder against the wire, with the iron touching the other side of the wire. The iron is used to heat the wire so that the wire melts the solder rather than melting the solder directly. To make a good joint, the wire must be hot enough to melt the solder, which should flow down into the wires. After soldering, inspect the joint closely in a good light. The solder should be smooth and a bit shiny; if it is dull and grainy, the chances are that a good joint has not been made. Reheat the joint until the solder flows again. Recheck the joint for mechanical strength after it has cooled.

When taping spliced and soldered joints, use enough tape to make the new insulation about as thick as the original. Use a good brand of plastic electrical tape. Wrap the tape diagonally along the joint, covering about an inch of the old insulation at each end. Plastic tape adheres better if it is kept taut during the wrapping. Make as many turns as necessary to build the tape insulation to the desired thickness. Then cut or tear the tape and press it around itself, finishing it as smoothly as possible.

1 Tinning

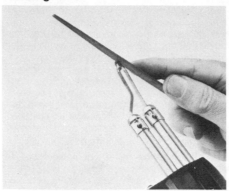

2

1 Soldering a splice

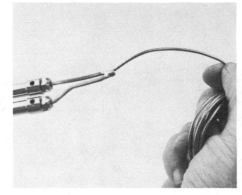

2

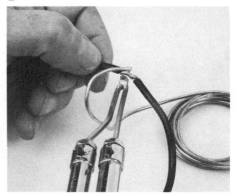

1 Taping a joint

2

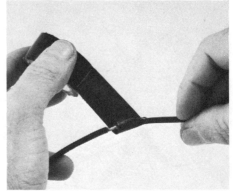

Solderless connectors

Solderless connectors of several types are used to make electrical connections between the wires inside appliances. Plastic screw-on connectors, called wire nuts, are the most common type and are satisfactory for most uses. They come in size to accomodate different wire thicknesses and different numbers of wires. If the connection is subject to vibration, as in motor-driven appliances, wrap tape around the wires and the base of the wire nut.

Wire nuts contain a tapered metal insert with spiral grooves that grip the ends of the wires when you screw on the wire nut. Trim the insulation from the wires so that when the wire nut is screwed down tight no bare wire shows.

Hold the wires together approximately parallel. Twist the wire nut clockwise onto the wires (no. 1, opposite, bottom). Check each wire to make certain it cannot be pulled free.

In high temperature areas inside appliances such as heaters and driers, ceramic wire nuts (no. 2, opposite, bottom) are used. They are installed in the same way as the plastic type.

1 Solderless connectors

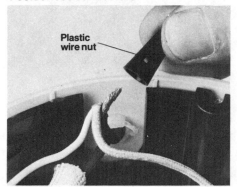

Plastic wire nut

2

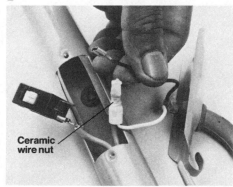

Ceramic wire nut

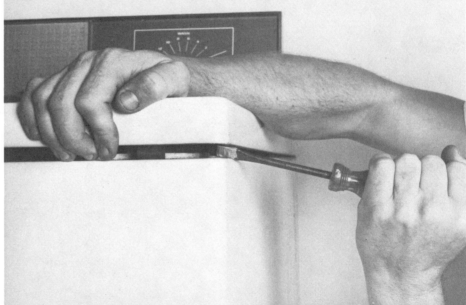
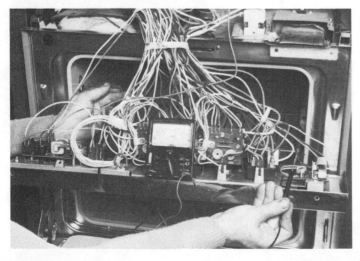
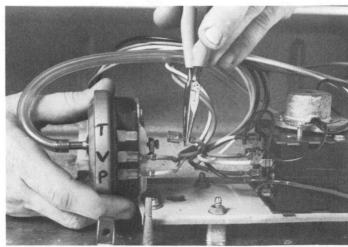

Large
Appliances

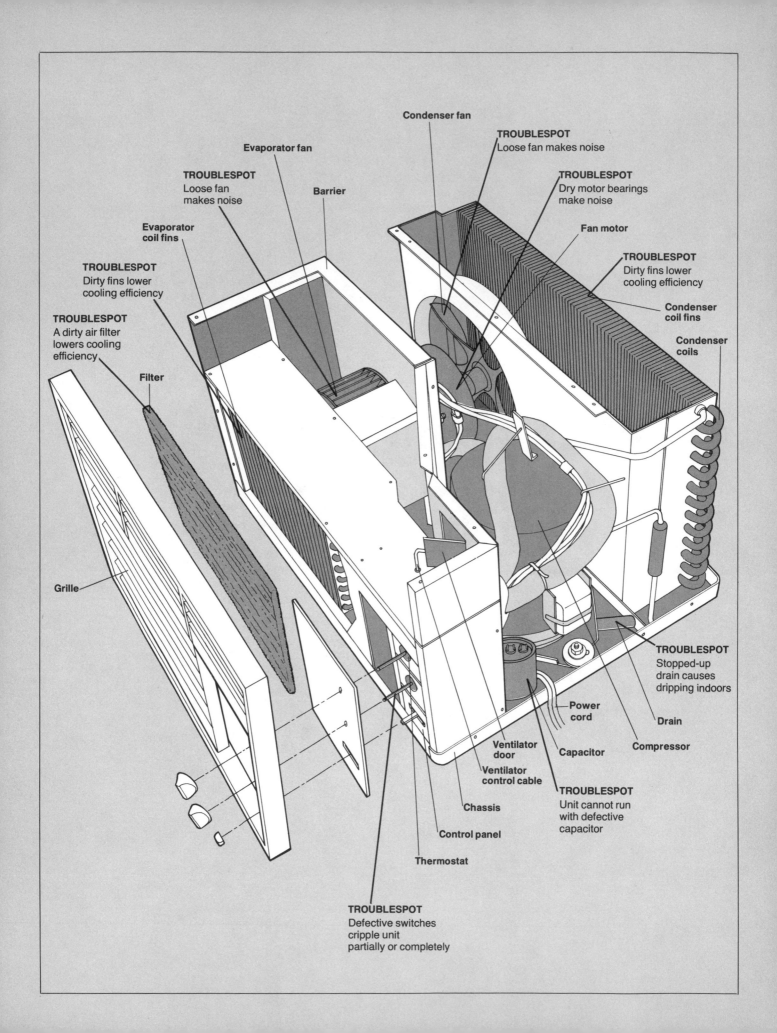

Condenser fan

TROUBLESPOT
Loose fan makes noise

Evaporator fan

TROUBLESPOT
Loose fan
makes noise

TROUBLESPOT
Dry motor bearings
make noise

Barrier

Fan motor

Evaporator
coil fins

TROUBLESPOT
Dirty fins lower
cooling efficiency

TROUBLESPOT
Dirty fins lower
cooling efficiency

Condenser
coil fins

TROUBLESPOT
A dirty air filter
lowers cooling
efficiency

Condenser
coils

Filter

Grille

TROUBLESPOT
Stopped-up
drain causes
dripping indoors

Power
cord

Drain

Ventilator
door

Capacitor

Compressor

Ventilator
control cable

TROUBLESPOT
Unit cannot run
with defective
capacitor

Chassis

Control panel

Thermostat

TROUBLESPOT
Defective switches
cripple unit
partially or completely

Air Conditioners

Air-conditioning units perform three comfort-making jobs in the home: they cool the air, dehumidify it, and filter out floating pollution. The cooling results from the constant circulation of a refrigerant around the unit (see diagram, below left). The refrigerant, usually known by its trade name, Freon, picks up heat inside the house and pumps it outside. Dehumidifying occurs at the same time but for different reasons (see diagram, below right). And the filter just behind the grille cleans the air—at least it does if you keep the filter clean! Other regular maintenance information is given here, as are simple mechanical adjustments. Some uncomplicated electrical tests and replacement procedures are explained step by step.

Anyone familiar with air conditioners knows that a problem can have several causes. Turn first to the troubleshooting chart at the end of the section for help in diagnosing the root of your unit's unhappy symptoms. Even if you would rather not do the repair suggested by the chart, you'll be ahead of the game when you discuss the matter with a repairman.

CAUTION   An air conditioner is a complicated, delicate machine. Testing and correcting problems in the cooling system itself requires tools and skills beyond the average homeowner's reach. It is better to let a trained technician handle the compressor and the refrigerant, sealed under pressure in its complicated set of tubing.

TIPS FOR ENERGY EFFICIENCY
Buy an air conditioner with a high Energy Efficiency Rating (EER).
Ratings range from 5 to 12. Any rating from 8 to 10 is good.
Buy a unit that fits your needs. The BTU rating of the unit should be appropriate for the size of the space it must cool. Consult your appliance dealer on what unit to buy.
Install a window unit on the shady side of the house. If the unit must be installed on the sunny side, provide a shade for it.
Keep air conditioner grilles and filters clean.
Keep the temperature set as high as possible. In a dehumidified room 78° F. is really not uncomfortable.
Close air ducts and chimney dampers so that cool air is not lost.
Close blinds and window shades when the sun shines in.
Don't make heat while the air conditioner is working. For example, don't run the dishwasher at the same time.

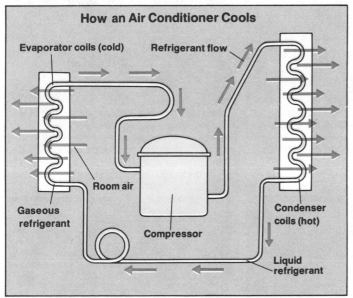

How an Air Conditioner Cools

Evaporator coils (cold) · Refrigerant flow · Room air · Gaseous refrigerant · Compressor · Condenser coils (hot) · Liquid refrigerant

The compressor continually pumps the refrigerant around the sealed cooling system. When pressurized refrigerant reaches the evaporator coils, an expansion valve lets it expand suddenly and change to a gas. It's a law of physics that a liquid changing to a gas absorbs a lot of heat. The squirrel-cage fan blows hot room air across the evaporator coils so the refrigerant has an endless supply of heat to absorb. Then the gaseous refrigerant flows toward the condenser coils, outside the room, where extreme pressure forces it to condense. Another law of physics says that a condensing gas releases a great deal of heat. The bladed fan continually forces a stream of outside air across the condenser coils, from which the air absorbs the unwanted inside heat carried there by the refrigerant.

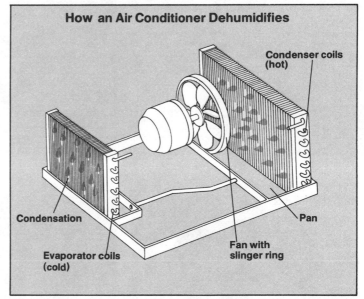

How an Air Conditioner Dehumidifies

Condenser coils (hot) · Condensation · Evaporator coils (cold) · Fan with slinger ring · Pan

Since cool air cannot hold as much moisture as hot air, the inside hot air must drop its moisture as it passes across the cooling evaporator coils. This condensed moisture drains through the unit to the pan under the hot condenser coils. There it evaporates and is blown outside. Many units have a slinger ring around the condenser fan that flips the water out of the pan onto the coils to hasten evaporation.

Getting inside

In most air-conditioning units, all the major components are mounted on a chassis that can be pulled straight out of the unit after the grille is removed. Be prepared to support the chassis on a bench or table close at hand. Some units have no mounting shell but have a removable cover and side panels. Never turn a unit upside down or on its side; something is bound to bend or break.

CAUTION Before starting to work near the wiring or the motor, discharge the capacitor to avoid the risk of shock. (See the box on discharging the capacitor, page 42.)

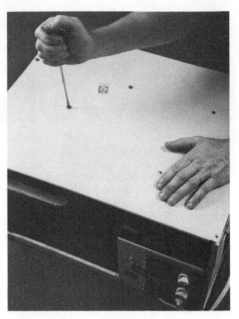

Pull the chassis out after the grille has been removed. Be careful not to damage the fragile aluminum fins or the tubing.

Top and side panels come off when retaining screws are removed. You may need a screwdriver, a Phillips screwdriver, or a hex nut driver. CAUTION Remove only those screws (if any) that hold the panels.

Regular maintenance

Do all five basic maintenance steps shown here at the beginning of every cooling season. Then clean or replace the air filter every month. Dirty filters cause more unnecessary service calls than any other complaint, and are the easiest to put right. As you work, keep an eye open for loose screws and bolts. Examine wiring for worn spots in the insulation. And at the end of the cooling season, cover the outside of the unit with a plastic sheet or the manufacturer's winter cover. It will prevent rust and save heat, too.

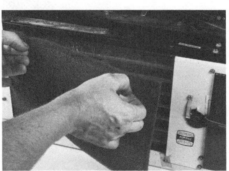

Clean the air filter at the beginning of the cooling season and once a month while the unit is being used. Wash a permanent filter in hot, sudsy water; replace other filters with exact duplicates.

Open clogged drain holes with a piece of stiff wire, so water dripping down on the evaporator side can flow through to the other side of the barrier. Check also for an outside drain hole on the condenser side. Bend the wire so that it can be turned like an auger, as shown above.

Clean condenser fins and surrounding cabinet area with the radiator attachment of a vacuum cleaner. Oily deposits should be removed with a solvent. The air filter should keep dust from accumulating on the evaporator fins, but check them to be sure.

Straighten bent fins on evaporators and condensers; they cut efficiency by blocking airflow and also cause whistling and dripping. Use a pencil, putty knife, or a fin-straightening comb. CAUTION Work carefully—the fins are fragile.

Lubricate the motor with one or two drops of SAE 10 oil in the oil holes or tubes found at both ends of the motor. Even permanently oiled motors benefit from seasonal oiling of the shaft.

Mechanical adjustments

Strange noises or unusual vibrations coming from the unit may signal the beginning of serious problems. Before sending for the repairman, check the troubleshooting chart on the following pages for possible causes. Often problems can be solved by making the simple mechanical adjustments shown here.

CAUTION Remember to discharge the capacitor first (see page 42).

The basic test (at right) is to hold the two fans, one hand on each fan, and try to turn them in opposite directions. You will discover at once if either fan is loose. Also, turn the fans in the same direction to be sure that they move freely. If the fans are hard to turn, the motor may need lubrication (see opposite page) or realignment.

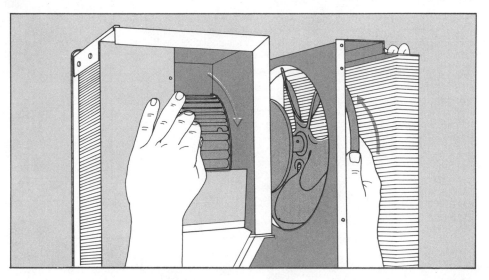

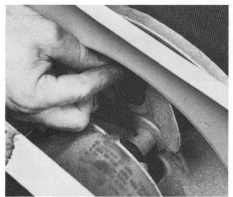

Tighten the bladed fan by turning the setscrew on its hub with a screwdriver or an Allen wrench. If your fan has a rubber hub, replace it when it is hard or cracked. A fan with broken or missing blades should be replaced, because the resulting vibration can damage the motor.

Tighten a squirrel-cage fan on its shaft with a long Allen wrench. To reach the screw on the fan shaft, insert the wrench through the hole in the fan blade.

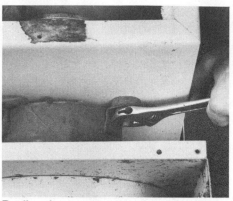

Realign the motor by first loosening the motor mounting nuts. When they are loose, the fans should turn freely. Tighten each nut a couple of turns in sequence around the mounting, testing the fans at each step, until all the nuts are tight.

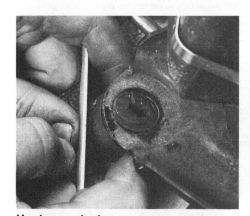

Hard or cracked compressor mounts magnify the compressor's sound. Replace deteriorated rubber mounts by unscrewing the mounting nuts and lifting the compressor to free the mounts. **CAUTION** Move the compressor as little as possible. A kinked refrigerant tube must be replaced by a repairman.

Silence a rattling exhaust vent by applying a few bits of self-sticking weather stripping around the opening. A thin layer will do the job.

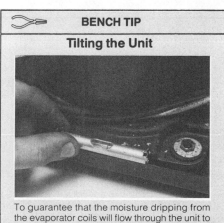

BENCH TIP

Tilting the Unit

To guarantee that the moisture dripping from the evaporator coils will flow through the unit to the outside, set the outside end of the unit about a quarter of an inch lower than the inside end. Use a level laid along the chassis to check this slight tilt. Or pour a little water beneath the evaporator coils and tilt the unit so it gradually flows toward the outside.

Electrical problems

Problems with the thermostat, the capacitor, or the selector switch cause the unit to fail completely or partially; for instance, the compressor may operate, but the fans fail, or the compressor may run continuously. Each electrical component can be tested and replaced if necessary.

CAUTION Before working inside the unit, always discharge the capacitor. (See box at right.)

When replacing any electrical part, always install an exact duplicate of the original. After finishing work and double-checking all wiring, take the added safety precaution of checking the unit for ground (see Blue Pages: *A word about safety*).

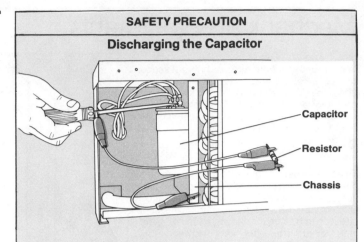

SAFETY PRECAUTION

Discharging the Capacitor

Capacitor

Resistor

Chassis

Before starting to work on the inside of any air-conditioning unit, always discharge the capacitor (there may be two). You can get a severe electrical shock if you touch a charged capacitor. With alligator clips, connect one lead of a 100,000-ohm, 2-watt resistor to the chassis, and the other to the shaft of a screwdriver. (**CAUTION** Hold the screwdriver by its insulated handle.) Then touch the screwdriver tip to each capacitor terminal in turn.

The thermostat

If the compressor runs continuously or not at all, test the thermostat. Unplug the unit, discharge the capacitor (see box above), and pull the knobs off the faceplate to get at the control panel where the thermostat is mounted.

Some older units have a sensing bulb mounted on the evaporator fins and connected to the thermostat by a thin tube; handle it carefully. All newer models have a bimetallic temperature-sensitive switch inside the thermostat. Label the leads to the thermostat and remove them. To prepare the thermostat for testing, disconnect one end of its resistor (if it has one) with a soldering iron.

1 **To test and replace a thermostat,** take out the screws that hold the thermostat to the control panel. Disconnect the leads to the thermostat, marking them so that you can connect the replacement properly. **CAUTION** If your unit has a sensing bulb, disengage it from the unit carefully.

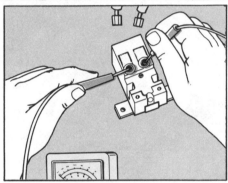

2 Attach probes from a VOM or a continuity tester to the thermostat terminals (see Blue Pages: *Electrical testers*.) With the thermostat in the OFF position, there should be no continuity; at any other setting there should be continuity. After this test, put the thermostat in the freezer for fifteen minutes and test again. The cold thermostat should show no continuity at any setting.

The capacitor

A faulty capacitor will stop the compressor dead, and the fans, too, if they are on the same circuit. Unplug the unit and look for the capacitor behind the grille. If it is not there, take the chassis out to get at the capacitor near the compressor or the fan motor.

CAUTION Discharge the capacitor before working on it. Read the box above.

If the capacitor vent is blown, or the capacitor bulges or leaks oil, replace it.

Test the capacitor with a VOM set at RX1 (see Blue Pages: *Electrical testers*). Disconnect one lead to the capacitor and touch the meter probes to the capacitor terminals. If the needle jumps to HIGH and then returns to 0, the capacitor is OK. If the needle holds at HIGH or does not move, the capacitor is bad. If your capacitor has three terminals, test the terminal at each side with the central terminal.

When replacing a defective capacitor, label the leads as you disconnect the old capacitor so you can connect the new one properly. Pull the leads straight off the terminals. Always use a capacitor of the same peak voltage and rated capacity as the original.

The selector switch

If neither fan nor compressor runs at any selector switch setting, and both thermostat and capacitor test OK (see opposite page), then the switch may be defective. A continuity tester will confirm this (see Blue Pages: *Electrical testers*). If the thermostat is OK and the fans run at one switch setting but not at another, examine all leads connected to the switch. If any terminal appears burned or any insulation on the wires is discolored, replace the switch and repair bad leads. If the compressor runs when the switch is set to COOL but the fans do not, the fan motor is probably bad.

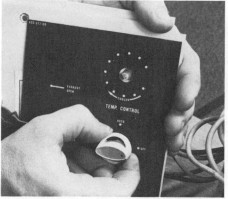

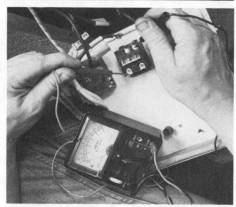

1 **To remove the selector switch,** pry off the control knobs, take off the faceplate, and remove the control panel. Label the switch relative to the faceplate so you can tell OFF from ON. Label the leads before you disconnect them from the switch.

2 Check the switch for continuity at all settings. All settings should show continuity except OFF. If any setting is defective, replace the entire switch.

Central air conditioning

Central air conditioners operate the same way single-room units do, but the components are separated by many feet of piping. The diagram at right shows central air conditioning installed in a home with a forced-air heating system. The evaporator (cooling) coils fit inside the furnace itself, so the furnace blower forces cool, dehumidified air through the same ducts that carry hot air in wintertime. The compressor and condenser coils stand outside the house in a separate cabinet that is connected to the evaporator (called the A-frame in such installations) by insulated tubing. You can't reach the evaporator coils because they're sealed inside the furnace, but don't forget to clean the air filter or replace it regularly. Keep the outside cabinet clean and unobstructed.

If your home has hot water heating, air ducts must be installed for central air conditioning, and the evaporator coils and blower are usually placed together in the attic. In this case, a hose leads the condensed water from the evaporator outside to a drain. Be sure this hose is open and running during the cooling season.

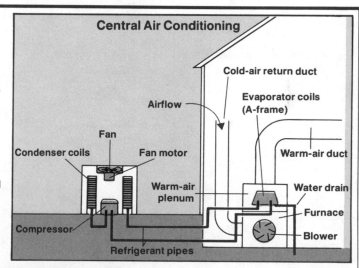

Central Air Conditioning

Cold-air return duct

Airflow

Evaporator coils (A-frame)

Fan

Condenser coils

Fan motor

Warm-air duct

Warm-air plenum

Water drain

Compressor

Furnace

Blower

Refrigerant pipes

Remove any debris

Clean the inside

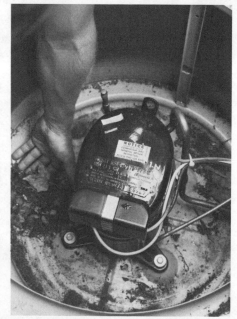

Remove any debris blocking the condenser coils in the outdoor section of the central air conditioning installation so airflow remains unobstructed. Anything on the coils—from leaves to spider webs—cuts down efficiency.

Clean the inside of the outdoor cabinet regularly. Dirt on the compressor makes it work harder and become hotter. See *Mechanical adjustments*, page 41, for procedures to use in checking the fan and fan motor. When the cooling season ends, protect the unit with a heavy plastic cover or a tarp.

Room Air Conditioners Troubleshooting Chart

WHAT'S WRONG	REASONS WHY	WHAT TO DO
Unit does not run at all.	No power reaching unit	Turn off unit; check for blown fuse or tripped circuit breaker; test outlet (see Blue Pages, *Electrical testers*).
	Defective line cord	Test cord and replace if necessary.
	Defective selector switch	Test switch.
	Defective thermostat	Test thermostat.
	Defective capacitor	Test capacitor.
	Low refrigerant level	Call repairman.
	Defective compressor	Call repairman.
Fans run but compressor does not (unit does not cool).	Defective thermostat	Test thermostat.
	Condenser fins clogged with dirt	Clean fins.
	Wrong voltage on line	Check line voltage.
	Defective overload switch	Check switch.
	Defective running capacitor	Check capacitor.
	Defective compressor	Call repairman.
	Defective selector switch	Check switch.
Unit continually blows fuses or trips circuit breaker.	Unit restarted too soon	Wait at least five minutes before restarting.
	Circuit overloaded	Don't run any other appliance on the air-conditioner circuit. Use only the recommended time-delay fuse.
	Short circuit in wiring	Make sure all electrical connections are tight and no exposed wires are touching metal.
	Defective compressor	Call repairman.
	Defective capacitor	Test capacitor.
	Low refrigerant level	Call repairman.
Unit runs but does not cool properly.	Thermostat set wrong	Turn thermostat to cooler setting.
	Filter clogged with dirt	Clean or replace filter.
	Dirty condenser	Vacuum condenser; use solvent to remove oily dirt.
	Unit too small for the job	Ask repairman or appliance dealer for advice. Write Ass'n of Home Appliance Manufacturers (20 N. Wacker Drive, Chicago, Ill. 60606) for a Cooling-Load Estimate Form for a room air conditioner.
	Outside temperature too cool	Don't operate unit when outside temperature falls below 70°F.
	Loose blower fan	Check and adjust fan.
	Air leaks around unit	Seal all joints around unit. Make sure nothing blocks front grille.
	Leaking refrigerant	Put thick soap suds on refrigerant line joints. If bubbles swell, refrigerant is leaking. Call repairman.
	Low refrigerant level	Call repairman.
Compressor turns on and off frequently.	Dirty evaporator	Clean evaporator.
	Dirty condenser	Clean and straighten condenser fins.
	Defective fan motor	Test motor. If motor hums but does not turn, check for obstructions around fan. Lubricate fan motor and fan bearings.
	Dirty filter	Clean or replace filter.
	Low refrigerant level	Call repairman.

Room Air Conditioners Troubleshooting Chart

WHAT'S WRONG	REASONS WHY	WHAT TO DO
Frost forms on evaporator.	Dirty filter	Clean filter and all air-flow areas.
	Outside temperature too low	Don't run unit when outside temperature is below 70°F.
	Leaking refrigerant	Call repairman.
Unit is noisy.	Loose panels, trim, screws, or supports	Tighten all screws and supports; if window rattles, use a wooden wedge to force it tight.
	Loose fan blades	Check and tighten fan screws.
	Worn compressor mounts	Check and replace.
	Dry fan motor bearings	Check and lubricate bearings.
	Tubing rattling	Carefully bend tubing so that it does not touch nearby parts.
	Bent evaporator fins (whistling noises)	Clean and straighten fins.
Water drips from inside unit. (NOTE: outside dripping is normal especially in humid weather.)	Clogged drain	Clean drain.
	Unit not installed correctly	Adjust unit so that outside is 1/4 inch lower than inside.
	Slinger ring needs adjustment	If your unit has a slinger ring, it should run 1/16 inch above the pan for best water pickup.
Unit smells.	Clogged drain holes (musty odor)	Open drain holes and clean pan.
	Dirty evaporator (oil or tobacco odors)	Vacuum fins; spray with deodorizer.

Central Air Conditioning Troubleshooting Chart

Most problems connected with central air conditioning systems are like those described above for room air conditioners. Problems peculiar to central air conditioners are given below. NOTE: Central air conditioning systems installed in forced-air heating systems have the condenser coil (A-frame) mounted inside the furnace – warm air plenum; it should be checked by a serviceman.

WHAT'S WRONG	REASONS WHY	WHAT TO DO
Water leaks into walls or ceiling.	Clogged drain hose from condenser pan (in attic installations)	Make sure hose can empty freely.
Unit cycles on and off.	Leaves and rubbish clogging evaporator unit; fan blocked	Keep evaporator unit clean.
	Hot sun beating on evaporator unit	Make shade for the unit (tree, wall, etc.).
	Insulation has fallen off feed line.	Secure insulation firmly to line; replace worn-out insulation.

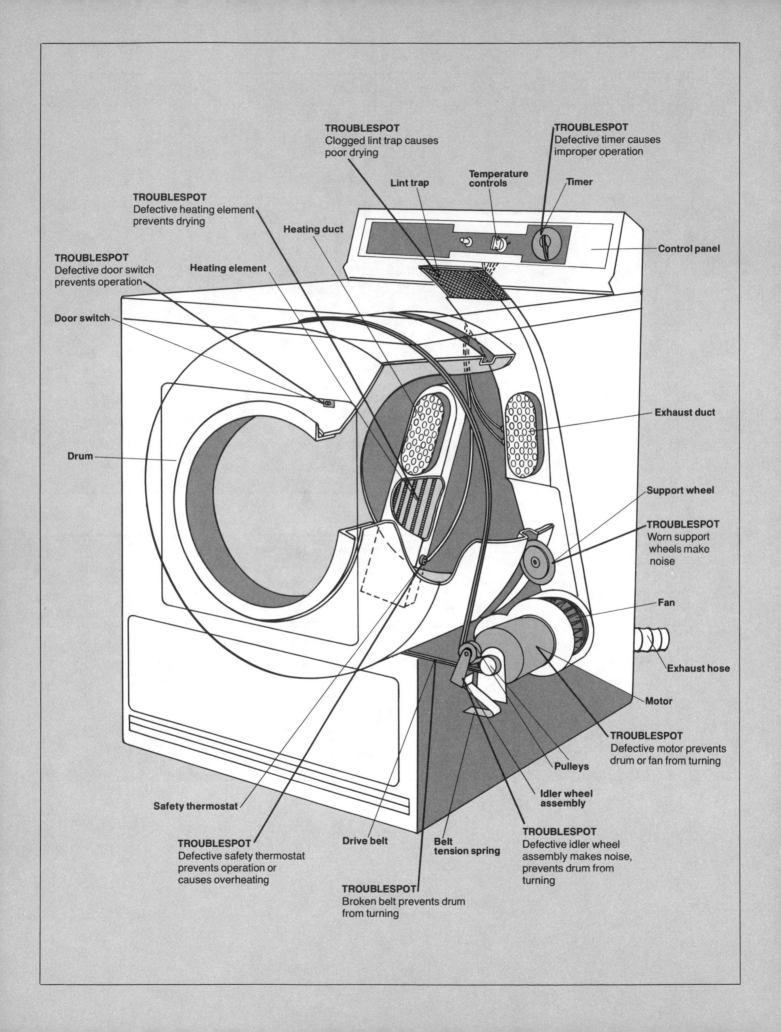

TROUBLESPOT
Clogged lint trap causes
poor drying

TROUBLESPOT
Defective timer causes
improper operation

Temperature
controls

Lint trap

Timer

TROUBLESPOT
Defective heating element
prevents drying

Heating duct

Control panel

TROUBLESPOT
Defective door switch
prevents operation

Heating element

Door switch

Exhaust duct

Drum

Support wheel

TROUBLESPOT
Worn support
wheels make
noise

Fan

Exhaust hose

Motor

TROUBLESPOT
Defective motor prevents
drum or fan from turning

Pulleys

Idler wheel
assembly

Safety thermostat

TROUBLESPOT
Defective idler wheel
assembly makes noise,
prevents drum from
turning

TROUBLESPOT
Defective safety thermostat
prevents operation or
causes overheating

Drive belt

Belt
tension spring

TROUBLESPOT
Broken belt prevents drum
from turning

Clothes Driers
Electric

Clothes driers are generally robust, long-lived machines. Their design and operation are based on simple principles. There is a source of heat, either an electric heating element or a gas burner; there is a motor that turns a drum to tumble the clothes and also turns a fan to circulate the hot air; there are a few controls, either a simple on/off timer or perhaps an elaborate panel offering choices in drying cycles and temperatures. Some safety switches and thermostats complete the electrical setup.

Most owners encounter few problems with the electrical parts of a drier until the appliance begins to wear out, after a long and useful life. Complaints of "poor drying" can usually be traced to clogged lint traps and exhaust systems, so the most important regular maintenance you can do is to keep the unit lint-free.

The most common mechanical problem usually involves a broken drive belt. On some models it may be possible to put a new belt on without taking the drum out, but it's a cumbersome process in any case. Read the suggestions on the next page for the easiest procedure. Take a good look at the diagram that shows how the belt is threaded around the drum, the motor, and the idler wheel, so you can get a new one on right.

A common complaint about driers is "too much noise." The bottom box at right gives hints for solving this problem.

Instructions are given on page 50 for testing the door switch and the centrifugal switch. If you can read your unit's wiring diagram, you can test and replace any other switches your model may have, as well as the timer. You must open up the back to make tests and repairs on the thermostat and the heating element. Before working on an electric drier, carefully read the Blue Pages, which describe electricity and electrical testing, and become thoroughly familiar with your volt-ohm meter (VOM). For information about a gas clothes drier's burner, turn to page 52.

CAUTION Most electric clothes driers operate on 240 volts AC, which is potentially deadly. Always pull the plug or turn the power off at the circuit breaker before starting to work inside the drier, and make sure no one turns the power on while you are working.

TIPS FOR ENERGY EFFICIENCY

Clean the lint trap after each drying.

Clean exhaust vent and hoses regularly.

Use the lowest temperature setting practical or recommended for fabric type.

Dry clothes only to damp-dry condition if you intend to iron them.

Do light drying in one load, heavy drying in another.

Do several loads consecutively to save heat stored up in the drier.

Don't overdry clothes. Natural fibers like wool and cotton need to retain a little moisture to avoid wrinkling.

Install the drier where it can get fresh, dry air.

In summer, vent the drier outside to reduce heat and humidity in the house. In winter, consider venting the drier inside, using a lint filter attachment, to keep heat and humidity levels up.

On a sunny day, try the clothesline.

Reducing Drier Noises

As driers grow older they may develop annoying noises. Here's how to reduce them.

Tighten loose drive belts. There should be about ¼ inch of play in a belt when it's pressed halfway between the pulleys.

Loosen tight belts. Tight belts put a strain on all moving parts, causing wear and noise.

Tighten loose fans, impellers, and pulleys by screwing the shaft setscrews in tight.

Make sure the drier sits level. Use a spirit level to check side to side and front to back.

Sometimes lint or an object becomes wedged between the drum and the cabinet. If the drum binds in any spot, check for an obstruction.

Replace worn support wheels (see page 49).

Cleaning air passages

Regular cleaning of lint traps, air vents, and exhaust hoses is a must: clogged air passages cripple the unit's capacity to dry clothes, thus wasting energy. In many models the lint trap is located on top of the unit, as shown below. For another location, see page 53.

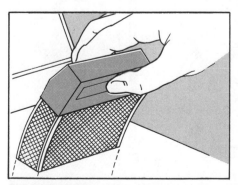

Pull the lint trap out of the drier after every drying session and remove the lint.

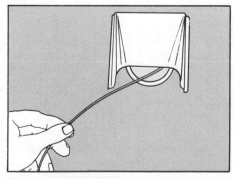

Check the outdoor air vent once a year to make sure there is no obstruction.

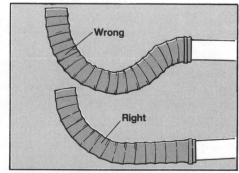

Remove the exhaust hose annually and clean it out. Don't let any dips or kinks develop, as they trap lint. Seal hose joints with duct tape.

Getting inside from the front

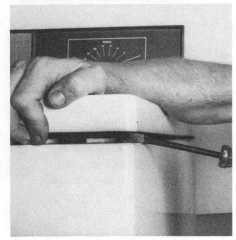

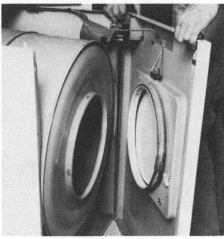

To open the top, pry it up carefully but firmly at the side (near the clips) with a screwdriver.

Wrap the screwdriver end with tape or paper to prevent damage to the finish. When the top pops off the clip, lift it up.

If your unit has screws at the back of the top, remove them, pull the top forward, and then lift it up at the front.

To get the front loose, snap it away from the sides and bottom. Some models may have screws to remove. If there is a front-mounted timer, be careful not to damage the wires attached to it. Label and disconnect them if necessary. On some models, the front panel supports the drum; in such a case, have a block of wood handy to prop up the drum.

To get the drum out, lift it slightly and pull it forward off the support wheels. Reach underneath the drum and slip the drive belt off the idler wheel assembly and motor drive shaft. Lift the drum out of the unit. NOTE: If the drum is supported on a center shaft; open the back of the unit and remove screws or rings holding the drum to the shaft. Then lift the drum out.

Replacing the drive belt

To replace a broken drive belt (or a broken idler wheel assembly), remove the drum as described above and remove the old belt. (In the model shown here, it's easier to install the new belt if you have first tipped the unit on its back.) Put the drum in, slipping it over the support wheels. Rotate the drum slowly to seat the gasket (if there is one). Slip the new belt around the drum, over the idler wheel, and over the motor drive shaft, so that it's in the S-pattern shown at near left. Some models have two drive belts, in the pattern shown below.

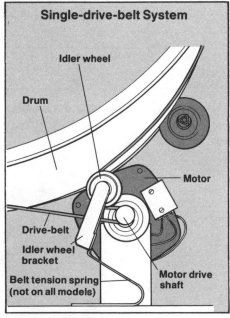

Install single drive belts in the S-pattern shown here.

Two-drive-belt systems look like the illustration at right. Remove the belt tension spring and the idler pulley first; then the belts come off easily. Replace both belts together.

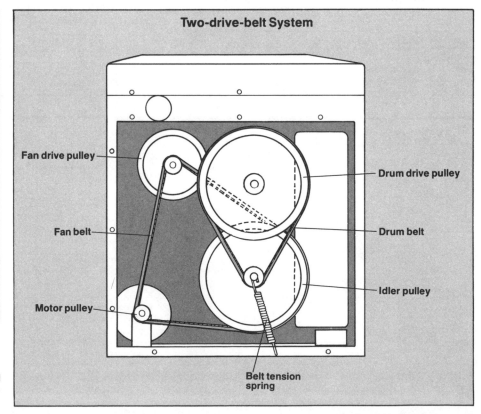

Replacing support wheels

Rumbling, bumping noises in the drier can be caused by worn support wheels. Turn the drum by hand and listen closely; if you hear several bumps for each revolution of the drum, the wheels are probably worn out.

To inspect or replace the wheels, turn off the power, lay unit on its back, open the unit from the front and take out the drum (see opposite page). Remove worn wheels and replace them.

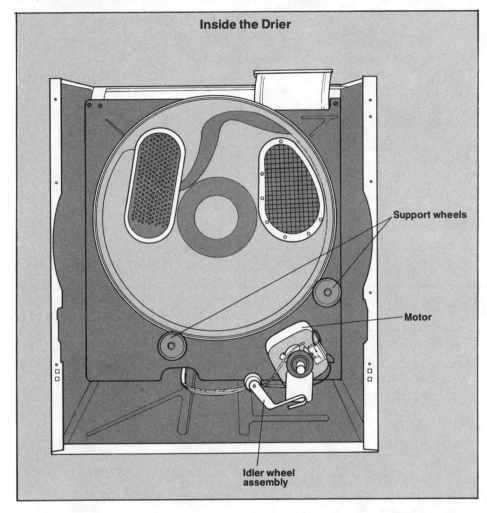

Inside the Drier

Support wheels

Motor

Idler wheel assembly

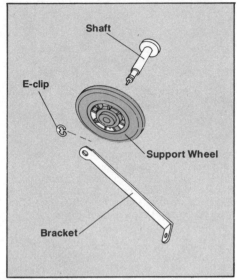

Shaft

E-clip

Support Wheel

Bracket

To remove a support wheel, pry off the retaining clip. Slip the wheel off its shaft and replace it with a new one. Some models may have a bracket screwed to the bottom of the cabinet and the shaft; take the screws out to get the wheel off.

Electrical problems

Some driers, have only a simple timer and one heat level. Others, like the one shown at the right, offer different heat levels and various heating and cooling cycles. In any case, defective timers and switches can be tested for continuity (see Blue Pages: *Electrical testers*) and replaced if defective (see instructions for replacing a timer under *Dishwashers,* page 62). Always install parts identical to those discarded; a nonmatching part can cause electrical failure.

To get inside the control panel, turn off the power, remove the screws that attach the panel to the cabinet and lay the panel down.

To test a push-button on/off switch in the control panel for continuity, pull one power lead off the switch and attach VOM probes to the terminals. There should be continuity with the button pushed in and no continuity with it out. Replace a switch that fails this test.

Door switch

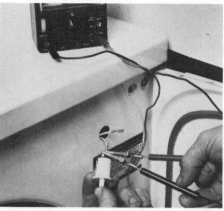

Testing the Centrifugal Switch

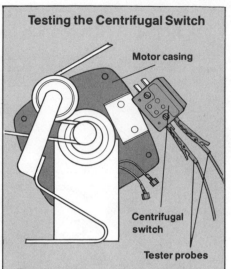

Motor casing

Centrifugal switch

Tester probes

1 **Check the door switch** if there's power to the unit, but it doesn't run. Pry the switch carefully out of the front panel with a screwdriver in order to test it for continuity (see Blue Pages: *Electrical testers*). On some models the switch may be screwed into the panel.

2 Turn off the power, disconnect one power lead to the switch, and attach VOM probes to the switch terminals. There should be continuity when the button is pressed and no continuity otherwise. Replace a switch that fails these tests.

Test the centrifugal switch for continuity if the door switch is OK and there's power to the unit but it doesn't run. Check your unit's wiring diagram to locate the connections. If the switch shows no continuity, replace it. This switch is sometimes mounted on the motor casing and sometimes inside the motor.

Getting inside from the back

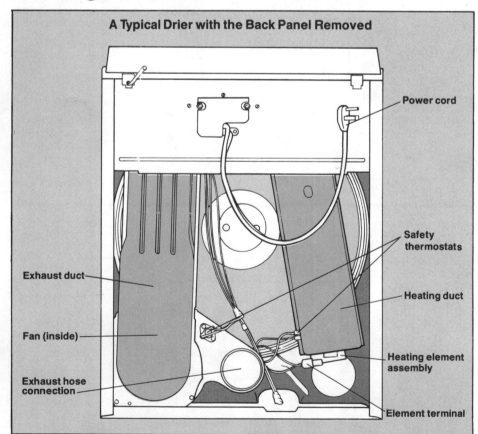

A Typical Drier with the Back Panel Removed

Power cord

Safety thermostats

Heating duct

Heating element assembly

Element terminal

Exhaust duct

Fan (inside)

Exhaust hose connection

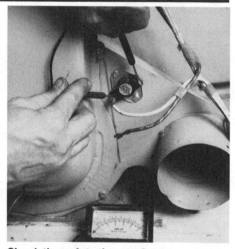

Check the safety thermostat (also called the overheat protector) for resistance if the drier doesn't heat. Turn the power off. Set your VOM at RX1. Disconnect one of the power leads to the thermostat, and attach VOM probes to the terminals. You should read 0 ohms. If the reading is high, the part is defective. Unscrew it from the cabinet and replace it with a duplicate.

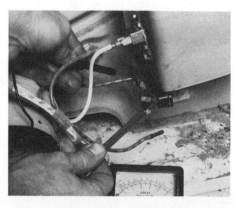

Check the heating element's resistance (right) if the drier heats poorly or not at all. Turn off the power and disconnect the leads to the element. Attach VOM probes to the element terminals. With the meter at RX1, it should read between 8 and 20 ohms resistance. A higher or no reading means a defective element. Then test the element for ground by touching one probe to the heating duct and one to a terminal; if there is low resistance (less than infinity) the element is grounded and defective. Replace it with a duplicate.

Replacing a heating element

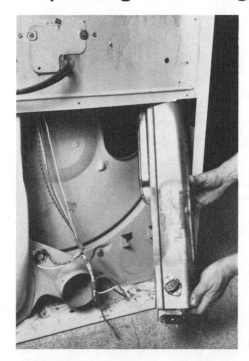

1 **To remove a heating element** (left), turn off the power and disconnect the power leads to the element. Remove the screws that attach the heating duct to the cabinet and lift it out. You may have to remove the top panels as well as the back to reach all the duct screws.

2 To remove the element from the heating duct, take out the screw that holds the element mounting bracket to the duct. Pull the element out. Element defects are shown at right. When installing an element, be very careful not to bend or stretch the coils; if they touch the heating duct they will ground the element.

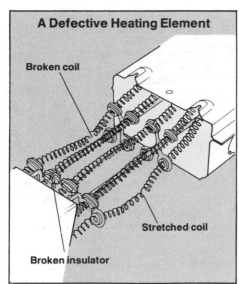

A Defective Heating Element

Broken coil

Stretched coil

Broken insulator

An element assembly with any of these defects must be replaced.

Electric Clothes Driers Troubleshooting Chart

WHAT'S WRONG	REASONS WHY	WHAT TO DO
Drier doesn't run at all.	Door open	Shut door tightly.
	No power at outlet	Check fuse box/circuit breaker.
	Loose wiring to motor	Tighten connections.
	Defective door switch	Check switch and replace.
	Defective centrifugal switch	Check switch and replace.
	Defective wiring between outlet and terminal block	Call electrician.
	Defective timer	Check timer and replace.
	Defective motor	Call repairman.
Motor runs, but drum doesn't turn.	Blocked drum	Open unit and check around drum to find obstruction.
	Broken drive belt	Replace belt
	Broken idler wheel assembly	Check and replace.
	Worn support wheel	Check and replace.
Drum turns, but drier doesn't dry.	Clogged lint trap or exhaust vent	Clean trap and vent.
	Defective safety thermostat	Check and replace.
	Defective heating element	Check and replace.
	Defective timer	Check and replace.
Drier dries poorly or takes too long.	Clogged lint trap or exhaust vent	Clean trap and vent.
	Overloaded drier	Reduce load.
	Clothes too wet	Wring clothes out first.
	Fan loose on shaft	Tighten fan setscrew.
	Worn-out door gasket	Replace gasket (not on all models).
Drier doesn't shut off at end of cycle.	Defective timer	Replace timer.
	Defective dampness-sensor system	If your unit has this type of electronic control, call a repairman.

CLOTHES DRIERS
Gas

Gas clothes driers are virtually the same as electric driers, except that the heat is made by a gas burner. This means that the mechanical and electrical matters (except for the element) discussed in the previous section on electric driers apply to gas driers as well. Read pages 47 to 51 for general information about driers, tips on energy efficiency, cleaning procedures, getting inside the unit, replacing a worn-out drive belt, and checking various switches.

Problems connected with the gas burner should be left to the gas company repairman, with two exceptions. If the pilot light goes out, relight it, following the directions in your owner's manual. If you have a flameless igniter instead of a pilot light, you can test and replace it if the burner fails to light (see the opposite page).

If the drier dries poorly, remove the grille over the burner and check the burner flames. If they are yellow or if there is a roaring sound, the air/gas mixture is incorrect. Call a serviceman to adjust it. Check the troubleshooting chart on the previous page for solutions to mechanical and electrical problems.

Don't attempt to move the drier; you may rupture a gas line or weaken a gas connection, inviting gas leaks. Call the gas company if the unit has to be moved.

CAUTIONS
If you smell gas around the drier, turn off the gas valve near the burner and call the gas company. Ventilate the room.
Whenever you work inside the unit, turn the gas valve off.
Don't smoke while working inside the unit.
If you can't reach a part you want to work on without moving the unit, call the gas company to help.

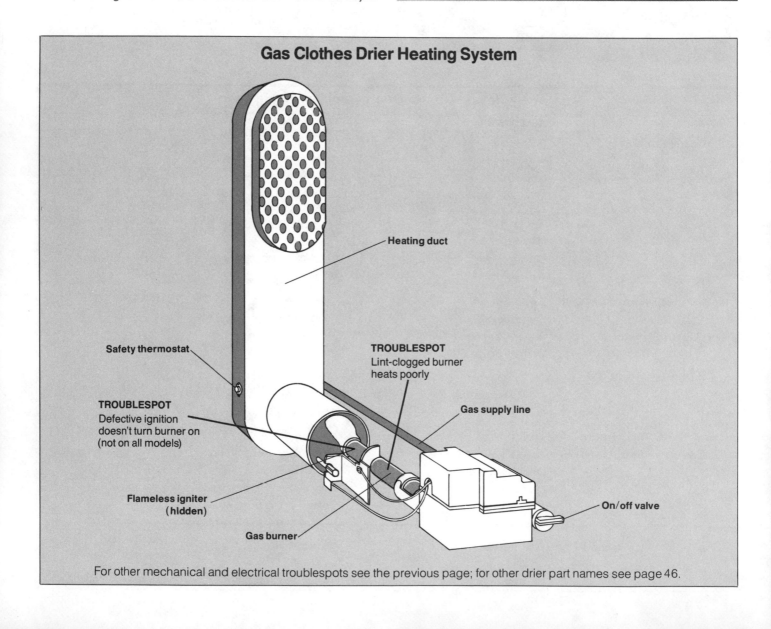

Gas Clothes Drier Heating System

Heating duct

Safety thermostat

TROUBLESPOT
Lint-clogged burner
heats poorly

Gas supply line

TROUBLESPOT
Defective ignition
doesn't turn burner on
(not on all models)

On/off valve

Flameless igniter
(hidden)

Gas burner

For other mechanical and electrical troublespots see the previous page; for other drier part names see page 46.

Cleaning air passages

Clean the lint trap after each drying cycle. A lint trap mounted just inside the door is shown at right; another type is shown at the bottom of page 47. Remove the grille over the burner occasionally and check to make sure that lint has not collected around the burner air intake. Also check the exhast hose and vent (see page 47) and make sure there are no obstructions.

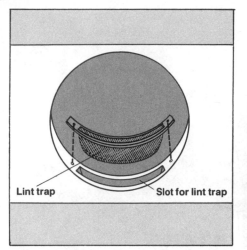

Lint trap   Slot for lint trap

Clean the lint trap after each drying cycle. If you don't keep the lint trap clean, the drier won't dry efficiently.

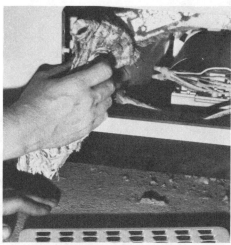

Remove the grille and wipe away any accumulations of lint and dust around the gas burner.

Checking the flameless igniter

If your drier's gas burner doesn't light and you have a flameless igniter (glow coil), first make sure there is electrical power reaching the unit (the drum will turn if there is). Then check the igniter, following this procedure: turn off the power and shut off the gas valve inside the drier. Remove the gas burner and test its igniter for resistance as described here.

After the burner has been reinstalled, check the connection for gas leaks: brush the connection with soapy water; if the bubbles expand, the connection is not tight enough.

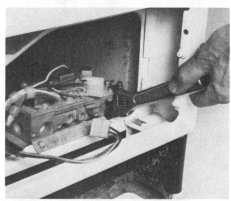

1 **Loosen the nut** that connects the gas line to the burner. Push the gas line gently aside.

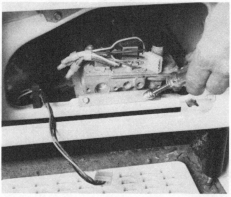

2 Remove the screws that secure the burner mounting bracket to the drier cabinet.

3 Disconnect the wires attached to the burner and lift it carefully out of the drier.

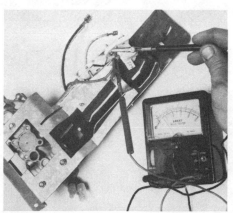

4 Lay the burner upside down and remove one wire to the igniter. Attach VOM probes to the igniter terminals. With the VOM set at RX1, you should read about 100 ohms resistance. If the igniter passes this test, the fault is elsewhere. Call a repairman.

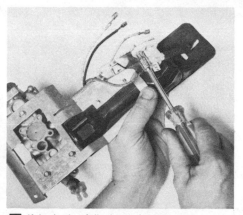

5 If the igniter fails the resistance test, unscrew it from the burner and take it to an appliance dealer for a duplicate to install.

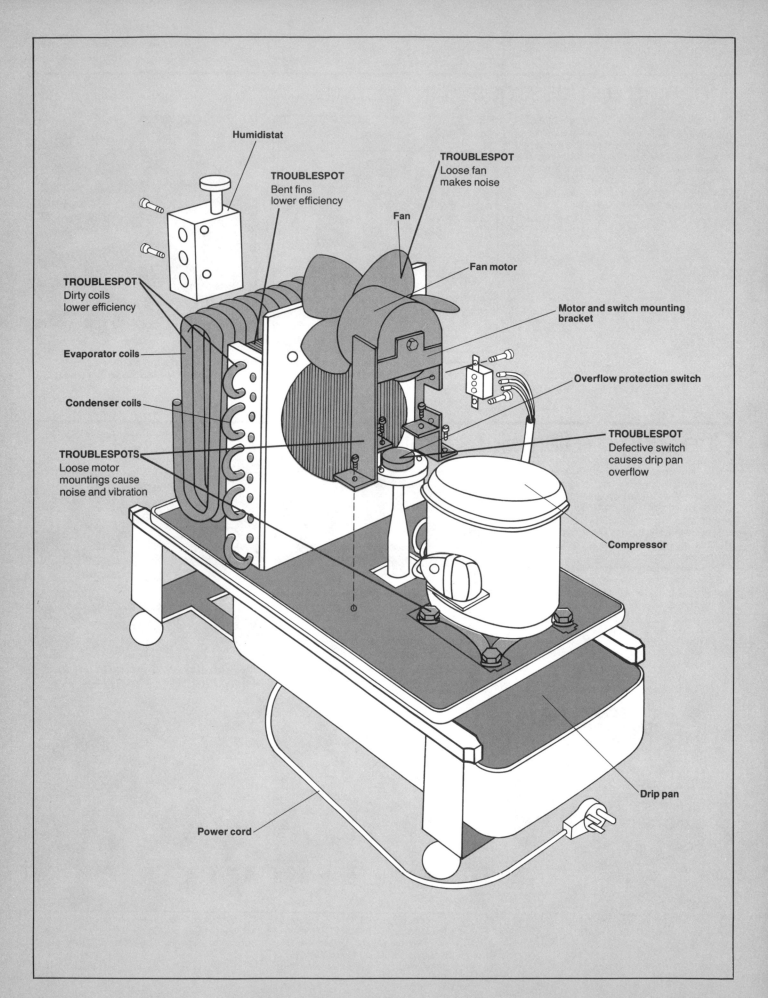

Humidistat

TROUBLESPOT
Bent fins
lower efficiency

TROUBLESPOT
Loose fan
makes noise

Fan

Fan motor

TROUBLESPOT
Dirty coils
lower efficiency

Motor and switch mounting bracket

Evaporator coils

Overflow protection switch

Condenser coils

TROUBLESPOT
Defective switch
causes drip pan
overflow

TROUBLESPOTS
Loose motor
mountings cause
noise and vibration

Compressor

Drip pan

Power cord

Dehumidifiers

High humidity produces not only discomfort but also musty odors, mildewed leather and fabrics, rusting tools, swelling wood (sticking drawers), sweating basement walls, dripping pipes, and peeling paint. Dehumidifiers get rid of these annoyances. A dehumidifier operates on the principle that cold air can't hold as much moisture as hot air. By blowing warm, moist room air across the cold coils of a refrigeration unit, the dehumidifier forces the air to drop its moisture, which collects in a pan beneath the unit. (For more information on the refrigeration cycle, see page 39.) Like air conditioners and refrigerators, dehumidifiers require a trained technician to work on the refrigeration components. But anyone can and should clean a dehumidifier regularly, and make the simple lubrication and bolt-tightening adjustments shown here. You will also find directions here for testing and replacing other components. If your unit doesn't have a safety thermostat to turn it off at low temperatures, read *When to use a dehumidifier*, below.

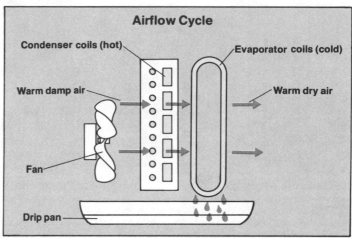

Airflow Cycle

Condenser coils (hot) Evaporator coils (cold)

Warm damp air Warm dry air

Fan

Drip pan

A dehumidifier has the same components as an air conditioner, running in the same refrigeration cycle. But the components are arranged in different order in a dehumidifier; they take moisture out of the air, like an air conditioner, but don't cool the air. The dehumidifier does not transfer the heat generated in the refrigeration cycle outside the room.

Getting inside

Dehumidifiers are easy to get into since most units have a one-piece cover. Sometimes there is a control switch attached to the cover, as on the model shown here; it must be removed before the cover can be pried off. Before opening the unit, unplug the power, then carefully pull the knobs off the grille.

1 **To get inside the humidifier,** check the grille for screws. If it has no screws, tip out the bottom far enough to get your hands in, then push the bottom back in to snap out the grille. If the grille has screws, remove them and lift it out.

2 If the unit has a humidistat mounted on the cover, remove the mounting screws and lift it away. If there is a grounding wire between the cover and the chassis, disconnect it. Then lift the cover straight up and off.

When to Use a Dehumidifier

Dehumidifiers are designed to work in warm, moist air—roughly above 65°F. and 60% relative humidity. The graph, right, gives more detailed limits. Don't run the unit if temperature and humidity fall in the colored area. If you do, the unit may ice up, blocking the refrigerant line and damaging the compressor. To protect against such damage, you can install an inexpensive de-icer thermostat—you will find them at stores that sell refrigerator parts—which will automatically shut down the unit if the line starts to freeze.

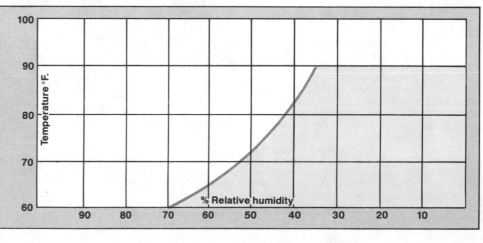

Temperature °F. / % Relative humidity

Regular maintenance

Clean and lubricate the dehumidifier every six months, or more often if its environment is particularly dirty. Dirt and dust on coils, fan, and motor reduce efficiency. Always unplug the unit when working inside, except as noted for cleaning the evaporator coils.

To clean the evaporator coils, remove the cover, plug in the unit, and turn it on. **CAUTION** Touch only the shaft of the switch. After a few moments of operation, the dirt will become soft enough to remove. Unplug the unit and scrape the coils with a wooden stick. Work quickly but don't damage the coils.

Clean the condenser coils and all other areas you can reach with a vacuum cleaner to remove dust and lint. Be very careful not to bend the evaporator coil fins. If there is a drain hole under the evaporator coils, make sure it is unclogged.

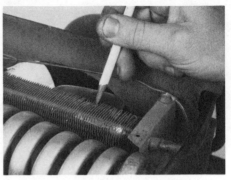

Straighten bent fins on the condenser coils. The easiest tool to use is a lead pencil, but whatever you use, be sure to work gently so as not to damage the fragile coils beneath.

Tighten the fan if it is loose on its shaft. In some models you may have to remove the fan motor from the chassis to work on the fan (see *Getting the motor out*, opposite).

Lubricate the motor with a few drops of light oil in the oil holes at both ends of the motor. If there aren't any holes, put a couple of drops of oil on the motor shaft where it enters the motor casing.

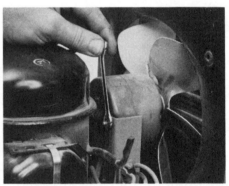

Tighten the motor mounting nuts during the twice-yearly cleaning of the unit, or whenever unusual vibration suggests that they might be loose. After tightening, give the fan a few turns by hand to make sure it doesn't strike anything.

Electrical problems

If the drip pan overflows, suspect a faulty overflow protection switch (if your unit has one) and test it for continuity.

Some models have a simple float switch instead of the electrical type shown here. The float raises a lever that opens a switch to stop the unit. This type should show no continuity when the float is up, continuity when the float is down (see Blue Pages: *Electrical testers*).

If the unit fails to turn on or runs all the time, you have a defective humidistat, which operates like a thermostat but responds to humidity in the air. In extremely humid conditions, the unit may of course run all the time. Before testing either switch, unplug the unit. Disconnect at least one power lead from the switch you are testing.

On the model shown, the motor, fan, and overflow protection switch come out as a single unit when the mounting bracket bolts are removed. Be careful not to damage the condenser coil fins or any tubing while removing the motor.

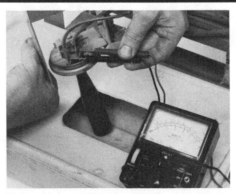

To test the overflow protection switch, attach VOM probes to the switch terminals. With the switch out of water, it should show no continuity. When you lower the switch's flexible tube into water, it should show continuity. If the switch shows continuity out of water, or no continuity in water, replace it.

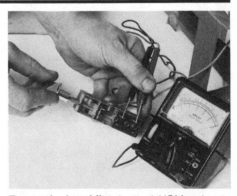

To test the humidistat, attach VOM probes to its terminals. With the humidistat in the OFF position, it should show no continuity. As you turn the humidistat through its range of settings, it should show continuity at some point (this will depend on the humidity when you make the test). If the humidistat shows either continuity or no continuity through the *entire* range, the switch is defective and should be replaced.

Getting the motor out

To remove the motor to replace it or to work on the fan, unplug the unit, open it up, and remove the motor mounting bolts. In the model shown here, you must pry out the rivets that secure the panel surrounding the fan to the chassis. In other models, the panel may be fastened with screws, or there may be no panel at all. Label the motor wires and disconnect them, then lift the motor, fan, and panel out together. In some models you may have to move tubing out of the way—be careful not to kink it. You can now tighten the fan on its shaft, or replace a bent one. The motor can be tested on the workbench by attaching leads from a 110-volt power source to it.

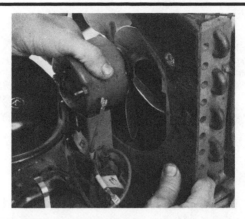

Dehumidifiers Troubleshooting Chart

WHAT'S WRONG	REASONS WHY	WHAT TO DO
Dehumidifier does not run.	No electricity at outlet	Check outlet with a lamp that works. Check fuse or circuit breaker.
	Defective cord	Check cord; replace.
	Defective humidistat	Check and replace.
	Defective fan motor	Check and replace.
	Defective overflow switch	Check and replace.
	Defective compressor	Call repairman.
Dehumidifier runs all the time.	Humidistat set too high	Reset humidistat.
	Defective humidistat	Test and replace humidistat.
	Excessive humidity	No problem
Unit blows fuses or trips circuit breaker.	Overloaded circuit	Run dehumidifier on its own circuit.
	Short circuit in cord or plug	Test cord and plug; replace.
	Short circuit in compressor, motor, or fan motor	Test and replace defective parts.
Unit turns on and off frequently.	Dirty coils	Clean coils.
	Fan not running	Check fan motor; replace.
	Low refrigerant level	Call repairman.
	Defective compressor motor	Call repairman.
Unit runs but does not dry air sufficiently.	Unit too small for job	Use in smaller area; buy larger unit.
	Fins clogged by dirt	Clean fins.
	Fan loose on shaft	Tighten fan.
	Fan motor defective	Test and replace fan motor.
	Fan bent or broken	Replace fan.
	Temperature too low	Operate unit above 65°F.
	Defective humidistat	Test and replace humidistat.
	Defective compressor	Call repairman.
Unit is too noisy.	Screws and panels loose	Tighten all screws.
	Fan loose on shaft	Tighten fan.
	Compressor mounts bad	Replace mounts (see Air Conditioners).
	Fan motor bearings dry	Lubricate bearings.
Unit frosts up.	Fins clogged with dirt	Clean thoroughly.
	Airflow blocked	Clean inside unit; remove obstructions.
	Air temperature too low	Operate above 65°F.
Unit leaks water.	Pan overflowing	Empty the pan.
	Defective overflow switch	Test and replace switch.
	Defective drain hose	Unkink hose; replace if necessary.

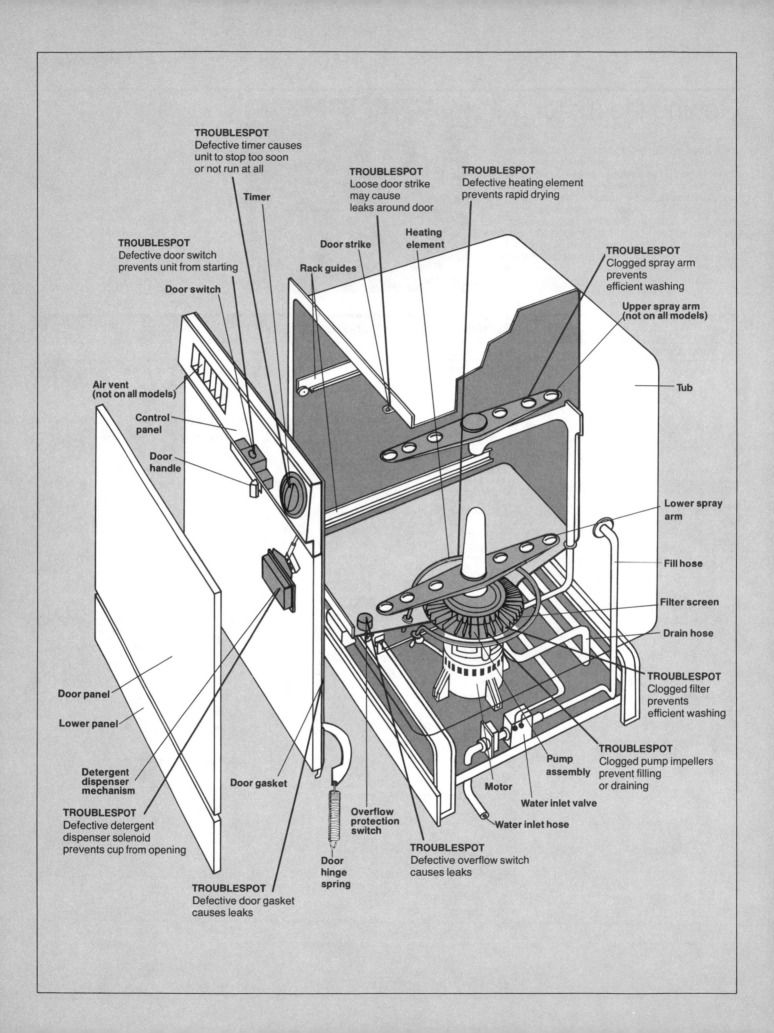

TROUBLESPOT
Defective timer causes unit to stop too soon or not run at all

Timer

TROUBLESPOT
Loose door strike may cause leaks around door

TROUBLESPOT
Defective heating element prevents rapid drying

TROUBLESPOT
Defective door switch prevents unit from starting

Door strike

Heating element

TROUBLESPOT
Clogged spray arm prevents efficient washing

Door switch

Rack guides

Upper spray arm (not on all models)

Air vent (not on all models)

Control panel

Tub

Door handle

Lower spray arm

Fill hose

Filter screen

Drain hose

TROUBLESPOT
Clogged filter prevents efficient washing

Door panel

Lower panel

Detergent dispenser mechanism

Door gasket

TROUBLESPOT
Clogged pump impellers prevent filling or draining

TROUBLESPOT
Defective detergent dispenser solenoid prevents cup from opening

Pump assembly

Motor

Water inlet valve

Overflow protection switch

Water inlet hose

Door hinge spring

TROUBLESPOT
Defective overflow switch causes leaks

TROUBLESPOT
Defective door gasket causes leaks

Dishwashers

An automatic dishwasher is not only an efficient and reliable machine, it is one of the few household appliances that does work more cheaply than you can do it by hand. Running a fully loaded dishwasher through a complete cycle costs less in energy than washing dishes and utensils in two or three batches by hand. But more than any other appliance, a dishwasher won't do its job satisfactorily unless you treat it right. You must prepare dishes properly for washing; you must use the right detergent, and make sure the machine gets water at the right temperature and pressure. In fact, most complaints result from improper use, not machine failure. Read the box at the bottom of this page very carefully.

There is a confusing variety of dishwasher models around. Some are simple, one-cycle models; others are elaborate multi-cycle machines with electronic controls. All of them, however, combine four basic functions (see box, right). The machines pictured here are typical late-model dishwashers. They may not look exactly like yours, but you will find parts on yours that correspond to the ones shown here. One basic tip: never turn a timer dial counterclockwise; it cannot survive such treatment.

CAUTION Electricity and water can be a fatal combination! Turn off the power before you start to work inside the unit. If you have to move the unit, you must also turn off the water and disconnect the plumbing connections. And remember that there's always some water left in the bottom of the unit. Drain it as much as possible before working around the bottom or turning it over.

TIPS FOR ENERGY EFFICIENCY
Operate machine only when it is fully loaded.
Don't use a "rinse and hold" cycle.
Don't use the unit as a plate warmer.
In hot weather, run the dishwasher at night to cut air conditioning expense.
If your operating instructions permit, eliminate the drying cycle. This saves one third of the energy cost. Open the door after the final rinse and let the dishes dry by themselves.

TIPS FOR WASHING EFFICIENCY
Scrape plates well before loading.
Use only fresh dishwasher detergent.
Load dishes carefully. Don't block spray arms or detergent cups; leave space between dishes for circulation.
Clean drains regularly.
Be sure the water temperature is at least 140°F. (see *Water Heaters*).
Make certain the unit sits level and doesn't wobble.

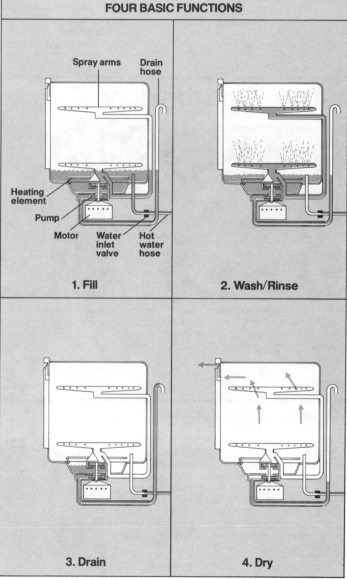

FOUR BASIC FUNCTIONS

Spray arms · Drain hose · Heating element · Pump · Motor · Water inlet valve · Hot water hose

1. Fill

2. Wash/Rinse

3. Drain

4. Dry

All dishwashers perform the four functions shown here, in various combinations. (1) When the door is locked, the timer opens the water inlet valve and hot water flows in. When the right level is reached, the timer shuts the water off and the unit is ready to wash or rinse. (2) The timer starts the motor that drives the pump, spraying water through the arms. During the wash cycle, a container opens, adding detergent to the water. (3) When washing or rinsing is finished, the timer starts the motor to pump water out. (4) When the tub is empty, the timer turns on the heating element to dry the load.

Regular cleaning and maintenance

About the only maintenance a dishwasher requires is regular and careful cleaning of drains, filters, and spray arms. Any obstruction of the water's constant flow greatly reduces washing efficiency.

If the rack wheels bind, try a little silicone spray on the axles. If the plastic covering on the racks wears, try a thin application of silicone caulking on the worn spots to stop rust.

To clean the filter and filter trap, lift them out of the dishwasher and scrub with a stiff brush. Some models, like the one shown here, have screens and filters in plain view. Others, like the one on page 62, require some disassembly for access to the filters.

To clear the spray arm holes of food particles or mineral sediment, take the spray arm out of the dishwasher (some simply lift out; others are screwed down at the hub). Ream out the spray holes with a stiff wire, then turn the spray arm over and shake out any debris.

Working on the door

If the door flops down hard, adjust the tension of the door hinge springs by slipping the end into a lower notch. You will have to remove the lower panel to get to the springs (see *Getting inside*, below).

If the door isn't snug when closed, adjust the door strike by loosening the screws and repositioning the strike forward or back as needed. A small adjustment is usually enough. The door shouldn't be too tight: this might damage the gasket.

If you notice leaks around the door, check the gasket. Replace a worn or hardened one. Mark the location of the old gasket before you remove it (or go by the stain on the tub), so you can put the new one in the same position. Some gaskets pop in, some screw in, and others are held in place by clips.

Getting inside

It's fairly simple to remove the three panels on the front of the dishwasher in order to make all the tests and repairs described here. If you have problems with the pump motor or with electrical or plumbing connections, you will probably have to move the unit out to work on it. This process may be complicated, depending on how permanently your unit has been installed. It may be better to call a repairman at this point.

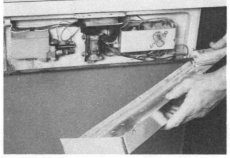

To take off the control panel, remove the screws that hold it in place. (You may have to pry off or unscrew a control dial first.)

To remove the door panel and lower panel, unscrew the door panel from the door. You can now work on the detergent dispenser and the rinse dispenser (if you have one). Remove the lower panel by loosening the screws at the bottom of the panel.

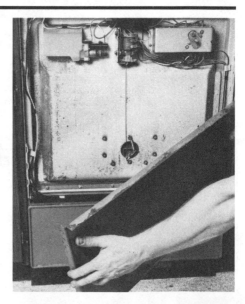

Electrical problems

Door switch

If the dishwasher won't start (and the fuse and power line are OK, and the door is locked), check the door switch.

Turn off the power and remove the top panel. In some models, a broken spring on the switch may prevent proper operation; if the catch on the switch has a broken spring, replace it. In others, an electrical failure may be the cause. Make the continuity test shown here (see Blue Pages: *Electrical testers*). In some models, the door switch is not a part of the door lock, as shown here, but is mounted on a corner or along the side.

1 **To test a door switch,** turn off the power, mark the wires running to the switch, and remove them from the terminals. Then unscrew the switch from the door and lift it out.

2 Test the door switch for continuity. With the switch button or contact up (door open), there should be no continuity. With the button pressed (door closed), there should be continuity. If the switch fails either test, replace it.

Heating element

Most dishwashers use a heating element to keep the wash water hot and to dry the load after the final rinse. If the unit won't dry dishes (and all other functions seem OK), test the heating element. Turn off the power and remove the bottom panel to reach the power connections to the element.

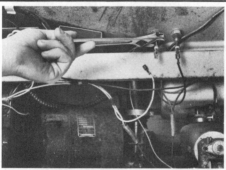

1 **To test the heating element,** disconnect one lead and attach the clips of a VOM set at RX1 (see Blue Pages: *Electrical testers*). The leads will be directly under the point where the heating rod meets the tub. The element should give a reading of 15 to 30 ohms. Higher readings mean it is defective.

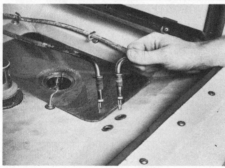

2 Disconnect all wires and retaining nuts from the element (see picture at left), and lift it out of the tub. Always make the replacement with a new element of the same size and electrical rating as the old one.

Other switch controls

Most dishwasher functions are controlled by switches (solenoids and microswitches) commanded by the timer. Two of these—the inlet valve and the drain valve—cannot be reached without moving the unit, a job that usually requires expert help. However, the detergent dispenser solenoid and the overflow protection switch are easy to test (see Blue Pages: *Electrical testers*) and replace through the front of the unit.

If the detergent dispenser fails to open (and it's not clogged with hardened detergent), test the dispenser solenoid as shown here.

If water leaks from the bottom of the door during the first filling, test the overflow protection switch. The switch is attached to the bottom of the tub; it is controlled by a float-type device mounted directly above it in the tub.

To test the detergent dispenser solenoid, clip the leads of a VOM (set at 250 volts AC) onto the solenoid terminals and, with the power on, turn the timer through a full cycle. If there is no continuity at any point, the timer is bad. If there is continuity, but the solenoid fails to click, then the solenoid should be replaced.

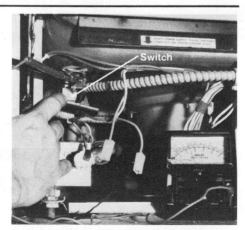

To test the overflow protection switch, turn the power off and disconnect one lead from the switch. It is operated by the float device in the tub. Attach leads from a VOM (set at RX1). There should be no continuity with the float up. If there is, replace the switch with a duplicate.

Timer

The timer controls every operation of the dishwasher except the overflow protection switch. Thus, if the dishwasher fails to run at all, or if it fails to finish its full cycle, the timer may be at fault. To test the timer, you need to be able to read the schematic diagram that comes with the unit and test the timer for continuity in every setting—quite a job! But you can identify the timer as the problem without testing for continuity by making the following checks: check the house circuit fuse, check the door lock and door switch, check that the selector button or dial is correctly set, and check for continuity in the push-button controls if your machine has any (see box, far right). If unit passes all these tests, you can assume the timer is bad. The timer cannot be repaired; it must be replaced with an exact duplicate, as shown here.

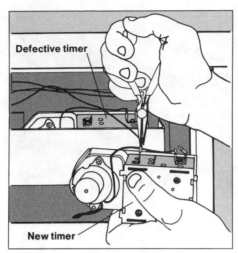

Defective timer

New timer

The easiest way to install a new timer is to hold the new and the old one next to each other in the same orientation and transfer the wires one by one from old to new. Go slowly and carefully—no mistakes allowed! When the wires are all moved, unscrew the old timer and screw in the new one.

Push-button Controls

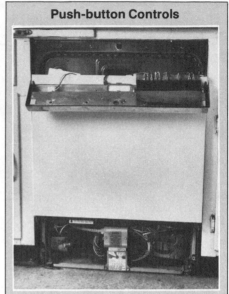

Some late-model dishwashers have an elaborate push-button control console at the top, while the timer itself is mounted at the very bottom. A bundle of wires connects the two. In this situation, all the push buttons must be tested for continuity before you can assume anything is wrong with the timer.

Pump problems

If the motor hums but doesn't pump water in or out, the impellers (which do the pumping) may be jammed. A complete spray arm assembly from a typical dishwasher is shown disassembled, right; this assembly sits atop the motor, which is at the very bottom of the tub. Since every model is different, yours may not look at all like this one, but you will find parts in your machine doing the same jobs these do.

Whenever you take this assembly apart, lay the parts down carefully in a row, so you can get them back together in the right order.

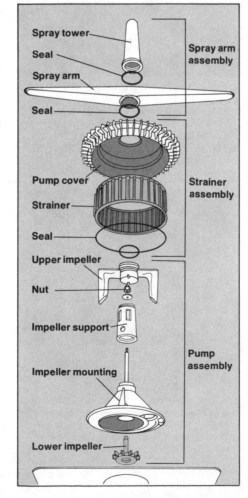

Spray tower

Seal

Spray arm

Seal

Spray arm assembly

Pump cover

Strainer

Seal

Strainer assembly

Upper impeller

Nut

Impeller support

Impeller mounting

Pump assembly

Lower impeller

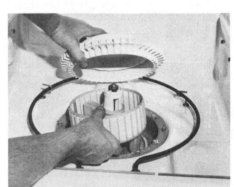

1 **After the spray arm comes off,** the cover can be unscrewed and the strainer (if any) removed for cleaning.

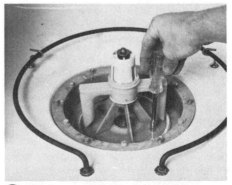

2 With the cover and strainer out of the way, the pump itself (the two impellers) can be unscrewed and taken out piece by piece. The drain pump (lower impeller) is the last part removed here.

Dishwasher Troubleshooting Chart

WHAT'S WRONG	REASONS WHY	WHAT TO DO
Dishwasher won't run at all.	Door not locked	Open the door and lock it again.
	Timer or selector button not properly set	Check timer and button.
	Power not reaching unit	Check fuse box/circuit breaker.
	Defective door switch	Check switch.
	Loose wires	Check all terminals on timer and motor.
	Defective timer	Replace timer.
Dishes don't get clean.	Water not hot enough	Check hot water at the tap; it should be between 140°F. and 160°F. Check hot water heater setting.
	Dishes not correctly prepared for washing	Scrape and rinse dishes before loading.
	Dishes not properly stacked	Dishes must not touch; they should face the direction of the spray.
	Wrong or outdated detergent	Use only fresh dishwasher detergent.
	Detergent dispenser fails to open	Check detergent cup; remove hardened detergent or mineral deposits. Make sure lid is not blocked. Check dispenser solenoid. Timer may be defective.
	Spray arms blocked	Make sure nothing blocks arms.
	No water in tub	See next section.
Dishwasher doesn't fill with water.	Defective water inlet valve or solenoid	Check valve.
	Clogged water filter	Some water inlet valves have filter; check and clean.
	Defective overflow switch	Check switch; if it freezes in FULL position, u nit will not fill.
	Defective timer	Replace timer.
Water doesn't shut off.	Water inlet valve stuck open	Check valve.
	Defective timer	Replace timer .
	Defective overflow switch	Check switch; if it freezes in EMPTY position, water will run on and on.
Water doesn't drain out.	Drain hose kinked or clogged	Check drain hose; disconnect it and blow through it to be sure it is open.
	Defective pump motor	Call repairman.
	Defective timer	Replace timer .
Dishes don't dry.	Mineral deposits on heating element	Clean off deposits with vinegar.
	Heating element wire loose	Check electrical connections.
	Heating element burned out	Replace element.
	Defective timer	Replace timer.
Dishwasher leaks water.	Defective gasket	Check gasket and replace.
	Defective overflow switch	Check switch.
	Door hinges broken	Replace hinges.
	Loose heating-element nuts	Tighten nuts that fasten element to the tub.
	Loose hose clamps	Check hose connections (you may have to move the unit).
Dishwasher is noisy.	Spray arm striking dishes	Load the unit properly.
	Defective water inlet valve (a knocking sound while unit is filling).	Replace valve.
	Insufficient water in tub	Don't open other faucets while dishwasher is filling.

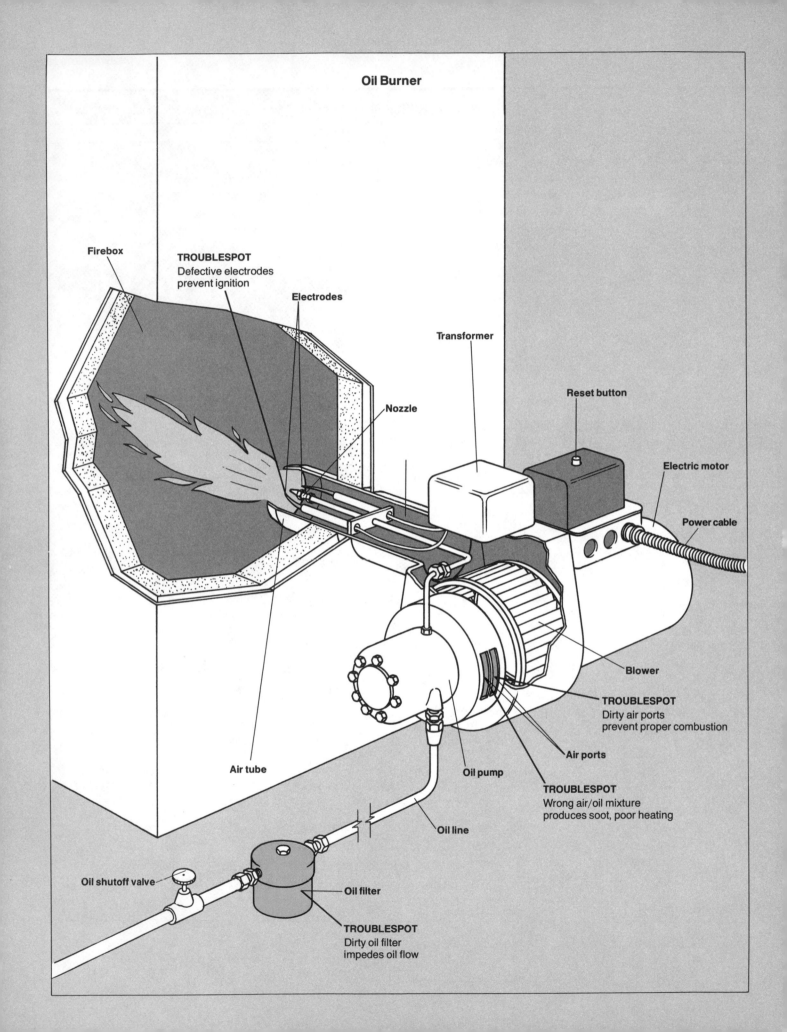

Oil Burner

Firebox

TROUBLESPOT
Defective electrodes
prevent ignition

Electrodes

Transformer

Nozzle

Reset button

Electric motor

Power cable

Blower

TROUBLESPOT
Dirty air ports
prevent proper combustion

Air ports

Air tube

Oil pump

TROUBLESPOT
Wrong air/oil mixture
produces soot, poor heating

Oil line

Oil shutoff valve

Oil filter

TROUBLESPOT
Dirty oil filter
impedes oil flow

Furnaces
Oil burners

A home heating system is easily the most expensive appliance to buy and operate. It's the most complicated, too, with controls, wiring, and pipes or ducts stretching all over the house. There are also numerous options. You can choose gas or oil to make heat for hot-air or hot-water systems.

To sort all this out, we've divided the subject into these separate sections: oil burners, forced-air systems, hot-water systems, furnace control systems, gas burners, and finally, some energy-saving options.

Long ago, when oil was cheap, the oil burner was a very efficient way to say good-bye to shoveling coal. Even today, it's still an efficient way to heat your home (and double as a water heater, too, if you have a hot-water heating system). An oil burner produces a very hot fire by forcing air and heating oil through a nozzle with a blower. This flammable mixture is ignited at the end of the nozzle by a spark that jumps between two electrodes.

A glance at the diagram opposite shows how complicated an oil burner really is; it requires sensitive adjustment to operate properly and safely, and that work is best left to a competent serviceman. You can, however, handle the cleaning jobs described at the bottom of this page. You should also keep alert for the following. (1) Turn the burner off and peer into the furnace through the peephole from time to time to check the firebox for broken bricks. Call the serviceman if you see any. (2) If you find accumulations of soot around the furnace, call a serviceman. (3) If there's a persistent smell of oil around the furnace or coming out the chimney, call the serviceman. (4) Keep the area around the furnace dry. (5) Have leaks in the oil line fixed immediately.

The procedure to follow if there's no heat is detailed at right.

What to do if your oil burner isn't making heat (and power is on).

1. Check the thermostat. Turn it up to maximum and wait thirty seconds. If nothing happens...

2. Check the two furnace switches. There should be one upstairs and one on the furnace. Both should be on red plates. They should be on. If nothing happens...

3. Check the fuse box/circuit breakers. If they're OK...

4. Check the oil tank to be sure there's enough oil. If there is...

5. Push the control panel reset button *once*. If nothing happens...

6. Push the reset button on the oil burner motor *once*. If nothing happens...

7. Push the reset button on the control panel once again, but *no more*.

If the burner starts and then cuts out, you have a problem in the burner or the control panel. Call the furnace man.

If the burner turns on, but the blower (hot-air system) doesn't come on, check the blower motor. If there is a reset button, push it. Check the belt. If it's OK, the problem is in the motor or the wiring to the motor. Call the furnace man.

If the burner turns on, but the circulator pump (hot-water system) doesn't run, listen for a broken coupling (see page 69). If the pump runs but there is no heat, turn your zone valves to manual (if you have them) and call a serviceman. (If one zone valve works and another doesn't, then the fault is in the nonworking thermostat or valve.) If the circulator motor hums or doesn't run at all, the problem is in the motor or motor wiring; that's another problem for the serviceman.

If nothing at all happens when you press the red buttons, call the serviceman. The problem is in the furnace switches or the burner itself.

Regular maintenance

Keep the area around the burner clean, so dirt doesn't obstruct the air ports. Keep the air ports on the burner clean; if the burner doesn't get enough air, it will make soot. You should replace the oil-filter cartridge and gasket twice a year; if dirt clogs the oil line or burner nozzle, the burner could fail to ignite.

To replace an oil filter, shut off the furnace and turn off the valve between filter and tank. Then loosen the nut on top of the filter with a wrench, while holding the filter with your other hand as it drops down. Steady! It's full of oil and gunk. Have an old paint can or other disposable container handy to put the dirty cartridge in. Clean the inside of the filter bowl, then slip the new cartridge and gasket in and put the filter in place, tighten the nut, and turn the valve on. Turn the furnace on.

Clean all air ports on the burner with the radiator attachment on a vacuum cleaner. Do this at least twice a year, and more often if the burner sits in a particularly dusty place. NOTE: Air ports (also called air shutters) are located in different places on different models.

FURNACES
Forced hot-air heating systems

In a forced hot-air heating system, the blower sends air through the heat exchanger that sits on top of the firebox. There, it is heated by the fires from an oil or gas burner. The hot air is forced through the ductwork to the room registers. Cold air returns by another set of ducts through filters to the blower. Although it's much more efficient than the old convection hot-air system, the forced air system remains very simple. There aren't any water pumps, plumbing, valves, or high pressure, and it operates at lower temperatures than do hot-water systems. In addition, you can easily add central air conditioning (see page 43), a humidifier (see page 80), and an electrostatic air cleaner to an existing hot-air system. See pages 70 to 72 for information on temperature controls.

Anyone can handle the basic cleaning and maintenance jobs described on the opposite page, although many people buy a service contract and leave these chores to a professional. Another job you can do (but most people avoid), is cleaning the stack and smoke pipes once a year. Before the heating season starts, number the smoke pipe sections and take them apart carefully. Carry them outside and empty the soot into a box or sack. A long-handled wire brush is a useful tool. Wash your hands thoroughly; most heating oils today contain sulphur, which stains and can burn your hands. Don't get any soot in the house; it makes an enduring mess.

NOTE: It's a good idea to leave the barometric damper on the smokestack alone; let the furnace man set it. If it's out of adjustment, combustion may be inefficient and soot may accumulate.

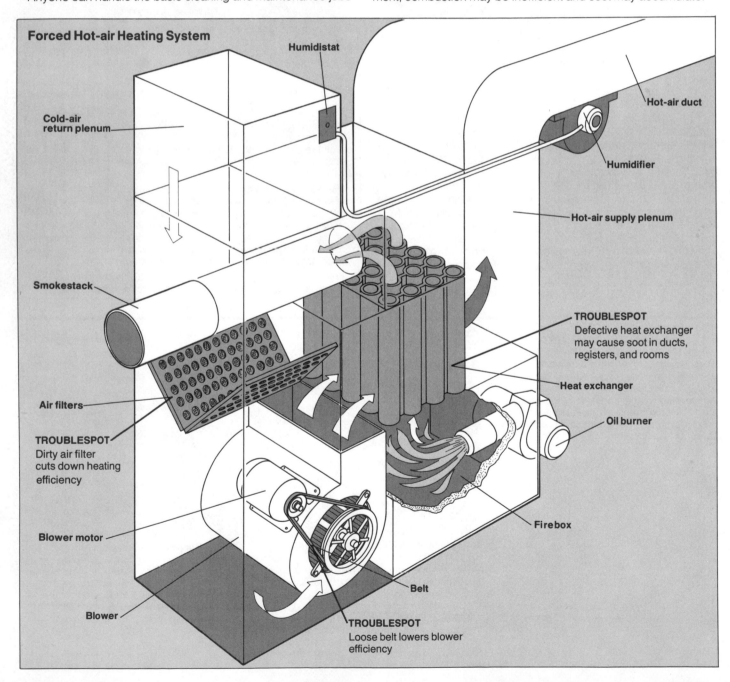

Forced Hot-air Heating System

Humidistat

Hot-air duct

Cold-air return plenum

Humidifier

Hot-air supply plenum

Smokestack

TROUBLESPOT
Defective heat exchanger may cause soot in ducts, registers, and rooms

Heat exchanger

Air filters

Oil burner

TROUBLESPOT
Dirty air filter cuts down heating efficiency

Firebox

Blower motor

Belt

Blower

TROUBLESPOT
Loose belt lowers blower efficiency

Adjusting and maintaining the system

A dirty forced-air system not only circulates dust and dirt all over the house, it also cuts heating efficiency. Change the air filter at the recommended intervals. Once a year, you should also clean the registers (take off the grille and use a vacuum cleaner), and the area in and around the blower, motor, and blower cabinet. If you see soot coming out of the chimney or find it on window panes, make the test described below. Soot in the house may mean a defective heat exchanger in the furnace; call a serviceman to check. Examine the blower drive belt once a year; make the necessary adjustment as shown at far right; replace a worn belt. NOTE: On some newer models, the motor shaft and the blower shaft are connected directly, eliminating pulleys and belt.

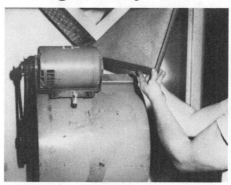

Replace the air filter once a month during the heavy heating season. Once every sixty days might be enough during light seasons. Some systems have two filters, as shown above; be sure to replace both. Install filters with the correct side toward the blower, as printed on the filter.

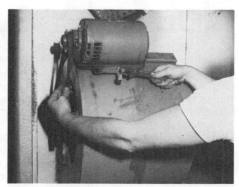

If there is more than half an inch play in the blower drive belt when you press it inward at the middle, adjust the tension by loosening the motor mount and pulling the belt up taut. Then tighten the mounting bolts. Check the belt twice a season and replace it when it becomes worn or cracked.

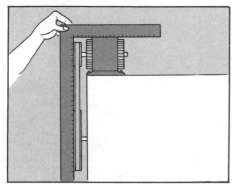

To check the motor and pulley alignment, place a large carpenter's square around the motor, motor pulley, and blower pulley. If the pulleys aren't in a straight line and at right angles to the motor, loosen the inside setscrew on the motor pulley. Adjust it until things are set up square. Then check belt tension and adjust it if necessary.

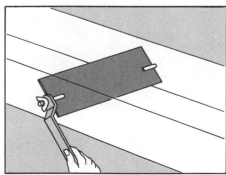

To "fine-tune" the individual dampers in the hot-air ducts, open them all completely. After a day or two of steady heating, walk through all the rooms. If one seems noticeably hotter, close the damper that controls that room about one third. Adjust the dampers until all the rooms are to your liking. NOTE: If you want to shut off the heat in one or more rooms, shut the dampers, not the registers, and take care that the pipes don't freeze.

If you find soot in the house (on window panes), and the filter is OK and the blower area is clean, tape a tissue or white handkerchief over a hot-air register. If soot collects inside, you probably have a defect in the heat exchanger of the furnace (see page 66). Call a serviceman.

Hot-air Furnaces Troubleshooting Chart

WHAT'S WRONG	REASONS WHY	WHAT TO DO
Furnace doesn't heat at all.	No power	Check fuse box/circuit breaker. (See also page 65.)
	Burner problems	See the sections *Oil burners* and *Gas burners*.
	Broken blower belt	Replace belt.
	Faulty blower motor	See Appliance Repair Basics, *How to test a motor*.
Rooms are not warm enough.	Dirty filters	Replace the filters.
	Dirty registers	Clean registers.
	Air leaks in ducts	Seal ducts with duct tape.
	Dirty heat exchanger	Call serviceman to clean.
	Blocked ducts	Remove obstructions.
	Blower belt loose	Tighten belt.
	Blower running slow	Call serviceman to adjust blower speed.
	Register closed	Open register.
	Blocked ducts	Remove obstructions.
	Incorrectly positioned duct damper	Adjust dampers.
Soot collects in house.	Dirty filter	Replace filter.
	Faulty heat exchanger	Call serviceman to check.
	Dirty ducts	Have professional clean them.
The blower makes noises (noticeable when burner is·off).	Loose pulleys	Tighten setscrews.
	Worn blower mounts	Replace mounts.
	Worn belt	Replace belt.
	Belt too tight	Adjust belt tension.
	Blower bearings need oil	Oil bearings.

FURNACES
Hot-water systems

In a hot-water system, the pump sends water into the heat exchanger inside the furnace, where it is heated by the fires of an oil or gas burner. The hot water is pumped through pipes around the house to baseboard heaters or separate convectors, which radiate heat into the room. The water travels back to the furnace via return pipes.

In addition to rather complicated plumbing, this system requires on/off valves controlled by thermostats, regulating valves to control water pressure and temperature, and a high operating temperature. Water must be heated to 180°F. if the convectors are to get hot enough to do their heating job. On the other hand, the heat in a hot-water system is steady; water holds heat a lot longer than air. Thus, less fuel may be consumed. Pipes take much less room than air ducts, and there are no drafts in the rooms.

Some simple maintenance steps and repairs are described on the opposite page. You'll need a plumber for any repairs to the pipes and a serviceman to do any work on the burner, whether it is a gas or oil burner.

Check the troubleshooting chart opposite for steps to take if there's no heat, and also read *Oil burners* or *Gas burners*.

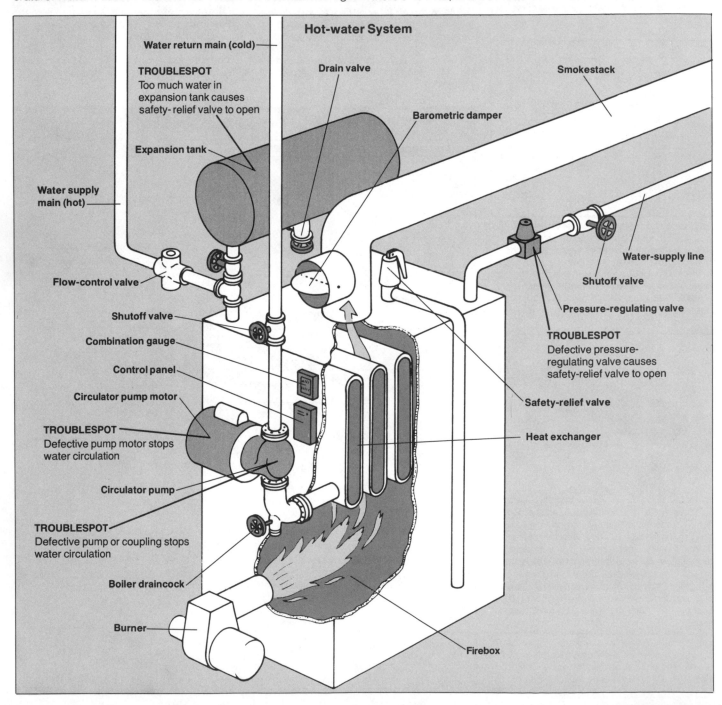

Hot-water System

Water return main (cold)

TROUBLESPOT Too much water in expansion tank causes safety- relief valve to open

Drain valve

Smokestack

Barometric damper

Expansion tank

Water supply main (hot)

Water-supply line

Flow-control valve

Shutoff valve

Pressure-regulating valve

Shutoff valve

Combination gauge

TROUBLESPOT Defective pressure-regulating valve causes safety-relief valve to open

Control panel

Circulator pump motor

Safety-relief valve

TROUBLESPOT Defective pump motor stops water circulation

Heat exchanger

Circulator pump

TROUBLESPOT Defective pump or coupling stops water circulation

Boiler draincock

Burner

Firebox

Maintenance and repairs

You don't have to do very much to maintain a hot-water heating system, except drain the expansion tank once a year. NOTE: Newer-model expansion tanks (much smaller than the one shown here) contain a rubber diaphragm; they don't need to be drained. You should also listen for a clattering noise in the pump; it signals a broken circulator coupling. Also, watch for a leaking safety-relief valve, which may indicate any number of problems (see box, below).

To drain an (old-type) expansion tank once a year, shut off power to the furnace and let the tank cool. Close the valve between the tank and the furnace and open the draincock in the tank. Have a pail ready to catch the water. When all the water has run out, close the draincock, open the valve, and turn on the furnace. A good time to do this job is just before the heating season.

Bolts

1 **To replace a broken circulator pump coupling** (or a burned-out pump motor), first turn off the power to the furnace. Then disconnect the electrical line on the pump. Then use an open-end wrench to remove the nuts that attach the motor to the pump. (To replace a defective pump, you'll have to shut down the whole system, a job best left to an experienced professional repairman.)

2 Loosen the motor end of the circulator coupling with an Allen wrench and then slip it off the motor shaft.

3 Loosen the pump end of the coupling with an Allen wrench inserted through an opening in the pump-mounting flange. Install the replacement coupling by following these steps in reverse order. Be sure you mount the motor with oil ports and connector wires on top.

When a Safety-Relief Valve Lets Go

If the safety-relief valve begins to spit, or a puddle appears beneath the valve drainpipe, turn off the furnace at once! Jot down the boiler temperature and the water pressure reading. Then check the expansion tank. If it's hot all over, it needs to be drained. See the instructions above.

If the expansion tank is OK, there are three possible reasons for a leaky valve. (1) If the water temperature is above the high limit (see *Setting temperature controls,* page 72), then the high-limit control is defective. (2) If the water pressure is below 30 psi (pounds per square inch), then the safety-relief valve is defective. (3) If the water pressure is above 30 psi, the pressure-regulating valve is defective. In *any* of these three cases, call the serviceman. Once you know what is causing the problem, you can intelligently discuss what repairs may be needed.

Hot-water Furnaces Troubleshooting Chart

WHAT'S WRONG	REASONS WHY	WHAT TO DO
Furnace doesn't heat at all.	Power off	Check fuse box/circuit breaker. (See also page 65.)
	No fuel	Call gas company; check oil tank.
	Improperly set thermostat	Adjust thermostat.
	Defective thermostat	Replace thermostat.
	Defective circulator pump	Call serviceman to replace pump.
	Defective motor or coupling	Replace motor or coupling.
	Zone valve problems	See page 65.
Pump makes clattering noise.	Broken circulator coupling	Replace coupling.
Circulator pump leaks.	Seal or impeller defective	Call serviceman to drain system and work on pump.
Safety-relief valve leaks.	Water in expansion tank	Drain tank.
	Valve problems	Call serviceman.

FURNACES
Control systems

No matter what kind of heating system you have—hot-air, hot-water, oil, or gas—they're all operated and controlled by electricity. All these systems require switches, thermostats, heat sensors, and safety circuits, all coordinated to make the system function evenly and continuously, and to produce exactly the heat level you want. Note also that while blowers, pumps, and burners need 120 volts, thermostats run on 24 volts. Thus, you'll always find trans-

formers working somewhere in the circuits to provide the right power for the thermostats.

The diagrams on these pages explain how heating systems are controlled. They are *not* wiring diagrams. (It takes an experienced electrician to handle heating-system wiring competently.) Rather, they outline how the various components are interconnected, both in simple systems and zone systems, and how they affect each other's operation.

Single-thermostat systems

A heating system with only one thermostat is the simplest of systems. Since it has the least amount of wiring and the fewest controls to adjust, there is the least likelihood of things going wrong electrically. On the other hand, it's not possible to vary the temperature in different parts of the house.

How it works. When it gets cold around the thermostat, the thermostat calls the control panel for heat. If the temperature in the furnace is above the blower's low limit (as reported by the temperature sensor) the control panel turns on the blower, forcing hot air out of the plenum, into the ducts, and on to the registers. If the furnace temperature is below the blower's low limit, the control panel turns the burner on first to make enough heat. The blower shuts off when the thermostat's temperature setting is reached. The burner operates only between its own high and low temperature limits.

How it works. When the area around the thermostat gets cold, the thermostat asks the control panel for heat. If the temperature in the furnace is above the cirulator pump's low limit, as reported by the temperature sensor, the control panel turns on the circulator motor. The circulator pump sucks cold water out of the return pipes, forcing hot water out of the furnace toward the convectors or radiators. If the furnace isn't hot enough, the control panel turns on the burner to heat the water in the furnace. The pump shuts off when the thermostat's temperature limit has been reached. The burner operates only within its preset high/low range.

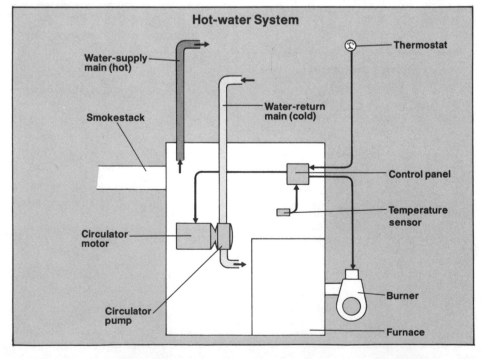

Forced Hot-air System

Cold-air return
Hot-air plenum
Thermostat
Smokestack
Control panel
Blower motor
Temperature sensor
Blower
Burner
Furnace

Hot-water System

Thermostat
Water-supply main (hot)
Water-return main (cold)
Smokestack
Control panel
Temperature sensor
Circulator motor
Circulator pump
Burner
Furnace

Zone systems

A zone control system divides the house into separate heating areas—upstairs versus downstairs, living quarters versus sleeping quarters—as many divisions as you want. Each area, or zone, has its own thermostat and other controls to bring heat just to that area. The zones can work independently or together, depending on what heat levels you demand from the thermostats.

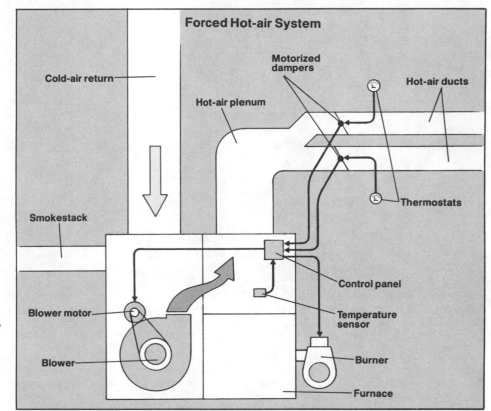

Forced Hot-air System

Cold-air return

Motorized dampers

Hot-air ducts

Hot-air plenum

Thermostats

How it works. When the thermostat calls for heat, it opens the motorized damper in the duct leading to that thermostat's heating area. When the damper is fully open, it signals the control panel. If the furnace is hot enough (as reported to the control panel by the temperature sensor) the control panel turns on the blower, sending hot air through the open duct (but not through the closed ducts). If the furnace isn't hot enough, the control panel turns on the burner to heat the air in the furnace. When the thermostat is satisfied, the damper closes, and the blower is shut off. The burner runs only between its high and low limits. The zones operate independently or together. (Two zones are shown here; more could be installed.)

Smokestack

Blower motor

Blower

Control panel

Temperature sensor

Burner

Furnace

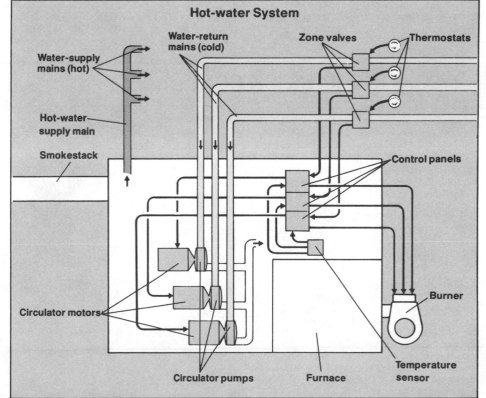

Hot-water System

Water-return mains (cold)

Zone valves

Thermostats

Water-supply mains (hot)

Hot-water supply main

Smokestack

Control panels

How it works. When a zone thermostat reaches its cold point, it opens the valve in the supply pipe that brings hot water to that thermostat's zone. The control panel is connected to a temperature sensor in the furnace. If the water is hot enough, when the valve is fully open the control panel for that valve will turn on the zone's circulator motor. If the water isn't hot enough, the control panel turns on the burner to heat the water. The circulator motor drives the pump, pulling cold water out of the zone's pipes and forcing hot water out of the furnace into the zone's convectors. When a thermostat is satisfied, its zone valve closes and the control panel shuts off that pump motor. The burner operates only between its preset high and low temperature settings. Each zone can operate independently, or in any combination with the others. (Three zones are shown here; there could be two or, rarely, four.) It is possible to hook up a multi-zone hot water system with a single circulator pump for all the zones. It's less expensive, but also less efficient.

Circulator motors

Burner

Circulator pumps

Furnace

Temperature sensor

Setting temperature controls

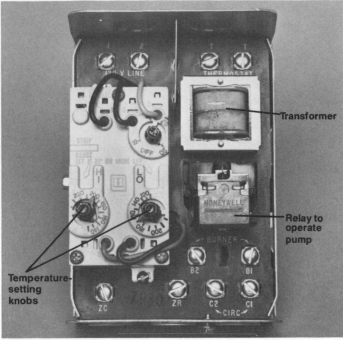

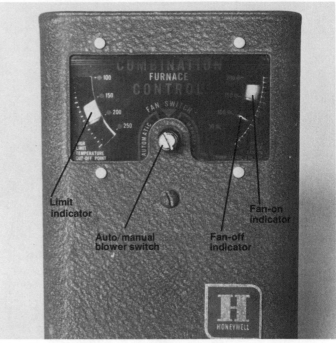

Hot-water systems. The temperature controls for a hot-water system are usually contained in one control panel mounted on the furnace. Behind the panel is a temperature sensor, mounted inside the furnace. The panel is connected to 120-volt power leads. There is a 24-volt transformer for the thermostat circuit. The panel turns the circulator pump and the burner on and off to satisfy the thermostats in the house, within the limits imposed by the high and low settings. For winter house heating, set the low dial at 170°F. and the high dial at 190°F.; set the differential dial at 20°F. This will give an average of 180°F., the temperature necessary for hot-water heating. For summer, if the furnace gives you domestic hot water, set the dials at 120°F. to 140°F. If the furnace makes hot water for a dishwasher in summer, set the dials at 130°F. to 150°F.

Forced hot-air systems. The temperature controls for forced hot-air systems are usually found in two places. One control panel is normally mounted on the burner. It contains the thermostat connection and the 24-volt transformer, and it controls the burner. There is usually a reset button on this panel. There are no temperature dials to set. A second panel, called the combination furnace control, is mounted near the top of the furnace so that its temperature sensor sticks into the hot-air plenum. There are three temperature-setting controls on this panel. The high-limit setting, normally 200°F., is a safety switch that turns the burner off if the temperature in the furnace reaches the high limit. The on/off settings control the blower motor. The ON setting should be about 130°F. and the OFF setting about 100°F. The air coming out of the ducts will be about 90°F. There is usually a separate auto/manual switch to control the blower on this panel.

Checking the stack control

The stack control is a safety device mounted in the smokestack of some furnaces. A metal tube containing a heat-sensing device (a bimetallic element, for example) projects into the smokestack from a control box mounted on it. If the heat in the smokestack reaches a preset upper limit, the stack control will turn off the furnace to prevent overheating. On most models, it is then necessary to push the reset button to start the furnace again. (In newer furnaces, this safety function is handled by a control panel mounted on the furnace itself.) Clean the stack control once a year.

To clean the stack control, turn the furnace off, loosen the mounting screw, and pull the sensor and control box straight out of the smokestack. Handle the control with care; the heat-sensing element is delicate. Use a small brush to remove the soot on the outside of the tube. If the tube is clogged with soot, it's a sign of poor furnace combustion, and you should call a serviceman. Clean the stack control just before the heating season starts.

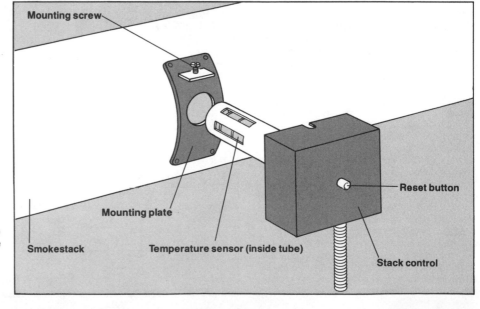

Gas Burner

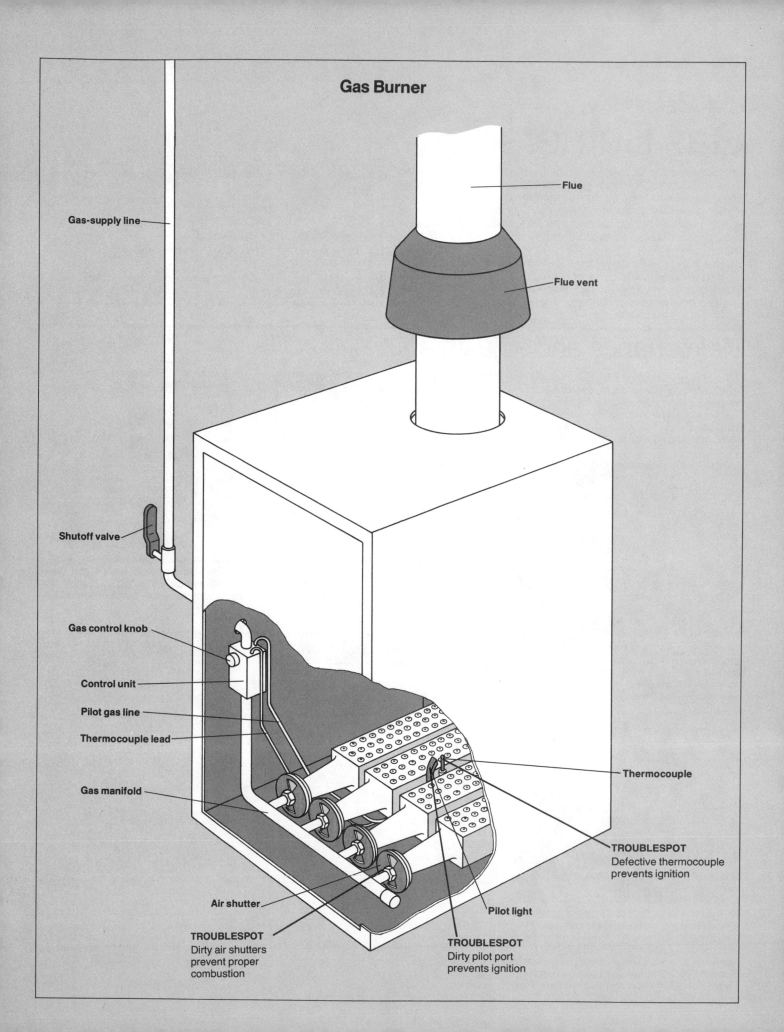

Flue

Flue vent

Gas-supply line

Shutoff valve

Gas control knob

Control unit

Pilot gas line

Thermocouple lead

Gas manifold

Thermocouple

TROUBLESPOT
Defective thermocouple
prevents ignition

Air shutter

Pilot light

TROUBLESPOT
Dirty air shutters
prevent proper
combustion

TROUBLESPOT
Dirty pilot port
prevents ignition

FURNACES
Gas Burners

Gas burners are probably the cleanest and most efficient burners for either hot-air or hot-water home heating systems. They cost less to install, and although gas costs more in some places than oil, more new gas burners are being sold than any other type. They can be made very compact, and a pipeline carrying gas into your home is generally a more reliable source of fuel than a truck that delivers oil.

A gas burner's efficiency depends on the careful adjustment of the air/gas mixture, and it is a job for a gas company serviceman. In fact, there's very little you can or should do to a gas burner. Simple adjustments and cleaning procedures are shown below.

If there's no heat from the burner (and the power is on), follow these steps:

1. Check the thermostat. Turn it to maximum. If the burner doesn't light...

2. Check the control dial on the burner. It should be on. If it is...

3. Check the pilot light; if it's off, relight it (see below). If it doesn't stay lit, call the gas company.

If you smell gas, shut off the furnace, close the gas valve, and call the gas company *immediately*.

Maintenance and adjustment

The only regular maintenance required on a gas burner is to clean the air shutters twice a year. If the pilot light goes out, relight it, following the directions given on your model. Two examples are shown below. You can also adjust the temperature setting on most models (see far right).

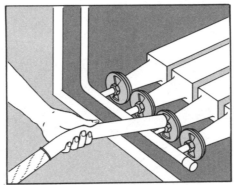

To clean the air shutters and the area around them, use the radiator attachment on a vacuum cleaner. Twice a year is usually enough unless the burner sits in a very dirty environment.

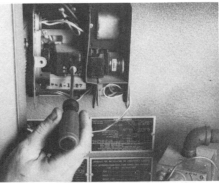

To adjust the maximum temperature setting of the furnace (either hot-air or hot-water system), use a screwdriver to turn the adjusting screw on the control unit. The normal setting is 190°F.

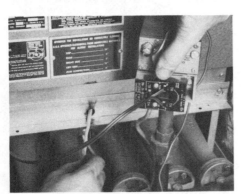

To light the pilot light on some models of gas burner, insert a lighted twist of paper or a long-stemmed match into the burner through a small port while holding the pilot lighting button down. Follow the directions printed on the face of the unit.

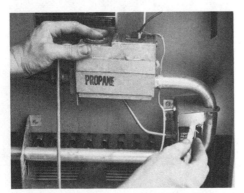

To light the pilot light on the type of burner shown here, hold a lighted twist of paper inside a shielded opening at the front of the unit while pressing down the pilot lighting button. The flame actually is drawn down into the unit to reach the pilot. If this method fails, try bending the shield out of the way and inserting the lighted twist into the burner itself. Avert your face.

Gas Burners Troubleshooting Chart

WHAT'S WRONG	REASONS WHY	WHAT TO DO
Furnace doesn't heat.	Pilot light out	Relight the pilot.
	No gas	Call the gas company.
Pilot light doesn't stay lit.	Dirty pilot port	Clean pilot port if you can reach it; if you can't, call serviceman.
	Defective thermocouple	Call gas company.
	Wrong-sized flame	Call gas company.
You can smell gas.	Pilot out	Relight the pilot light.
	Possible leak	Turn off the gas supply; call the gas company; ventilate the room.

FURNACES
Energy-saving options

Multifurnaces

A multifurnace can heat your home with either of two fuels. The forced hot-air furnace shown here works with an oil burner or a wood fire. Both burner and fire heat a common heat exchanger (see page 66). The furnace can also be set up to use a gas burner or a coal fire. It is also possible to combine a wood- or coal-burning furnace with a preexisting hot-water furnace that is heated by either gas or oil.

In all of these setups, the idea is to save money by burning less expensive fuels, like coal and wood, while holding the gas or oil burner on standby. The burner turns on automatically when the wood fire burns down and the house temperature falls below your thermostat setting.

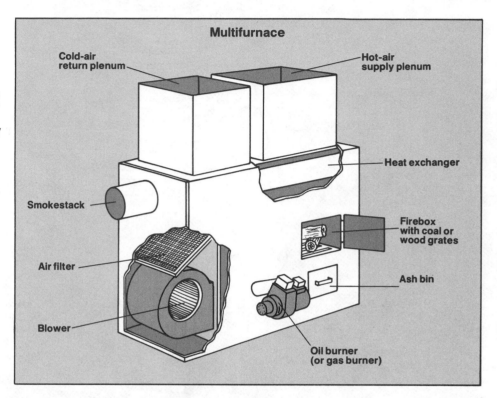

Multifurnace

Cold-air return plenum

Hot-air supply plenum

Heat exchanger

Smokestack

Firebox with coal or wood grates

Air filter

Ash bin

Blower

Oil burner (or gas burner)

Automatic flue dampers

Much of the heat generated in any furnace is simply lost up the chimney. Of course, the chimney has to be open while a burner is on to take waste gases outside. But what about when the burner is off? You can install an automatic flue damper that stays closed while the burner is off, preventing heat in the furnace and surrounding areas from escaping out the smoke-stack. When the thermostat calls for heat, the damper is opened by a small motor and only then does the burner come on. (If the power fails, a strong spring opens the damper.) Believe it or not, there can be a 20% fuel savings on furnaces equipped with this heat miser.

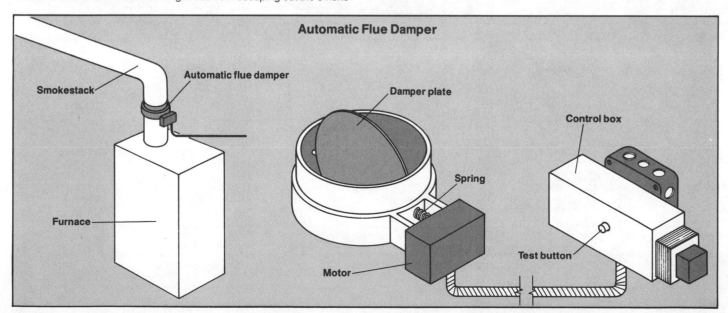

Automatic Flue Damper

Smokestack

Automatic flue damper

Damper plate

Control box

Spring

Furnace

Motor

Test button

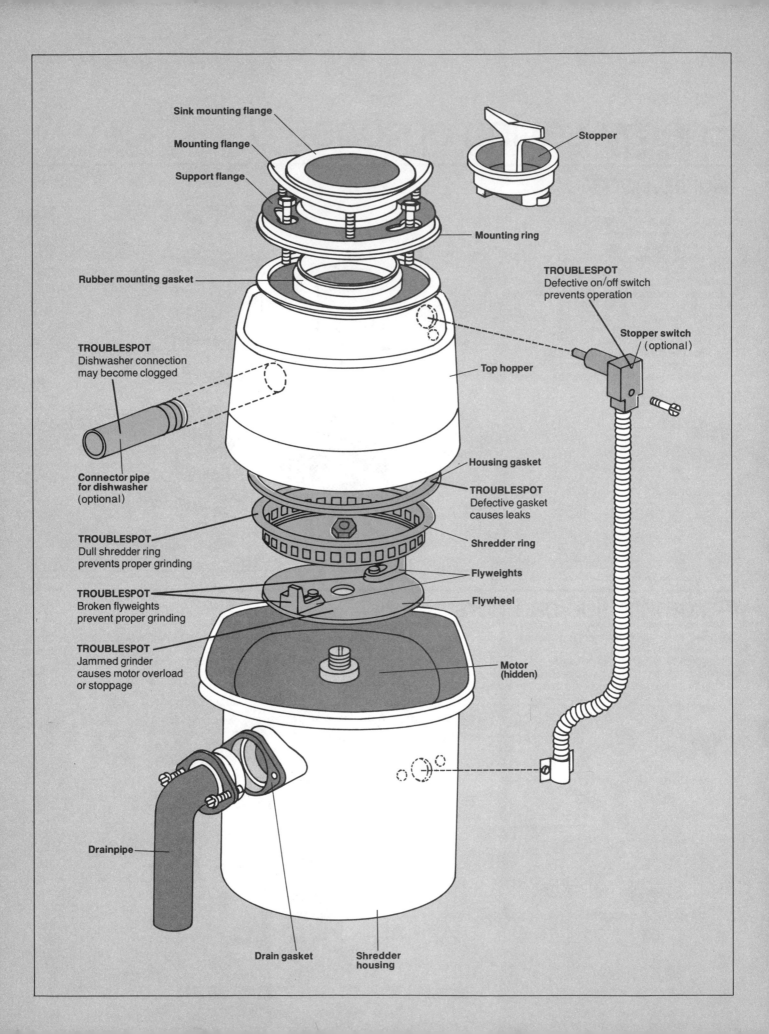

Sink mounting flange

Mounting flange

Support flange

Stopper

Mounting ring

Rubber mounting gasket

TROUBLESPOT
Defective on/off switch prevents operation

TROUBLESPOT
Dishwasher connection may become clogged

Top hopper

Stopper switch (optional)

Housing gasket

Connector pipe for dishwasher (optional)

TROUBLESPOT
Defective gasket causes leaks

Shredder ring

TROUBLESPOT
Dull shredder ring prevents proper grinding

Flyweights

TROUBLESPOT
Broken flyweights prevent proper grinding

Flywheel

TROUBLESPOT
Jammed grinder causes motor overload or stoppage

Motor (hidden)

Drainpipe

Drain gasket

Shredder housing

Garbage Disposers

A garbage disposer—a set of rotary jaws under the sink—turns soft food wastes into a slurry that disappears down the drain. A disposer will give you service for five years or longer, if you don't mistreat it. Read your owner's manual and the suggestions in the box at right to find out what kinds of garbage your unit can take.

There are two kinds of disposers. The continuous-feed type has an on/off switch, mounted on a nearby wall, which, when left on, lets you feed garbage into the unit continuously. The batch-feed type has its switch in the mouth of the unit. You must load the disposer up and put in the stopper. As you turn the stopper in tight, the switch starts the motor. Nothing can be added until that batch has disappeared. Either kind of switch can be tested for continuity and replaced if faulty (see Blue Pages: *Electrical testers*).

There are only a few repairs that can be made inside a disposer. Gaskets, worn-out shredder rings, and broken flyweights (the parts that do the actual grinding) can be replaced as described here. Plumbing connections sometimes leak because they just need tightening. If plumbing connections are worn out, however, you will have to buy a new disposer. The disposer motor is sealed up tight. It usually cannot be repaired, so if it burns out, you must replace the whole unit. Before buying a garbage disposer, consider the following. Disposers are prohibited in many towns, because local authorities don't want the sewer lines clogged with ground-up garbage. If you have a septic tank system, you should check its capacity before installing a disposer. A family of four should have a drainfield of about 750 gallons capacity to handle a disposer's contribution. With eight occupants in the house, a 1,000-gallon capacity is needed.

CAUTION Always turn the power off at the fuse box or circuit breaker before starting to work on the disposer. *Never* put your hand into the unit. Even if the motor doesn't accidentally start up, the shredder ring is sharp enough to cut.

TIPS FOR EFFICIENT OPERATION
Put into the disposer only materials it can handle. Putting glass, bottle caps, rubber, dishrags, silverware, and paper in the unit will only bring you grief. Consult your owner's manual for further details.
Do not pack waste into the unit; just drop it in.
Use lots of cold water when running the disposer.
Never use hot water; it melts grease, which then clogs the drain.
After the unit has finished grinding, run the cold water for twenty or thirty seconds to clear the drain. Don't use chemical cleaners; they may damage the unit.
Never put your hand into the disposer; the machine will shred it just as fast as it shreds the garbage.

If the disposer jams

If the motor hums when you turn it on, but the disposer doesn't grind, the flywheel is probably jammed. If your unit has a reversing switch, try running it backwards for a few seconds to dislodge the obstruction. If you hear metallic noises, a piece of silverware may have fallen in. Try fishing it out with a pair of tongs.

If these procedures don't work turn the power off and use a wooden rod (not your hand) to try to turn the flywheel as shown at right. Use rotary pressure; don't press down. After freeing the flywheel, turn the unit on and put in a handful of ice cubes to help flush it. If you can't free the flywheel, you'll have to open the unit up (see page 78 for instructions); try freeing it from inside, or check if the flyweights are broken.

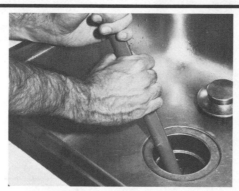

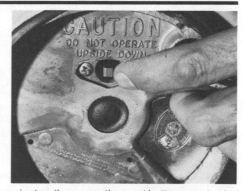

If your unit's motor has an overload protector, the motor will cut out automatically when the unit jams. Some units eventually turn back on automatically. Other units have a reset button, near right. Remove the obstruction. Wait about 15 minutes; then press the reset button once to start the motor again, as shown above. If it doesn't start, the protector switch or the motor may have burned out. Call a repairman if you have to replace the motor, the switch, or the entire unit.

Solving a plumbing problem

If you have a dishwasher installed near your garbage disposer, the drain line from the dishwasher may be connected directly to the hopper of the disposer (see drawing, far right). Waste material from the disposer can back up into the dishwasher line and clog it. You can avoid this problem by connecting the dishwasher drain line (see drawing, near right).

Disconnect the dishwasher drain line from the disposer and plug the hole in the disposer with a cork, sealed with epoxy. Buy a T-elbow connection at a plumbing supply store and install it as shown (near right). Connect the dishwasher drain line to the T-elbow, bypassing the disposer.

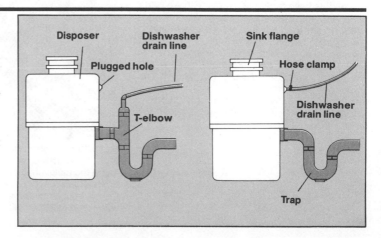

Disposer · Dishwasher drain line · Sink flange · Plugged hole · Hose clamp · T-elbow · Dishwasher drain line · Trap

Getting inside

The only repairs you can practically make on a disposer are to replace a worn-out shredder ring, or a flywheel with broken flyweights, or to tighten plumbing connections. Directions for these repairs are given below. Getting into a disposer is a tedious process, complicated by the cramped quarters where it is installed. Be sure to turn off the power before starting to work. Have lots of old newspapers on hand; you will probably find a mess inside the unit. When reassembling the disposer, always install a new housing gasket (see opposite page).

1 **To get inside the unit,** first remove the trap in the drain line from the disposer to the house plumbing system. Use a wrench to loosen the slip nuts.

2 Remove the flexible bottom outer cover (if your unit has one) and the sheet of sound-muffling insulation you may find wrapped around the unit.

3 Loosen the screws or bolts that hold the unit to the support flange. Rotate the unit slightly; the mounting screws will slip out of the flange and the unit will drop down.

4 On this model you must remove the mounting ring to get the top outer cover off. Pull the ring off over the rubber mounting gasket. Then pull off the flexible outer cover (if your unit has one).

5 Remove the screws that secure the top hopper to the shredder housing. On some models that may be a clamp ring (instead of screws) that fits around the hopper and housing. The clamp will be secured with a screw in its edge. You can now remove the top hopper and inspect the shredder ring inside the flywheel.

Replacing the shredder ring and flywheel

If, after some years of service, your disposer begins to take forever to grind the garbage, the shredder ring has probably grown dull or the flyweights have broken. To replace these parts, open the unit up as shown above. A dull shredder ring can then be lifted out and a new one dropped in. Look closely at the flywheel; if the flyweights are broken, the flywheel must be replaced. Look for a nut that holds the flywheel to the motor shaft. If there is one, use method 1 at right to remove the flywheel. If there is no nut, try method 2. Take the defective parts and your model number to the dealer to get duplicates.

METHOD 1: To remove a flywheel secured with a nut, insert a screwdriver into the slot on top of the motor shaft and grip the nut with an adjustable wrench. Hold the shaft rigid and turn the nut counterclockwise. When the nut is off, the wheel can be lifted out.

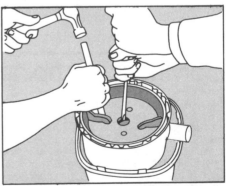

METHOD 2: To remove a flywheel that has no nut, put a screwdriver into the top slot and hold the shaft rigid. Strike the flyweights sharply with a hammer to move the wheel counterclockwise. The wheel will come loose from the shaft and can be lifted out. Force the new flywheel onto the shaft, applying pressure evenly around it.

Stopping leaks

Leaks from a disposer are a signal that the plumbing connections are not tight enough or that the connections have disintegrated. In the first case, follow the instructions given here for repairing a connection or replacing a gasket. Replace a housing gasket whenever you open the unit for inspection or repairs.

If the connections are worn out, buy a new disposer. The test for any new or repaired connections is simple: plug the disposer mouth and fill the sink with water. Then pull the plug. The pressure built up by that amount of water should reveal any leak.

To remove a housing gasket, just lift it off the rim at the top of the housing. Apply a thin layer of silicone caulk all around the top edge of the new gasket before screwing or clamping the hopper down tight.

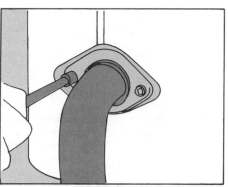

If you notice water leaking from the drain-pipe connection, tighten the screws that secure the flange to the unit. If the gasket breaks or deteriorates, replace it.

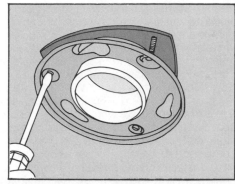

If water leaks from the sink connection, tighten the screws that secure the support flange to the mounting flange. If the leak doesn't stop, try putting a layer of plumber's putty on the top side of the mounting flange.

Garbage Disposers Troubleshooting Chart		
WHAT'S WRONG	**REASONS WHY**	**WHAT TO DO**
Motor does not turn on.	No power	Check fuse box/circuit breaker. If disposer is plugged into wall outlet check the outlet.
	Defective switch	Check wall switch (for continuous-feed models) and stopper switch (for batch-feed models) for continuity.
	Overload protector switch tripped	Free flywheel if jammed. Press reset button.
	Defective motor	Call repairman.
Motor hums but unit doesn't grind.	Flywheel jammed	Free flywheel.
	Motor bearings frozen	Call repairman; you'll probably have to buy a new unit.
Disposer blows fuses.	Too many appliances on circuit	Install disposer on its own 15-amp circuit.
Disposer doesn't shut off.	Defective switch	Call repairman.
Disposer grinds too slowly.	Not enough water	Use more cold water.
	Improper waste put in unit	Put in only materials allowed by manual.
	Dull shredder ring or broken flyweights	Replace defective parts.
Disposer drains slowly.	Not enough water	Use more cold water.
	Drain line clogged	Flush with hot water to remove grease plug; remove drainpipe and clear. (Don't use harsh chemical agents.)
	Unit not grinding fine enough	Replace dull shredder ring or broken flyweights.
Disposer makes noises.	Metallic object in unit	Fish it out with tongs or forceps.
	Loose mounting screws	Tighten screws.
	Broken flyweight	Replace flywheel.
	Defective motor	Call repairman.
Disposer leaks.	Loose sink connection	Tighten flanges holding gasket or replace gasket.
	Loose drain connection	Tighten drain flanges or replace gasket.
	Defective housing gasket	Replace gasket.

Humidifiers
Hot-air furnace

People, plants, and objects made of porous materials such as wood and leather need a certain amount of moisture in the air. People are generally aware not of any actual amount of moisture in the air, but of the relative humidity level. Since hot air carries much more moisture than cold air, people are comfortable at 75°F. when the relative humidity is about 20%—less comfortable if the relative humidity is 40%. At 70°F. we don't mind 40% relative humidity. And at 65°F. even 55% is pleasant. This means that in hot weather we want to take water out of the air to be comfortable. Air conditioners do this at the same time they cool air. In cold weather, however, we often need to add moisture for comfort indoors. Cold outdoor air seeping into the house may have a relative humidity level of 40% or so, but when the air is heated to 70°F. and expands, that humidity level drops to only 5% or 10% (see chart below). This is much too low for health or comfort. Mucus membranes dry out, causing respiratory ailments; skin becomes dry; carpets generate static electricity when you walk across them; wood and plaster shrink and crack; leather dries out and crumbles; plants die.

Homes in northern states that are heated by forced-air furnaces are particularly liable to low humidity levels in winter and the accompanying problems. A humidifier installed directly in the hot-air supply plenum of your furnace solves these problems easily. Surprisingly, there is no standard type of humidifier. Many mechanical methods can be used to get moisture into the air. Two of the most common types are described here. If you buy a unit with a capacity suited to your home, it will keep the humidity at a pleasant 35% to 40%, regardless of outside temperature.

NOTE: If your home is not well insulated, or if it was built without a vapor barrier, it is pointless to try to humidify the house or even a single room. The moisture will leak through the walls and roof to the outside just as fast as a machine can generate it. Consult a home heating expert for advice in this case.

Both types of furnace humidifier described here require a small flexible tube connection to a cold water supply pipe and a 120-volt AC power connection to operate their motors or pumps. Some units require a 24-volt transformer to provide stepped-down electrical power to operate the motors or pumps.

To operate at top efficiency, all humidifiers need regular—almost constant—cleaning. Evaporating water leaves mineral deposits behind, which clogs the unit, and water always attracts dust, dirt, and airborne bacteria, which can cause unpleasant odors. Be prepared to clean your humidifier monthly during the heating season, and even more often if you use well water.

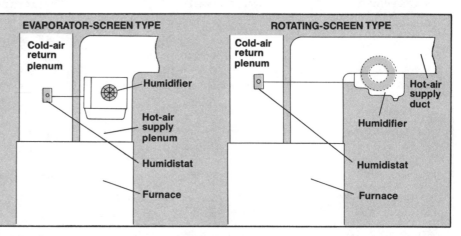

Two Types of Furnace Humidifier

Two types of furnace humidifier are described on the following pages. 1) The evaporating-screen type (see opposite page) is usually mounted on the side of the hot-air supply plenum. 2) The rotating-screen type (see page 82) is usually mounted under a hot-air supply duct, but it can also be mounted on the side of the plenum.

EVAPORATOR-SCREEN TYPE

Cold-air return plenum

Humidifier

Hot-air supply plenum

Humidistat

Furnace

ROTATING-SCREEN TYPE

Cold-air return plenum

Hot-air supply duct

Humidifier

Humidistat

Furnace

TIPS FOR EFFICIENT OPERATION

Buy a unit with sufficient capacity for your needs. Take into consideration the size of the area to be humidified, the type of insulation and tightness of construction of your home, and your own sensitivity to the relative humidity level. Higher relative humidity lets you be more comfortable at lower inside temperatures; this also saves heating costs during the winter.

Keep your unit clean. Accumulations of minerals and scum prevent proper humidifying. Follow the manufacturer's suggestions and those given here. Clean at least twice during the heating season, and more often if you use well water.

If your home water supply has a water softener, the humidifer water supply tube must be connected to the cold-water supply pipe before it reaches the water softener. Softened water contains salts that clog the humidifier.

RELATIVE HUMIDITY LEVELS IN WINTER

OUTDOOR TEMPERATURE	OUTDOOR RELATIVE HUMIDITY	*INDOOR RELATIVE HUMIDITY	**RECOMMENDED INDOOR RELATIVE HUMIDITY
−10°F.	40%	1%	20%
	80	1	
0°	40	3	25
	80	6	
10°	40	5	30
	80	10	
20°	40	7	35
	80	14	
30°	40	9	35
	80	18	

*Without using a humidifier.   **Set your humidifier at this level.

Evaporator-screen furnace humidifiers

An evaporator-screen humidifier is mounted on the side of the hot-air supply plenum of the furnace. A motor-driven pump lifts water from the water pan to the top of a metal mesh or foam rubber screen. As the water slowly trickles down the screen, a fan blows air across the screen, carrying moisture into the plenum. This type of humidifier is controlled by a humidistat mounted in the cold-air return plenum. See page 87 for testing instructions. The fan motor is similar to those used on dehumidifiers (see page 57). The fan operates only when the furnace is on. Oil the motor as your owner's manual recommends. Clean the water pan, evaporator screen, and water inlet valve regularly. When the pan is removed, examine the bottom opening of the pump and clean it if it is clogged.

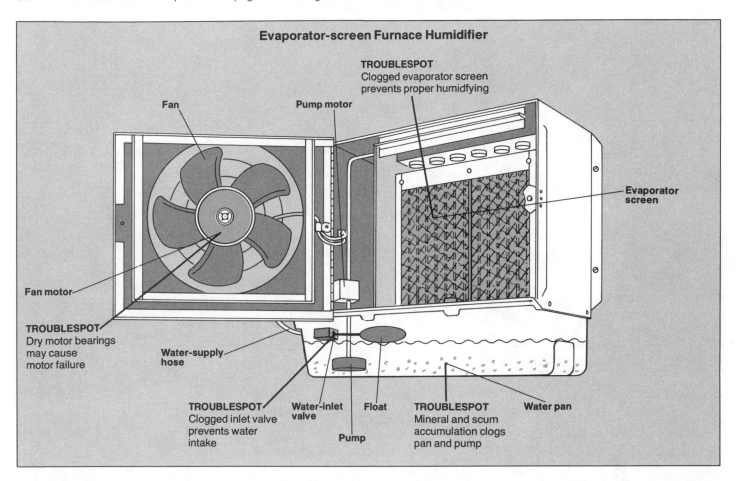

Evaporator-screen Furnace Humidifier

Fan

Pump motor

TROUBLESPOT
Clogged evaporator screen prevents proper humidfying

Evaporator screen

Fan motor

TROUBLESPOT
Dry motor bearings may cause motor failure

Water-supply hose

TROUBLESPOT
Clogged inlet valve prevents water intake

Water-inlet valve

Float

Pump

TROUBLESPOT
Mineral and scum accumulation clogs pan and pump

Water pan

Maintenance

To clean the evaporator screen, loosen the fan mounting screws and swing the fan door open. Lift the screen out. If it's dry, rap it sharply against a hard surface to dislodge mineral accumulations. To remove stubborn accumulations, soak the screen in a solution of 1 cup vinegar to 1 gallon water.

To remove the water pan for cleaning, loosen the mounting screws and lower the pan. Wash it in hot water and detergent.

To clean the water-inlet valve, remove the water pan and insert a thin wire into the valve port. Work the wire back and forth and the float up and down until the port is clear. A small amount of water will spit out as you clean.

Rotating-screen furnace humidifiers

The rotating-screen humidifier is mounted on the underside of the furnace's hot-air supply duct so that its screens project up into the plenum. A motor slowly turns the screens so that they pick up water from the container at the bottom of the unit. As warm air passes over the screens it readily absorbs moisture from them. No fan or pump is needed for this kind of installation. On this model, a humidistat mounted on the cold-air return plenum controls the unit.

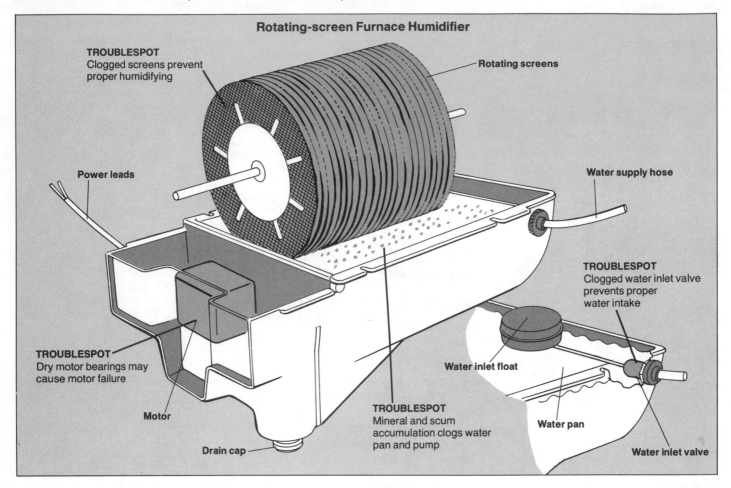

Rotating-screen Furnace Humidifier

TROUBLESPOT Clogged screens prevent proper humidifying

Rotating screens

Power leads

Water supply hose

TROUBLESPOT Clogged water inlet valve prevents proper water intake

TROUBLESPOT Dry motor bearings may cause motor failure

Water inlet float

Motor

TROUBLESPOT Mineral and scum accumulation clogs water pan and pump

Water pan

Drain cap

Water inlet valve

Maintenance

At the end of the heating season, take the unit apart. Clean the screens and the water pan. Check the water inlet valve to be sure it is clear. Oil the motor. Drain the unit during the season whenever there is an accumulation of scum and mineral deposits, and keep the unit dry during the off-season.

To drain and clean the water pan, open the drain cap. Have a bucket ready to catch the drainage, or connect a garden hose to take the water to a floor drain.

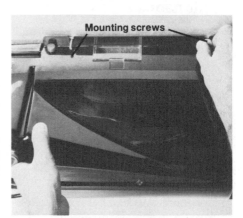

Mounting screws

To remove the unit from the furnace for cleaning or repair, first turn off the power and the water supply. Disconnect the water supply hose. Loosen the mounting screws and lower the water pan while lifting the motor out.

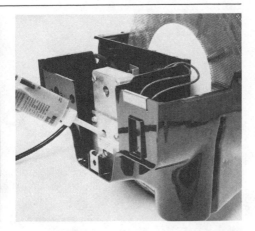

To clean the screens (right), pull the screen shaft carefully out of the motor socket and lift the screens out of the unit. Wash them in hot water and detergent. Remove stubborn deposits by soaking the screens in a solution of 1 cup vinegar to 1 gallon hot water.

To oil the motor (far right), remove the motor cover and locate the motor oil port. It may be on the outside or on the inside of the motor. There may be two ports. Apply a few drops of light oil to each port.

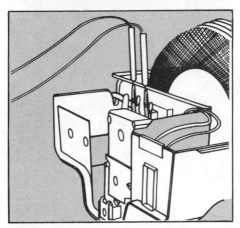

Test the motor if the unit fails to operate and there is power at the unit (right). Turn off the power, disconnect one motor power lead, and connect VOM probes to the motor terminals. You should have between 30 and 100 ohms resistance. Any other reading indicates a defective motor, that should be replaced.

To clean the water inlet valve (far right), loosen the mounting screw and take the float and valve assembly out. Use a thin wire or needle to probe the valve port carefully and clean it out. Work the float arm back and forth and blow through the inlet tube to clean out obstructions.

Humidifiers Troubleshooting Chart

WHAT'S WRONG	*REASONS WHY	WHAT TO DO
Unit doesn't run at all.	No power to unit	Check fuse box/circuit breaker; check power leads to unit.
	Defective humidistat	Test and replace if defective.
	Defective motor	Test motor; replace if defective.
Unit runs all the time.	Unit capacity too small for normal conditions	Buy a larger unit.
	Defective humidistat	Test and replace if defective.
	Humidity level set too high	Adjust controls.
Unit doesn't humidify properly.	Water supply cut off	Check supply hose and pump; clean water pan.
	Clogged float valve	Clean valve.
	Clogged screens, pads, plates, etc.	Clean unit thoroughly.

*If your unit does not have the part mentioned, ignore the entry.

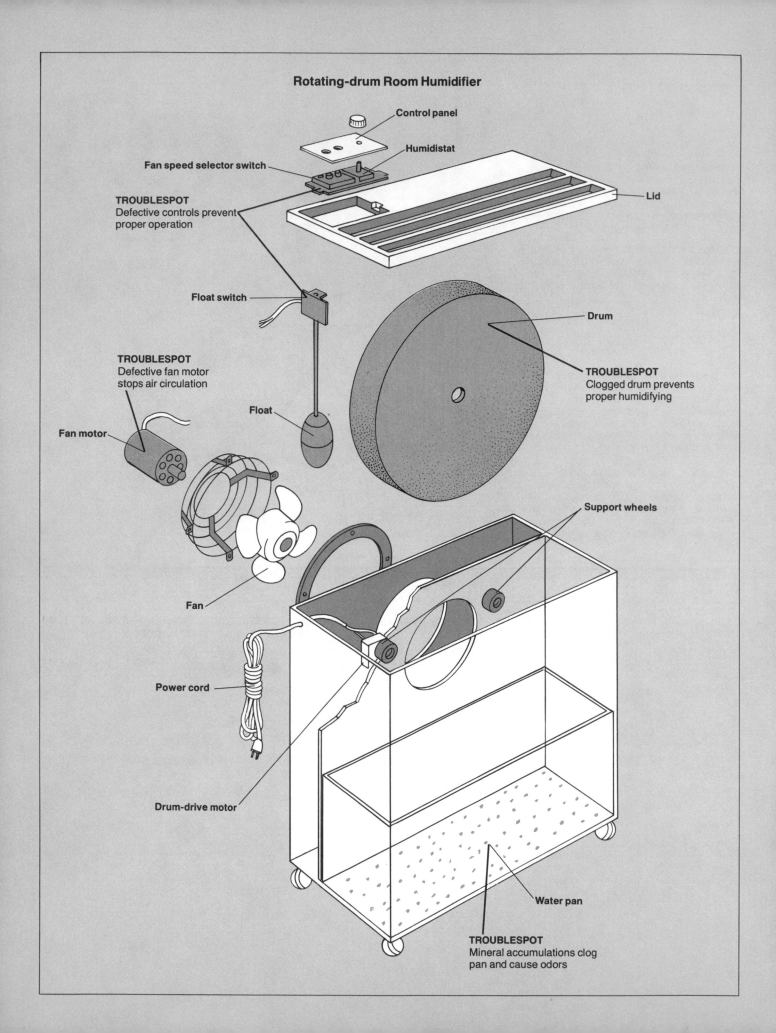

Rotating-drum Room Humidifier

Control panel

Humidistat

Fan speed selector switch

TROUBLESPOT
Defective controls prevent
proper operation

Lid

Float switch

Drum

TROUBLESPOT
Defective fan motor
stops air circulation

TROUBLESPOT
Clogged drum prevents
proper humidifying

Fan motor

Float

Support wheels

Fan

Power cord

Drum-drive motor

Water pan

TROUBLESPOT
Mineral accumulations clog
pan and cause odors

HUMIDIFIERS

Room

If your home needs humidifying during the winter season and you don't have a forced-air heating system, use a room humidifier to ease the discomforts of dry air. (See page 80 for information and charts on the need for humidifiers in the home, and for tips on efficient operation.) Room humidifiers are portable cabinet units that use fans to blow dry room air through wet plastic filters. The air picks up moisture from the filters as it circulates through the machine. The units differ in how they wet the filters; three types are described on these pages. Unlike hot-air-furnace-mounted humidifiers, which are hooked up to a water supply pipe, room humidifiers must be filled with water by hand.

Some room humidifiers have very simple controls—just an on/off switch. Others, like the one shown on the opposite page, have a humidistat for automatic operation, fan speed selector switches, and a signal light that indicates when the unit is running out of water.

The main problem encountered with a humidifier is the accumulation of mineral deposits and scum. The deposits clog the unit, preventing efficient humidification and causing unpleasant odors. Clean the unit often to avoid both problems. Check the troubleshooting chart on page 83 for procedures to follow when the unit doesn't run properly.

Rotating-drum room humidifiers

A rotating-drum humidifier has a large plastic-mesh drum that is partially submerged in a pan of water. As the drum slowly turns, it continually picks up water from the pan. A fan blows room air through the drum, evaporating the water and circulating the moisture around the room.

The model shown opposite has several electrical controls, which can be tested when the unit does not run properly. Instructions for finding and solving electrical problems are given on page 86. As with all humidifiers, the most important maintenance requirement is to keep the unit clean.

Maintenance

To clean the water pan, pull it out of the unit and scrub it in hot water and detergent. Stubborn mineral deposits can be removed with a solution of ¼ cup of vinegar to 1 quart of hot water.

To clean the evaporating drum, lift it off the support wheels. Remove the plastic mesh from the metal frame (if instructions in your owner's manual call for it). Use hot water and detergent to remove mineral deposits; soak in a solution of ¼ cup vinegar to 1 quart water in stubborn cases.

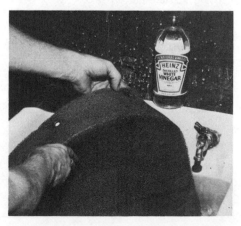

Electrical problems

If the humidifier doesn't run when you turn it on, first check that power is reaching the unit and that there is water in the pan. To find the problem in the electrical circuit, you must do a series of continuity checks (see Blue Pages: *Electrical testers*). Check the float switch; any control switches (they're push buttons on this model); the humidistat, see opposite; and the motors. The fan motor is like the one found on dehumidifiers (see page 57). The drum-drive motor, shown here, is a combination motor and gearbox. If the motor passes a resistance test (see below) but the unit still doesn't run, something in the gearbox has probably failed. The motor and gearbox assembly will have be replaced.

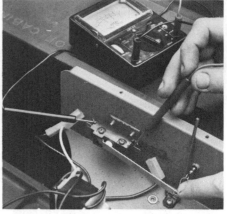

To get inside the unit for tests and repairs, turn off the power and remove the screws that secure the back panel to the cabinet. On the model at right, the panel and fan swing out together. Be careful not to break any electrical connections between the panel and the cabinet.

To test the float switch (far right), turn the power off, disconnect one lead from the switch, and touch VOM probes to the switch terminals. With the float down (no water in pan) the switch should be open and there should be no continuity. With the float up there should be continuity. If the switch fails either test, replace it.

To test the push-button controls (right), read the wiring diagram that comes with the unit to identify the wires and their functions. Turn off the power and test each control for continuity. If there are any faulty controls, the entire control panel will probably have to be replaced.

To test the drum-drive motor (far right), turn the power off, diconnect one lead from the motor, and attach VOM probes to the motor terminals. You should read about 200 ohms resistance. A reading much higher or lower than this means the motor is defective. If the motor runs or hums but the drive shaft doesn't turn, the gearbox is defective. The motor and gearbox assembly must be replaced as a unit.

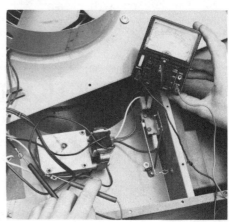

Roller-belt room humidifiers

A roller-belt humidifier is very similar to the rotating-drum type described on the preceding page, except that a belt of plastic mesh takes the place of the drum. When the unit is running, the belt, which is partially submerged in the water pan, is continuously turned by a small motor. The belt picks up water from the pan. A fan blows dry room air through the belt, carrying moisture into the room. Switches and motors can be tested like those on the rotating-drum humidifier. Clean the water pan and the belt regularly to stop mineral accumulation and to prevent odors.

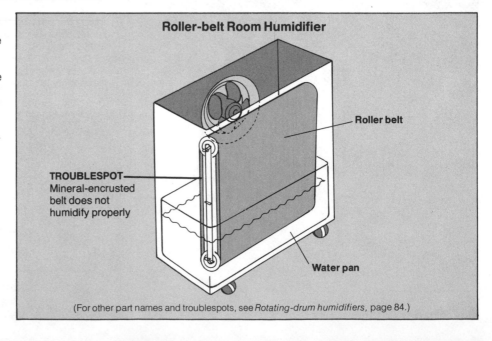

Roller-belt Room Humidifier

Roller belt

TROUBLESPOT
Mineral-encrusted belt does not humidify properly

Water pan

(For other part names and troublespots, see *Rotating-drum humidifiers*, page 84.)

To clean the roller belt, turn off the power, open the lid (or the back panel) of the unit, and lift out the belt and its frame (right). Don't try to take the belt off the frame; wash frame and belt in hot soapy water or soak in a solution of 1 cup vinegar to 1 gallon water.

To test the humidistat for continuity (far right), turn the power off and disconnect one power lead to the humidistat. Clip VOM probes to the power terminals. As you turn the control shaft toward high humidity, at some point the humidistat should click on and show continuity (unless you're in a very humid room). As you turn the shaft toward low humidity, the humidistat should click off and show no continuity (unless you're in a very dry room). If it fails this test, replace it.

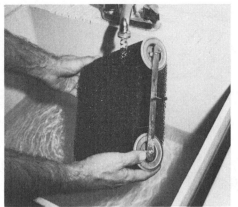
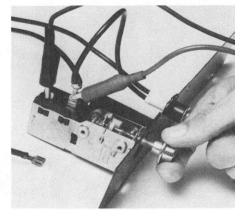

Drip-pad room humidifiers

In a drip-pad humidifier, a plastic-mesh pad sits above a water pan. A pump lifts water from the pan to a drip trough above the pad. Water drips through the trough, soaking the pad. A fan blows room air through the pad to carry moisture into the room. To test the motor and switches, follow directions for the rotating-drum unit described opposite. Test the humidistat as shown above for the roller-belt model. Keep the water pan, fan, drip trough, and pump clean for efficient humidifying.

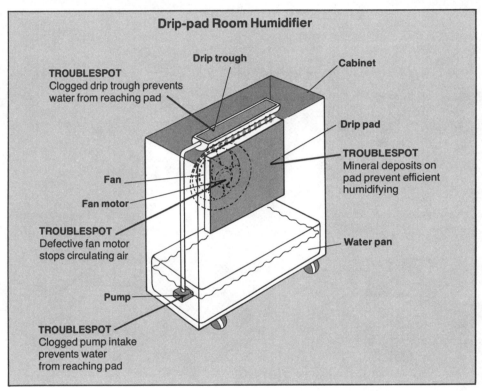

Drip-pad Room Humidifier

Drip trough

Cabinet

TROUBLESPOT
Clogged drip trough prevents water from reaching pad

Drip pad

TROUBLESPOT
Mineral deposits on pad prevent efficient humidifying

Fan

Fan motor

TROUBLESPOT
Defective fan motor stops circulating air

Water pan

Pump

TROUBLESPOT
Clogged pump intake prevents water from reaching pad

Maintenance

To clean the pump, turn off the power, remove the bottom panel of the unit, and take off the C-clamp that holds the two halves of the pump column together (right). You can now clean the inside of the column, the impeller, and the bottom opening.

To clean the drip trough, lift it out of the unit and scrub it with steel wool. Poke a pencil point or thin wire through all the holes in the bottom of the trough (far right).

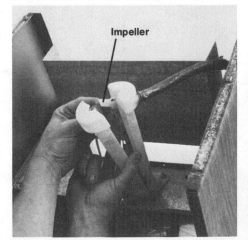

Impeller

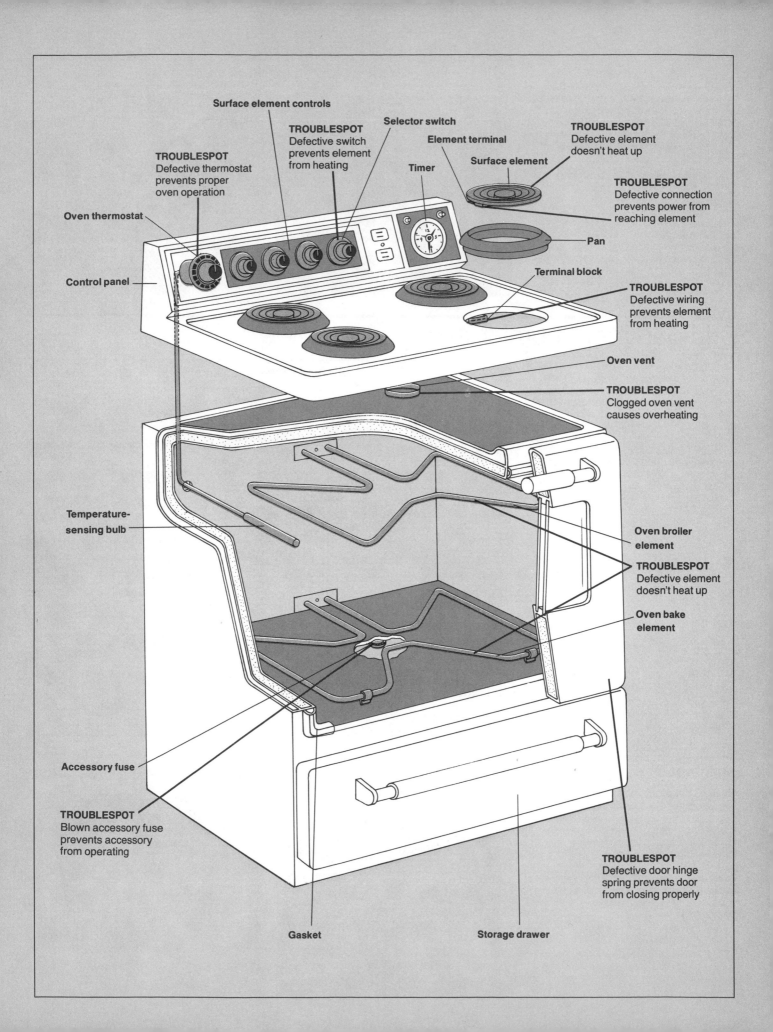

Surface element controls

TROUBLESPOT
Defective switch
prevents element
from heating

Selector switch

Element terminal

Timer

Surface element

TROUBLESPOT
Defective element
doesn't heat up

TROUBLESPOT
Defective thermostat
prevents proper
oven operation

TROUBLESPOT
Defective connection
prevents power from
reaching element

Oven thermostat

Control panel

Pan

Terminal block

TROUBLESPOT
Defective wiring
prevents element
from heating

Oven vent

TROUBLESPOT
Clogged oven vent
causes overheating

**Temperature-
sensing bulb**

**Oven broiler
element**

TROUBLESPOT
Defective element
doesn't heat up

**Oven bake
element**

Accessory fuse

TROUBLESPOT
Blown accessory fuse
prevents accessory
from operating

TROUBLESPOT
Defective door hinge
spring prevents door
from closing properly

Gasket

Storage drawer

Ranges

Electric

An electric range cooks by the heat generated when a high-voltage current passes through metal coils of low resistance, called elements. Basically, a range consists of these elements and the switches to turn them on and off. Thus, there is very little mechanical work involved in maintaining a range, but repairs require a great deal of electrical testing and wiring. Carefully read the Blue Pages, which describe electricity and electrical testing, and become thoroughly familiar with your volt-ohm meter (VOM) before working on a range, and Appliance Repair Basics, which describes different types of heating elements.

Modern ranges have been made more complicated by the many controls added to make things easier for the cook. Selector switches, thermostats, timers, accessory switches and motors, meat temperature controls—all these mean more wiring, more connections, and more things to go wrong. The maze of wires inside an elaborate control panel (see page 92) can look daunting at first, but if you have the patience and aptitude for solving puzzles, you can make the tests and repairs explained here without difficulty. When in doubt, however, call an electrician.

The self-cleaning oven deserves special mention because of the high wattage required to do the pyrolitic (heat) cleaning and the high temperature attained in the oven. Everything about a self-cleaning oven must be heavier and stronger to withstand the 5,000 watts and 1,000°F. heat that do the work. Most important, is the fail-safe door lock: the cleaning cycle will not start if the door is not locked, and the oven door cannot open at high heat.

You can test the cleaning efficiency visually: if there's some gray ash left over, the cleaning cycle was successful. If brown deposits remain, call a repairman.

CAUTION Electric ranges operate on 240 volts AC. This is a lethal dose of current. Make absolutely certain that the power is shut off at the fuse box/circuit breaker before you start any repairs or tests. Take steps to prevent anyone from turning the power on while you're working.

TIPS FOR ENERGY EFFICIENCY

Turn the range off as soon as you're through cooking. In fact, an electric range can be turned off *before* cooking is finished, since it holds heat for some time.

Be sure the pot or pan covers the element. An exposed element wastes energy. A pot too wide for the element may cause uneven cooking.

Pressure cookers save time and energy.

Defrost foods before starting to cook them.

When heating large quantities of water, start with hot water from the tap; it's much cheaper. For long cooking, the oven is more efficient than the burners, since it's insulated and holds heat longer.

Open the oven door as little as possible. Every time you open the door the temperature drops about 50°F. Cook by time and temperature, not by peeking.

Self-cleaning ovens consume large amounts of energy, so wipe up spills when they occur. When self-cleaning is necessary, start immediately after cooking, to save energy.

Adjustments to door and hinge

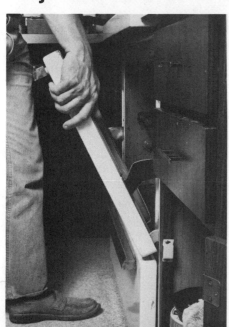

To work on the door handle or hinges (left), you must remove the door. Grasp it on both sides and pull up firmly. When the door has moved an inch or so, it will fall forward off the top hook of the hinge. Continue pulling and the door will slip off the bottom hook.

To tighten or replace the door handle (below), remove the screws holding the door liner panel. Hold the insulation in the panel as you lift the panel out of the door. The screws holding the door handle will now be accessible.

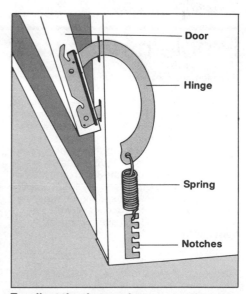

- Door
- Hinge
- Spring
- Notches

To adjust the door spring, remove the door and take out the storage drawer. The notches that hold the end of the spring will be accessible on both sides at the bottom.

Problems with the heating elements

If an element doesn't heat up at any switch setting, it is probably defective. To make sure, turn the power off and remove and test the element, as shown here. If the element is OK, check the switch or the wiring. If none of the elements work at all, check the fuse box/circuit breaker. If that's OK, call an electrician; you may have a problem in the power line that leads to the range.

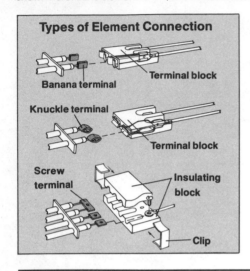

Types of Element Connection

Banana terminal
Terminal block

Knuckle terminal
Terminal block

Screw terminal
Insulating block
Clip

Remove a surface element by pulling it gently out of the terminal block (power is off). If it is screwed on, pull it out as far as you can and remove the screws with your free hand.

Test a doubtful element for resistance with a VOM, set at RX1. If there is either no resistance or infinite resistance, replace the element. If the element is OK, check the wiring and switches (see below).

Checking the oven elements

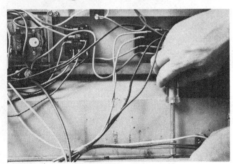

1 **To reach the oven element connections,** you'll probably have to unscrew the back panel. It may be possible to remove the elements from inside.

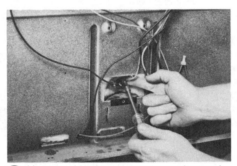

2 Unscrew the wires connected to the terminals of the oven heating elements at the rear of the oven.

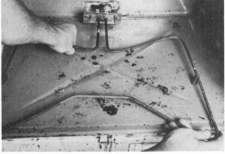

3 Pull the element out of the oven. It may be screwed to a mounting bracket. Test an oven element the same way as a surface element (above).

Problems with switches and wiring

If an element does not heat at any switch setting and the resistance in the element itself is OK (see above), the problem is in either the wiring or the switch. To test these parts, remove the panel that covers the back of the switches (power is off). First, check all connections to be sure they're tight and not burned. If they're OK, make the tests described in the Blue Pages under *Electrical testers*. If both the switch and the wiring between the element and the switch are OK, then the problem lies in the wiring between the switch and the fuse box/circuit breaker. Better call an electrician to make the necessary power tests.

Test the wiring from switch to element. Place one VOM probe on one point in the terminal block and the other on one hot wire terminal on the back of the switch (red and black wires carry power in). Test the other pair of terminals. With the switch off, there should be no continuity in either circuit. With the switch on, there should be continuity in both.

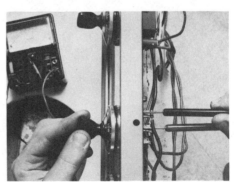

To test a switch, compare it to a working duplicate from your range. Check continuity between all terminals at all switch settings. If the suspected switch does not match the good switch in its responses, replace it with a duplicate.

To work on surface elements, wiring, and terminal blocks, remove the screws that hold the stove top and lift it up. (Elements and reflector pans will have to come out first—see opposite page) When replacing defective wiring, always do one wire at a time, to avoid any wrong connections. Any defective wiring must be replaced with No. 14 solid asbestos-covered wire, marked 105°C. Never use ordinary electrician's tape in a range.

If a terminal block is broken, unscrew it from the bottom side of the stove top, label the wires, unscrew them from the block, and take the block out. (The block is also called *terminal guide* or *porcelain receptacle*). Replace the bad part with a duplicate.

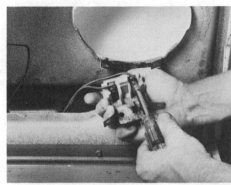

Problems with the oven thermostat

If the oven thermostat works at only one temperature, or doesn't keep the oven at the temperature you set, call a repairman to check the calibration of the thermostat. If the oven doesn't work at all but the top elements work OK, then check the oven elements (see opposite page). If they pass a continuity test, check the wiring from the elements to the thermostat for continuity. Next, test the wiring from the thermostat to the selector switch (if your oven has one). Then check the selector switch itself. If all these parts check OK, then the problem lies in the thermostat itself and its sensing bulb. Replace them as shown below.

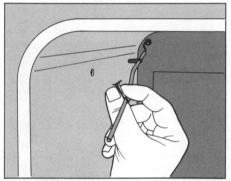

1 **To replace a defective thermostat,** first remove the temperature-sensing bulb from inside the oven by squeezing out the clips that attach the bulb and its tube to the side or back of the oven.

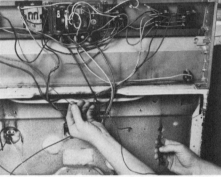

2 Pull the sensing bulb and tube out of the back of the oven. Note how the tube is attached to the oven wall, and how it finds its way from thermostat to oven, so you can install the new one correctly.

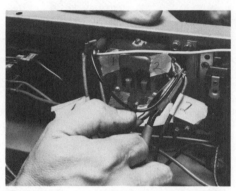

3 Label the wires attached to the thermostat with bits of masking tape and remove the wires from the defective part.

4 Remove the knob from the front of the thermostat and unscrew it from its mounting inside the panel. Replace it with an exact duplicate, installing first the sensing bulb and tube and then the thermostat.

Occasional Problems

If your oven begins to overheat or to burn food, lift out the top elements and reflector pans to locate the oven vent. There is usually a heat deflector that sits above the vent and directs the exhaust out the element hole in the top of the range. Clean this deflector, the space beneath it, and the vent hole.

If your range has an outlet in the control panel for an accessory (such as a coffee pot or waffle iron) there will be a separate fuse somewhere for this independent circuit. On this model it's underneath the oven in the top of the storage drawer. On some models you must lift the stove top (see directions at top this page) to find the fuse underneath at the back. If the fuse blows, replace it with a 15-amp fuse only.

Electric range accessories

Some late-model electric ranges offer a large number of accessories for alternate ways of cooking. By slipping interchangeable parts in and out you can have a broiling grill on top of the range, a motor-driven shish kebab cooker, a deep-fat fryer, a rotisserie, a flat grill, and a ceramic cook top, besides the usual circular elements. There may also be a ventilation system to keep smoke and odors out of the kitchen and a grease collection system to make cleaning up easier. If your range has these parts, be sure to install them according to your instruction manual to prevent electrical problems, and keep them clean to avoid fire hazard from the accumulation of grease.

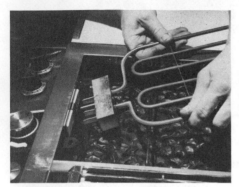

To install and remove interchangeable electric parts, follow the instruction book strictly. Treat the terminals especially carefully so as not to bend them out of shape. Be sure the control panel switches are turned off.

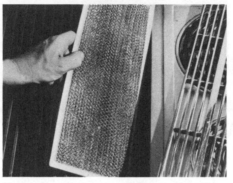

If your range has a ventilation system, there will be a metal air filter somewhere inside. On this model it's just below the ventilation grille. Clean air filters frequently.

If your range has a grease collection system, there will be a grease trap somewhere inside the range. Empty the trap frequently. This model uses a glass jar identical to an ordinary mayonnaise jar.

A range with solid-state components

Some late-model electric ranges that offer elaborate temperature and time controls use solid-state components to conserve space in the control panel. Elaborate controls mean elaborate wiring systems, however, as this model shows. Even if you can't read the wiring diagram, you can, with patience, make the same tests and replacements of elements as on an ordinary range. Just be prepared to spend more time tracing the wiring. You can also test and replace a solid-state component such as the oven's meat temperature control, as shown below.

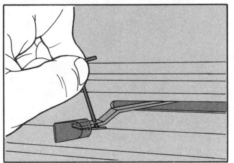

1 **To get inside the control panel,** you must remove the knob of the oven door lock lever. On this typical model, use a small Allen wrench to press the retaining clip just behind the knob. Press and pull at the same time and the knob will slip off.

2 Remove the screws that attach the control panel to the oven. Then pull the panel straight forward until it clears the door lock lever. Let the panel fall gently down; the wires will support it.

Checking the meat temperature control

1 **If the meat temperature control doesn't work** but the rest of the oven seems OK, first check the meat probe (the metal rod that you insert into the roast to take its temperature). When cold the probe should show about 100 ohms resistance. When hot (put the probe tip in boiling water) the resistance should be much lower.

2 If the probe is OK, then test the wiring between the probe socket in the oven and the meat temperature control unit in the control panel for continuity. It's mounted right behind the meat temperature dial. If the wiring is OK, the problem is in the control unit, a small solid-state control board in this model.

3 To replace a faulty meat temperature control unit, first remove the dial from the front of the panel. Label the wires leading to the unit, disconnect them, unscrew the unit from its mounting, and take it out. Replace it with an exact duplicate.

Electric Ranges Troubleshooting Chart

WHAT'S WRONG	REASONS WHY	WHAT TO DO
Nothing works.	No power to range	Check fuse box/circuit breaker. If OK, call electrician.
One top element doesn't heat.	Defective element, wiring, terminal block, or switch	Check each part for continuity and replace if defective.
Top element doesn't cook properly.	Wrong size pot or pan	Use flat-bottomed utensil that just covers element.
	Defective element	Replace element.
Oven doesn't heat.	Defective element, wiring, thermostat, or selector switch	Check each part for continuity and replace if defective.
	Timer not set properly	Reset timer.
	Defective timer	Replace timer.
Top rear element doesn't heat.	Oven in self-cleaning cycle	(Extremely high power requirement during cleaning may prevent top element from working.)
Oven overheats.	Clogged vent	Clean vent.
Oven does not hold set temperature.	Defective door gasket	Replace gasket.
	Thermostat not properly calibrated	Call repairman.
Oven lamp doesn't light.	Bulb burned out	Replace bulb with special oven-type bulb.
	Defective switch or wiring to bulb socket	Test wiring and switch; replace if defective.
Timer doesn't work.	Timer not set properly	Reset; check instructions.
	Timer fuse blown	Check 15-amp fuse in timer circuit.
	Loose connections	Turn power off and check all timer connections for continuity.
	Timer worn out	Replace unit.
Oven door doesn't stay shut.	Defective hinge or spring	Replace defective part.
Condensation forms in oven.	Clogged vent	Clean vent. If there is an air filter, clean or replace it.
	Door not closing properly	Check gasket and door hinge springs.
	Improper preheating	Preheat oven with door ajar.
Accessory receptacle on control panel doesn't work.	Blown fuse	Check 15-amp fuse in accessory circuit.
	Defective wiring	Check wiring and replace.
Oven doesn't self-clean.	Door not locked	Try again.
	Defective door switch, wiring, or thermostat	Call repairman.

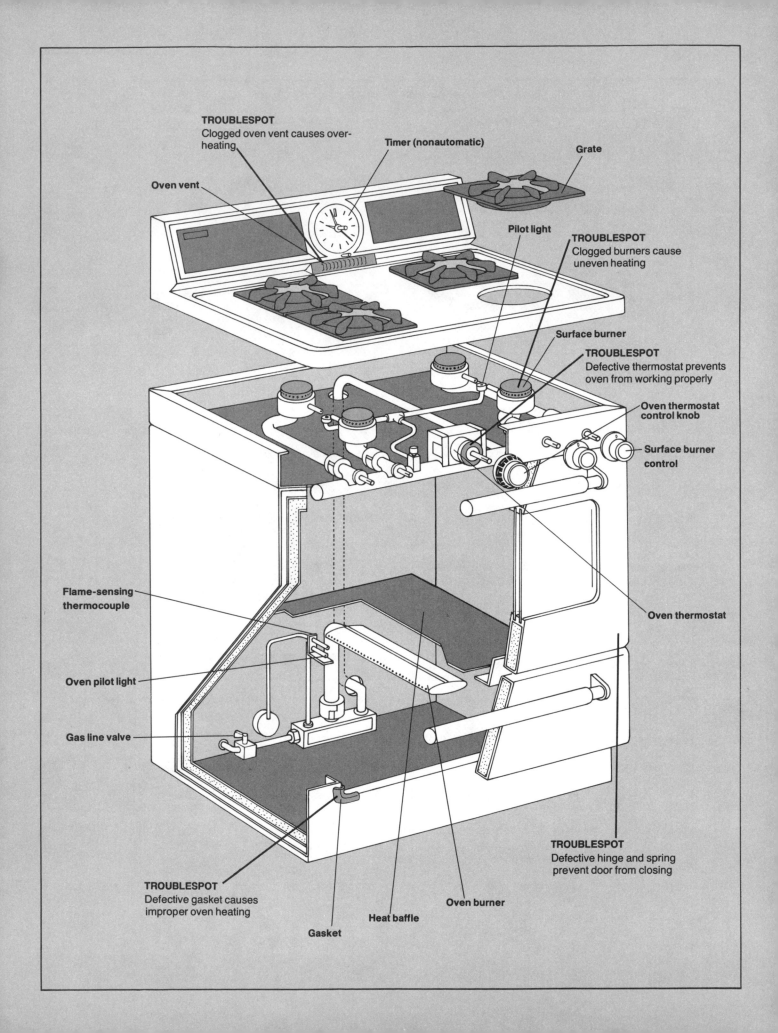

TROUBLESPOT
Clogged oven vent causes over-heating.

Timer (nonautomatic)

Grate

Oven vent

Pilot light

TROUBLESPOT
Clogged burners cause uneven heating

Surface burner

TROUBLESPOT
Defective thermostat prevents oven from working properly

Oven thermostat control knob

Surface burner control

Flame-sensing thermocouple

Oven thermostat

Oven pilot light

Gas line valve

TROUBLESPOT
Defective hinge and spring prevent door from closing

TROUBLESPOT
Defective gasket causes improper oven heating

Gasket

Heat baffle

Oven burner

RANGES
Gas

Gas ranges are probably the simplest large appliances in the home: a few pipes carry gas to the burners, and hand valves turn the gas on and off. The lack of numerous switches and complicated wiring means that there is little to go wrong and little for the owner to work on. In fact, you should not attempt any adjustment of the gas pipes or the gas/air mixture. This means you should never move the range itself or move the air shutters on the burners. These are all jobs for trained personnel from the gas company.

There are a few mechanical problems you can take care of: a sagging door or broken hinge spring (see page 89); a clogged oven vent (see page 91); or a worn-out door gasket—replace it with a duplicate.

A new feature of gas ranges is pilotless ignition. A red-hot coil ignites the gas instead of the ever burning pilot flame. This adds the complications of electrical components and wiring to the gas range. See page 96 for instructions for testing and replacing an ignition coil.

TIPS FOR ENERGY EFFICIENCY

Turn the range off as soon as you're finished cooking.

Pressure cookers save time and energy.

Defrost foods before starting to cook them.

When heating large quantities of water, start with hot water from the tap.

For long cooking, the oven is more efficient than a burner; it's insulated and holds heat longer.

Open the oven door as little as possible. Every time you open the door the temperature drops about 50°F.

Self-cleaning ovens consume large amounts of energy, so wipe up spills when they occur. If self-cleaning is necessary, start right after cooking to utilize the heat.

Cleaning a Clogged Burner

If the burner flames are uneven, clean the burner ports with a small, stiff wire. If the flames are yellow instead of blue, call the gas company to adjust the air/gas mixture.

Safety Precautions

If you smell a slight odor of gas, check the surface and oven pilot lights. Ventilate the room and relight any pilot that has gone out. If no pilot flames are out, there must be a leak elsewhere in the gas line. Call the gas company.

If there is a heavy, oppressive odor of gas, ventilate the house and call the gas company immediately. Do *not* light any flames and do not turn any electrical switches on *or* off. Never search for a gas leak with an open flame.

Gas ranges are adjusted for either LP or natural gas. If you want to change fuel type, call the gas company.

Relighting an oven pilot light

If the oven doesn't light, check the pilot light. You will probably have to remove the heat baffle, which sits above the burner, to reach the pilot. If the pilot is burning, then there is probably something wrong with the safety thermocouple, which must sense the pilot flame before the gas will come on. The thermostat may also be faulty. Call the gas company to deal with these problems.

1 **To reach the pilot light to relight it,** first remove the heat baffle that covers the oven burner. You may have to unscrew a wing nut to free the baffle.

2 Clean all the ports in the oven burner with a small, stiff wire while the baffle is off.

3 Relight the oven pilot flame while the oven is turned off. Keep your face out of the oven, just in case.

Checking a pilotless ignition system

Some late-model ranges have eliminated the wasteful pilot light and substituted electric ignition. In this system there is a small coil near each burner that glows instantly when the control knob is turned. The heat from the coil ignites the gas. If none of the pilot coils work, check the fuse box/circuit breaker; if that's OK, call an electrician to check the power cable to the range. If one pilot coil is out (and you have gas), test and replace it as shown here.

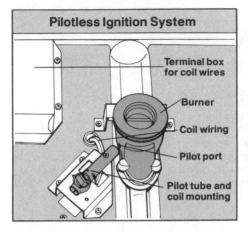

Pilotless Ignition System

Terminal box for coil wires

Burner

Coil wiring

Pilot port

Pilot tube and coil mounting

1 **If a burner doesn't light,** first be sure the pilot port at the side of the burner is open. Use a very thin wire to probe and clear the tiny hole.

2 Test the wiring between the coil and the terminal box for resistance (see Blue Pages: *Electrical testers*). Turn the power OFF. Remove the cover from the terminal box and disconnect at the box one of the two wires leading to the suspect coil. Place the probes on the terminal ends of the two wires. You should read very low resistance, about 1 ohm. If resistance is high, replace the coil.

3 To replace a defective pilot coil, disconnect its wires in the terminal box and unscrew the coil mounting bracket. Pull the coil and wires out of the range and take them to an appliance store for a duplicate.

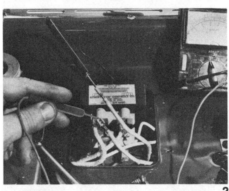

2

3

Gas Ranges Troubleshooting Chart

WHAT'S WRONG	REASONS WHY	WHAT TO DO
Surface burner doesn't light.	Pilot light out	Relight pilot; follow instructions for your range.
	Gas supply shut off	Call the gas company.
Pilot flame doesn't stay lit.	Clogged pilot port	Clean port with small wire.
	Drafty location	Prevent drafts around range.
Burner burns erratically.	Clogged burner	Clean burner ports.
	Improper gas/air mixture	Call gas company to adjust.
Oven does not light.	Oven pilot light out	Relight pilot.
	Defective safety thermocouple	Call gas company.
	Gas supply off	Call gas company.
Oven heats poorly.	Improper gas/air mixture	Call gas company.
	Defective thermostat	Call gas company.
Oven bakes unevenly.	Defective door gasket	Replace gasket.
Oven overheats.	Clogged exhaust vent	Clean vent.
	Defective thermostat	Call gas company.
Burners make soot.	Improper gas/air mixture	Call gas company.
Burners are noisy.	Improper gas/air mixture	Call gas company.
Gas odor	Pilot out	Ventilate room; relight pilot.
	Possible leak in gas line	Call gas company to check for possible leak. Ventilate room. Extinguish all flames. Don't fip any electric switch.

Microwave ovens

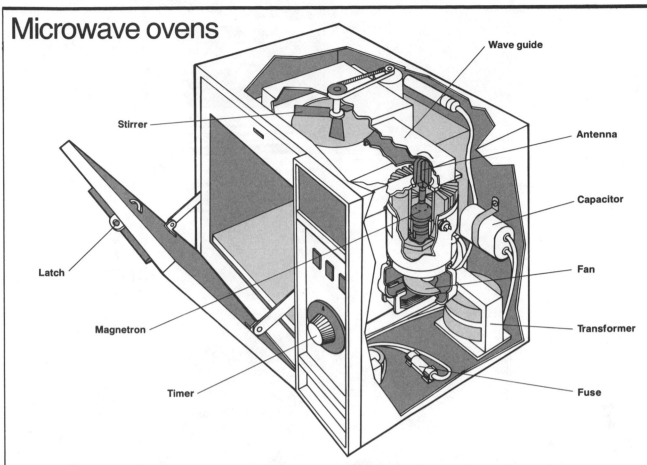

Stirrer

Latch

Magnetron

Timer

Wave guide

Antenna

Capacitor

Fan

Transformer

Fuse

"Cooking with gas" used to be the newest thing. Today, cooking with microwaves is becoming increasingly popular. Microwaves have three important properties: they are reflected by metal; they can pass through glass, paper, plastic, and similar materials; and they are absorbed by foods.

How microwave ovens work

Microwave ovens use a special type of electron tube called a magnetron. The tube is fitted with a magnet whose magnetic field acts on the electron flow to produce electromagnetic radiation in the microwave frequency range.

When the oven is turned on, a step-up transformer raises the normal household power of 120 volts to 4,000 volts. This high voltage is converted to direct current and applied to the magnetron, which then generates the microwaves. The microwaves, fed by an antenna, are then channeled by a metal conduit, called a wave guide, into the oven chamber. A fanlike device, called a stirrer and located at the top of the oven, disperses the microwaves as they leave the wave guide.

The magnetron is cooled by a fan and protected from overheating by a thermostatic switch that cuts off power if the magnetron becomes too hot. A fuse protects the entire oven from damage if there is a sudden surge of current—a short circuit, for example.

Microwave ovens and safety

All microwave ovens made after October 1971 are covered by a radiation safety standard enforced by the Food and Drug Administration. The safety standard limits the amount of radiation leakage allowed for an oven over its lifetime. This limit is far below the level of radiation known to be harmful.

A double interlock system—also required by law—stops the production of microwaves the moment the latch is released or the oven door is opened. In addition, a monitoring system stops oven operation if one or both of the interlocking systems fail. The FDA monitors the manufacture of microwave ovens to assure adherence to these standards.

No documented cases of radiation injury from microwave ovens have been reported. Injuries that have occurred could happen with any oven or cooking surface—burns from heated plates, steam, hot food, and the like.

How food is cooked in microwave ovens

Microwaves cause the water molecules in food to vibrate, producing heat from friction, which cooks the food.

Glass, paper, ceramic, or plastic containers can be used in microwave cooking because the microwaves pass through them. Metal pans or aluminum foil should not be used since they reflect microwaves, causing food to cook unevenly. The instructions that come with each oven tell you what containers to use, and how to test others for possible use in the oven.

Installing the oven

To install a microwave oven, follow these three steps.(1) Remove all packing material from the oven interior. (2) Place the oven where you want it, but be sure to leave 1 inch clearance at the top and rear and 6 inches on the sides to assure proper ventilation. (3) Plug the oven into a standard 120- to 240-volt household outlet. Be sure that the oven is the *only* appliance on that circuit.

Maintaining the oven

Because of the strict safety standards on microwave ovens, owner service is strongly discouraged, and little disassembly is possible. In fact, manufacturers will usually void their warranties if they see that the oven has been taken apart. Maintenance is thus limited to cleaning.

Clean the oven cavity, door, and seals frequently with water and a mild detergent. A special cleaner is not necessary. Don't use a scouring pad, steel wool, or other abrasives. To remove odors in the oven, boil a solution of a cup of water and several tablespoons of lemon juice in the oven for five to seven minutes.

Recommendations for Operating a Microwave Oven

Examine a new oven for evidence of shipping damage.

Follow the manufacturer's instruction manual for operating procedures and safety precautions.

Never operate an oven if the door does not close firmly or if the door is bent, warped, or damaged.

Never insert objects through the door grille or around the door seal.

Never turn on the oven when it is empty.

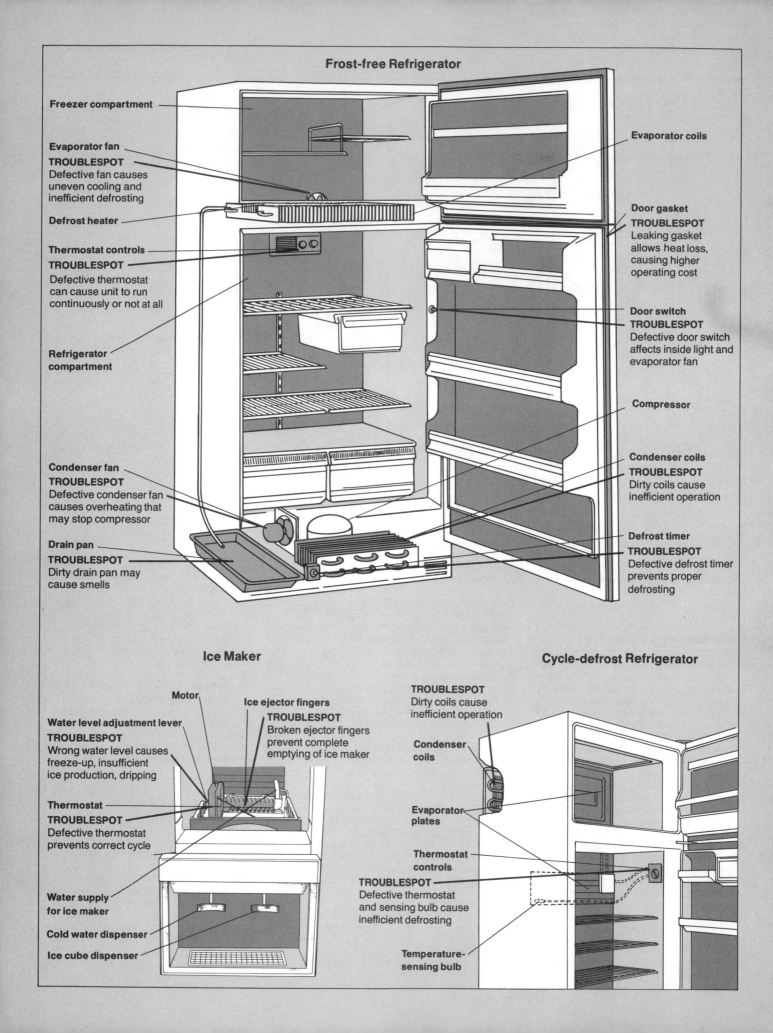

Frost-free Refrigerator

Freezer compartment

Evaporator fan
TROUBLESPOT
Defective fan causes uneven cooling and inefficient defrosting

Defrost heater

Thermostat controls
TROUBLESPOT
Defective thermostat can cause unit to run continuously or not at all

Refrigerator compartment

Condenser fan
TROUBLESPOT
Defective condenser fan causes overheating that may stop compressor

Drain pan
TROUBLESPOT
Dirty drain pan may cause smells

Evaporator coils

Door gasket
TROUBLESPOT
Leaking gasket allows heat loss, causing higher operating cost

Door switch
TROUBLESPOT
Defective door switch affects inside light and evaporator fan

Compressor

Condenser coils
TROUBLESPOT
Dirty coils cause inefficient operation

Defrost timer
TROUBLESPOT
Defective defrost timer prevents proper defrosting

Ice Maker

Motor

Ice ejector fingers
TROUBLESPOT
Broken ejector fingers prevent complete emptying of ice maker

Water level adjustment lever
TROUBLESPOT
Wrong water level causes freeze-up, insufficient ice production, dripping

Thermostat
TROUBLESPOT
Defective thermostat prevents correct cycle

Water supply for ice maker

Cold water dispenser

Ice cube dispenser

Cycle-defrost Refrigerator

TROUBLESPOT
Dirty coils cause inefficient operation

Condenser coils

Evaporator plates

Thermostat controls
TROUBLESPOT
Defective thermostat and sensing bulb cause inefficient defrosting

Temperature-sensing bulb

Refrigerator-freezers

A refrigerator is an expensive necessity. Its purchase price represents only about one fifth of its ten-year cost, the rest being the cost of electricity to run it. Thus, sensible operating practices that can improve efficiency are important (see box below). Regular cleaning procedures (see below) also help the unit to run more easily and cheaply. A refrigerator uses the same kind of cooling components as an air conditioner. They are described on page 39. As with the air conditioner, you should leave all repairs to the pressurized refrigerant system to a trained service person. Take care when you are working around a refrigerator not to bend or break any of the refrigeration lines.

There is always some moisture in the air in the refrigerator. Since cold air can't carry much moisture, it collects as frost on the evaporator coils, the coldest surface. The refrigerator has to have a way of getting rid of the frost that accumulates inside. On manual-defrost models, you have to turn the unit completely off and let the ice melt away. Several years ago, cycle-defrost units were developed in which the frost accumulates on evaporator plates in plain sight inside the unit. Every so often a timer turns on a heater that melts the frost, which drains down and out the bottom into a drain pan. In the latest frost-free models the place where the frost accumulates—the evaporator coils—is hidden so you never see any frost. Again, a timer turns on a heater occasionally to melt the frost.

The refrigerator-freezer combination is used by almost everyone today. Separate freezer units, however, are really just like refrigerators in terms of basic components and functions, except that the whole machine runs at near-zero temperatures, not just a section. The mechanical and electrical problems found in freezers and refrigerators are virtually identical, even if the components are arranged somewhat differently.

If your refrigerator develops any suspicious symptoms, turn first to the troubleshooting chart at the end of this section. You can eliminate the possible causes of your trouble one by one until you find the culprit. Very often a simple adjustment—such as cleaning the coils—will take care of the problem.

NOTE: There are probably hundreds of models of refrigerators. Our pictures show typical late-model frost-free units. Some of the components in your refrigerator may be in a different place, but they're doing the same jobs and are repaired the same way.

Basic maintenance

Refrigerators require a minimum of regular maintenance, but a thorough cleaning and disinfecting once a year, inside and underneath, makes the unit run more efficiently and prevents bad odors. The coils underneath are not easy to reach, and to get to those in back you must move the unit (see page 104). But the effort is worth it: dirty coils can make a unit run continuously or stop altogether. The drip pan should be cleaned more often, perhaps once a month in hot weather.

 Don't put the pan in the dishwasher; it may bend out of shape.

Clean the drip pan in soapy water to prevent bad odors. To get at the pan, snap out the bottom grille. If the pan rattles while the refrigerator is in operation, move it slightly so it's not touching the unit at the sides. If that doesn't help, try putting a flat stone in it.

Clean the coils underneath with the crevice attachment on your vacuum cleaner. On older models, the coils hang on the back of the unit. To do an honest job on many late models, you have to lay the unit on its side (see page 104).

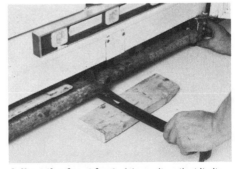

Adjust the front feet of the unit so that it sits level from side to side, and tilts backward just enough so that the doors will close slowly by themselves. A crowbar on a piece of two-by-four gives the necessary lift. Older units may have four adjustable feet; on later models only the two in front are adjustable.

Clear the drain holes with a screwdriver or a piece of wire. You'll find a drain at the bottom of both refrigerator and freezer compartments. (On late models, the freezer drain cannot be reached without extensive dismantling.) After you have opened the drain, force water through the passage with a baster or syringe.

⚙ TIPS FOR EFFICIENT OPERATION

Do not open the door any more often than necessary.

Clean the coils regularly.

Check the gasket for tightness.

Keep liquids and damp foods sealed up, especially in frost-free units.

Never put hot food into the unit.

Place containers to allow air circulation.

Never block circulation vents in a frost-free unit.

Set the thermostat so the unit runs at 5°F. in the freezer and 35°–40°F. in the refrigerator.

Mechanical problems

To adjust a sagging door, hold it steady with one hand while you loosen the hinge screws with the other. Lift the door to the proper position and tighten the screws. To adjust the bottom door you may have to open or sometimes even remove the top door.

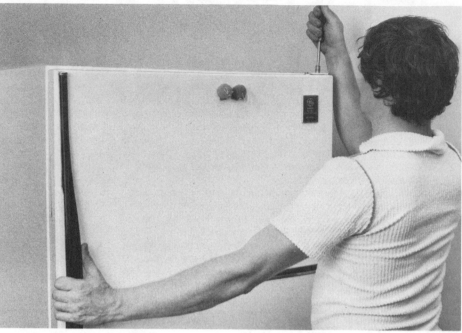

To adjust a loose magnetic catch, screw the door magnet all the way down, until there is space between door and body. Then loosen the door magnet little by little until it just touches the body.

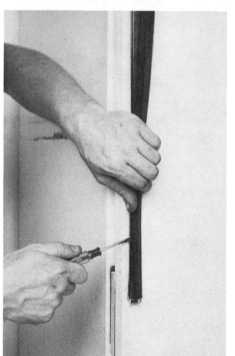

1 **To replace a damaged door handle,** first pry out the metal or plastic insert that most models have covering the screws. Some models have a small movable socket at the bottom of the handle into which the insert fits and which can be forced down with a screwdriver.

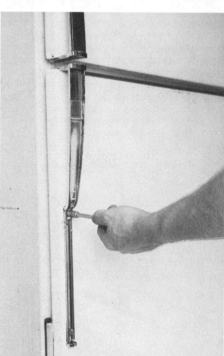

2 Unscrew the damaged handle from the unit body and replace it with a duplicate.

Replacing a defective gasket

A worn or hardened gasket leaves gaps between the door and the body of the refrigerator. This allows warm air and moisture into the unit, forcing it to work harder and longer, making it frost up. If a test shows gaps, make sure the door is not just sagging or warped (opposite). Before you start, be sure you have an exact duplicate of your old gasket.

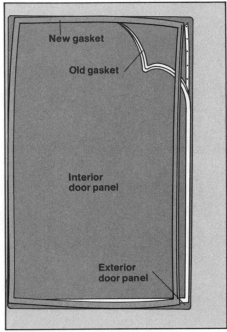

Always replace a gasket in steps. To begin with, remove the old gasket from one top corner and put in the new one there. Follow the same procedure for the other top corner. Finally, take the rest of the old one off the bottom and finish installing the new one.

If you take the entire gasket off in one piece, on most models the door panel comes off, the insulation falls out, and the door sags out of shape (it may even kink). Getting it all back together is a real problem.

When you have finished installing a new gasket, examine the door carefully to make sure the door has not slumped out of shape. If it has, loosen the retaining screws, press the door (not the door panel) up into true shape, and tighten the screws. You may have to loosen and tighten them several times.

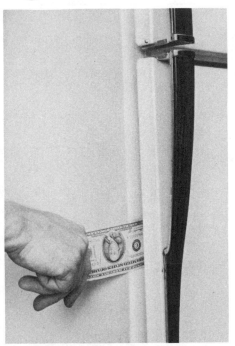

To test a gasket, try to push a crisp bill under the gasket all the way around with the door closed. If the bill slides under, the gasket is defective. Another test is to shut the door on a bill; there should be moderate resistance when you pull it out.

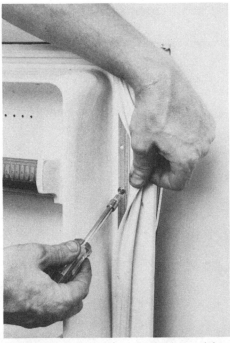

1 To replace the gasket, loosen the retaining screws under the gasket around one corner of the door. If you can get the gasket off the retaining metal strips without removing the screws entirely, so much the better. If not, you may have to take both screws and strips out entirely.

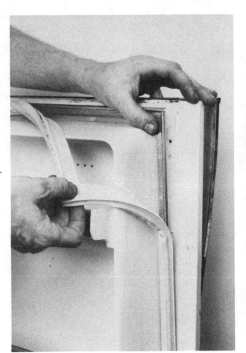

2 Pull the gasket off the retaining strips, going only halfway across the top and about halfway down one side.

3 Slip the new gasket over the retaining strips while the old gasket hangs out of the way, and put the screws back in halfway. Proceed with the other corner, then the bottom. After the new gasket is in, hold the door up square and tighten the screws all around.

Electrical problems

Fixing a door switch

If a bad door switch leaves the inside light burning, the resulting heat may force the unit to run continuously. On frost-free models, the same switch may control the evaporator fan, shutting it off when the door is open; on other models (like the one shown here) there are two identical-looking switches, one for the light and the other for the fan. If the evaporator fan switch fails, the freezer will frost up.

If the light does not turn off when you depress the switch button with your finger, or if it does not turn on when you open the door (and you've made sure the bulb is good), unplug the unit and proceed as shown here. If the evaporator fan doesn't work (see *Checking the evaporator fan*, opposite, to tell whether it's operating) check its switch as shown here.

1 **To test a door switch** it is usually necessary to pry off the side panel. (The switch pulls forward out of the panel, but the wires are often too short to let the switch drop completely out of the hole.) Hold the wall insulation in place with masking tape.

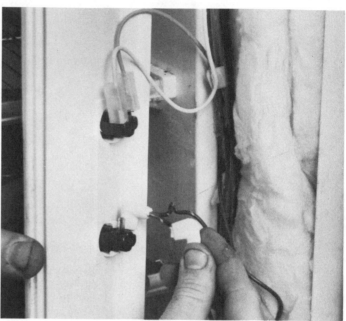

2 Unclip the leads from the switch. Pull the leads straight off so as not to bend the terminals.

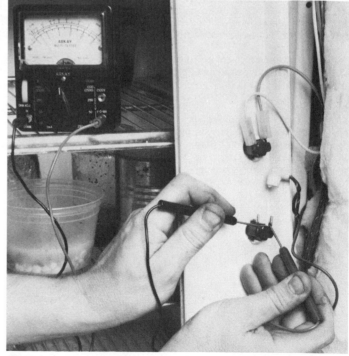

3 Test the switch for continuity (see Blue Pages: *Electrical testers*). On the light switch there should be continuity with the button out, and no continuity with the button pushed in. (The results for the fan switch should be exactly the opposite.) If the switch is defective, replace it .

Testing the thermostat

If the refrigerator won't maintain the right temperature (and you've made sure the coils are clean and the door gasket is tight), check the thermostat or "temperature control." In a frost-free unit, this control is easy to get at. In a cycle-defrost refrigerator, it's more complicated, since there is a sensing bulb that must be removed from behind the compartment liner. When replacing the new bulb, be careful not to kink the tubing; place the new bulb exactly where the old one was. **CAUTION** Turn off the power before starting to work.

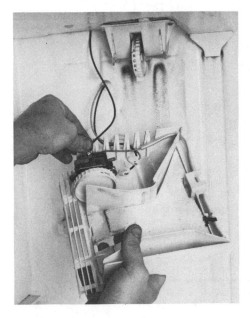

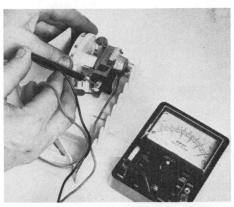

1 **To reach and test the thermostat,** unscrew the cover or pry it off. On some models, first pry off the control knob and then take out retaining screws to get to the thermostat. Label and disconnect the wires. (Be sure that the power is off!)

2 Test the thermostat for continuity (see Blue Pages: *Electrical testers*). At OFF, there should be no continuity. As you turn the shaft to ON it should start to show continuity at some point (depending on how much it has warmed up) and continue to show continuity through the coldest setting. If it's defective, replace it with a duplicate.

Checking the evaporator fan

If you find frost in the freezer of your frost-free refrigerator, and if you're sure the air circulation vents aren't blocked and there are no open food containers in the unit, the evaporator fan may have failed. Open the refrigerator door and listen for the compressor. When it's running, press any buttons on the door jamb. The fan should go on and there should be a draft through the air ducts. If this does not happen, unplug the unit and check the evaporator fan door switch (see opposite page). If the door switch is OK, unscrew the bottom plate or other covers in the freezer; lift them and any insulation out to expose the fan. Check the blades first; they may be blocked. If they turn freely, turn the power off, then check the motor as shown here.

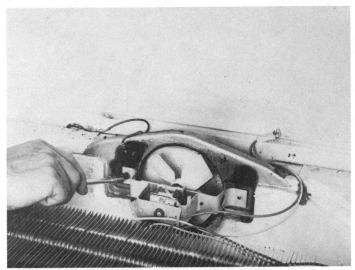

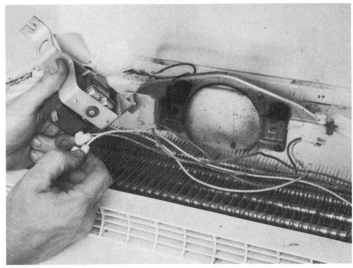

1 **To test the evaporator fan motor,** unscrew the fan mounting and lift the fan and motor out. (If you can reach the motor terminals without removing the fan, make the test with the motor in place). ☞ Lay a towel over the sharp evaporator fins to avoid cutting yourself or damaging the fins.

2 Disconnect the leads and attach VOM probes. With the meter set at RX1, you should read between 50 and 200 ohms resistance. A higher or no reading means a defective motor. Save the fan blades and mounting and replace the motor.

Getting into the unit from the back

Moving the refrigerator out of its usual spot takes some muscle, but it's the only way to check the condenser fan, the water connections to the cold water dispenser and ice maker, and (on some models) the defrost timer. It's also the only way to clean the condenser coils properly, and if you want your unit to operate efficiently you should make the extra effort.

To get inside the back, unplug the power cord from the outlet and take out the screws that hold the rear cover. You may have to disconnect the power cord from the cover.

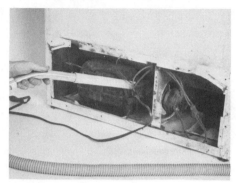

Clean the condenser coils and as much of the bottom compartment as you can reach with the radiator attachment on a vacuum cleaner.

Checking the condenser fan

If your frost-free refrigerator runs all the time or cools poorly (and you've kept the coils clean), check the condenser fan. It should run when the compressor does. With the back of the refrigerator off, plug in the unit and watch to see whether the fan turns. If it doesn't, unplug the unit and make sure the blades are not obstructed or bent, then make the following test. CAUTION Be sure the refrigerator is unplugged.

1 **To check and adjust the condenser fan and motor,** remove the assembly by taking out the screws that hold the mounting bracket in place.

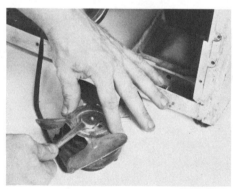

2 If the fan blades are loose, tighten the nut (or screw) that holds them in place. If the blades are bent or broken, replace them.

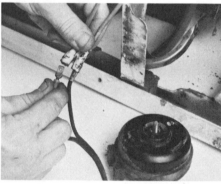

3 If the fan blades are tight, test the motor. Disconnect the motor leads and attach VOM probes to the terminals. With the meter set at RX1, it should read between 50 and 200 ohms resistance. If the reading is higher, the motor is defective and should be replaced.

A Difficult Cleaning Job

Many late-model refrigerators must be laid on their sides for proper cleaning of the condenser coils; the coils are mounted on the bottom and there's no other way to get at them.

Reaching under from the front will not do the job. Be sure to empty the unit before you turn it over! Put down a rug or old blanket to avoid scratches. Once a year should be often enough for this job, and the extra effort will be repaid in lower operating costs and less strain on the compressor.

Replacing a defective defrost timer

When a frost-free refrigerator starts frosting up (and the evaporator fan is OK), the defrost timer may have failed. (The timer turns on the heater in the evaporator coils to melt the frost accumulated there.) On most units, the timer is at the bottom in front. On some, it's mounted at the bottom in the rear.

Remove the timer bracket from the refrigerator, then take the timer off the bracket and take the cover off the timer so that you can see into the gears. With the power on, turn the thermostat to the coldest setting. Don't touch the timer. You should see at least one gear turning. If not, turn the power off, disconnect the leads, and make the test in step 3. If the gears *are* turning, turn the power off, disconnect the leads and, as shown in step 4, make these tests. NOTE: The circuit schematic, usually pasted on the back of the refrigerator, explains which terminal is which. If you can't read it, stop and call a repairman. (1) Between the motor terminal and the common there should be between 500 and 3,000 ohms resistance. (2) Between the heating terminal and the common there should be continuity for only about 10 degrees of the circle as you turn the timer adjustment dial completely around. The timer clicks at this point. (3) Between the cooling terminal and the common there should be continuity for the remaining 350 degrees of the circle. If the timer fails *any* of these tests, replace it.

1 **To test the defrost timer,** unscrew the bracket attaching it to the refrigerator and lift off the bracket and timer.

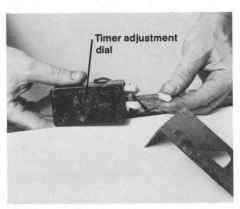

2 Take the timer off the mounting bracket and disconnect the power leads. (Label them first, for identification.)

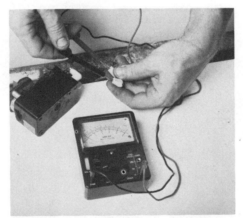

3 Attach VOM probes to the power leads (see Blue Pages: *Electrical testers*), turn the thermostat all the way up, and turn the power on. You should read about 120 volts. If you don't, the problem is elsewhere.

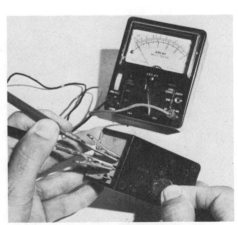

4 Use a VOM to make the three electrical checks listed at the left. All the leads must be disconnected for these tests.

Checking the cold water dispenser

Refrigerators that have a cold water dispenser mounted on the front have a water supply pipe coming into the unit at the bottom rear. The pipe is connected there to a solenoid-operated valve. (There may be a second valve for an ice maker.)

If you're not getting cold water, first check the valve. Unplug the unit and pull the refrigerator out carefully. Remove the rear panel, and unscrew the valve mounting bracket to get the valve out. Disconnect the cold water line (on the refrigerator side of the valve).

Put a pan under the valve. Plug in the unit, being careful to keep any wires away from the pan and water. Then press the dispenser lever. The solenoid should click and water should flow out of the valve. If it doesn't, the solenoid is defective and the valve can't function. If it *does*, the problem is in the unit itself. Check the cold water line on the unit for kinks or blockage.

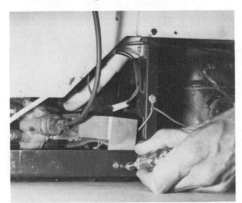

1 **To check and replace the solenoid water valves,** unscrew the valve mounting bracket from the body of the refrigerator and carefully pull the valves out of the unit. Be sure not to break any wire connections.

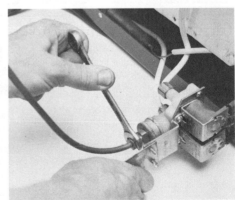

2 If the solenoid valve is bad, unplug the refrigerator, turn off the water supply, and disconnect the valve with a wrench, taking care not to bend any copper tubing. Disconnect the refrigerator tubes and power leads, and replace the entire valve assembly.

Ice makers

Automatic ice makers use the cold in the freezer compartment to freeze ice in a tray. The ice is then momentarily heated to loosen it so that rotating fingers, driven by a small motor, can eject it from the ice maker. Some units dump the ice into a container in the freezer from which you pick the ice out by hand. Others, like the model shown here, dispense the ice through the front. (This requires a second motor hidden below the freezer.) If the ice maker unit doesn't make ice, check the water supply solenoid valve to be sure water is flowing into the unit. If ice covers the ice ejector fingers, adjust the water level adjustment screw (see box below) before starting any repair.

Getting inside

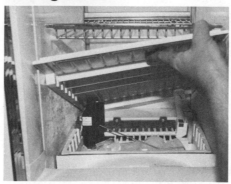

1 To get inside a dispensing ice maker, remove the bottom plate in the freezer unit. The plate usually lifts out; there may be screws to remove in some models. (A nondispensing unit will be visible inside the freezer.)

2 Take out the ice container (in dispensing units), to clean it or to remove ice that has frozen solid inside, by disengaging a retaining lever on the side and then lifting the container up out of the freezer.

A Common Problem

If the ice maker freezes solid or if water runs into the ice container or down into the compartment below, reduce the water flow by moving the adjustment lever on the ice maker. (This model has a lever and a screw for finer adjustment.) Water should just fill the individual ice slots in the ice maker, and go no higher.

Repairing an ice maker

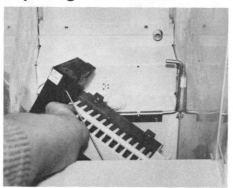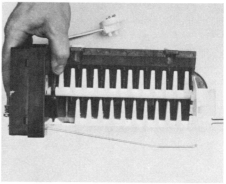

To get the ice maker out of the freezer, take out the ice container (see step 2, above), take off the water supply pipe, remove retaining screws, unplug the unit and lift off the long thin arm that hangs down in front (it operates the on/off switch). Then you can lift the ice maker out.

To replace broken ice ejector fingers, take out retaining screws and clips on the end of the ice maker opposite the motor, and lift the broken parts out for replacement.

Checking the thermostat

If the ice doesn't eject (and the ice maker isn't overfilling) the thermostat that controls the heating cycle may be defective.

To get to the thermostat, unscrew the retaining nuts from the back of the motor housing. Lift the cover off, taking care not to break any connections (the motor will come away attached to the cover).

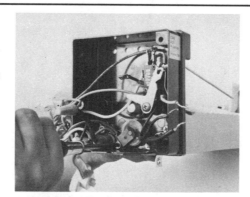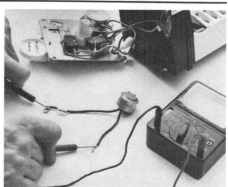

1 To test the thermostat, disconnect its leads and remove it from the motor housing. Put the thermostat in the freezer for at least half an hour; it must be well below freezing to test. (The one shown must be below 18° F.)

2 Quickly attach probes from a VOM or continuity tester to the thermostat leads. The thermostat should show continuity; as it warms up, it should show no continuity. If the thermostat shows no continuity when cold, or does show continuity when warm, replace it.

Refrigerator-freezers Troubleshooting Chart		
WHAT'S WRONG	**REASONS WHY**	**WHAT TO DO**
Refrigerator does not run; no sound can be heard; light is out.	No power at outlet	Check fuse box/circuit breaker. Check outlet with VOM or a lamp. If refrigerator blows fuses, put it on its own circuit.
	Defective power cord	Test cord; replace if defective.
Refrigerator does not run; light is on; occasional clicking may be heard.	Dirty condenser coils	Clean coils.
	Defective condenser fan (frost-free type)	Check fan.
	Incorrect voltage	Check voltage with VOM; call power company if not between 105 and 125 volts.
	Defective thermostat	Test thermostat; replace if defective.
	Defective compressor	Call repairman.
Refrigerator cycles on/off.	Incorrect voltage	Run unit on its own circuit; check voltage at outlet (see above).
	Defective compressor	Call repairman.
	Refrigerant leak	Call repairman.
	Dirty condenser coils	Clean coils.
Refrigerator cools poorly or runs all the time.	Thermostat set wrong	Adjust the thermostat.
	Dirty condenser coils	Clean coils.
	Defective door gasket	Check gasket.
	Sagging door	Straighten door.
	Heavy frost accumulation	Defrost unit more often; if frost-free type, see under "Refrigerator frosts up rapidly...."
	Door open too much	Open door as little as possible.
	Hot, humid weather	If unit runs continuously but cools well, there is no problem.
	Light on inside	Check door switch.
	Wet insulation in door and sides	Open unit on a dry day and let it dry out; repair or replace cracked door jambs and panels.
	Room too warm	Move to a cooler place, or air-condition room.
	Defective evaporator fan	Check fan.
	Defective condenser fan	Check fan.
	Defective defrost timer	Check timer.
	Refrigerant leak	Call repairman.
Refrigerator frosts up rapidly or does not defrost at all.	Door open too much	Open door as little as possible.
	Sagging door	Straighten door.
	Defective door gasket	Test and replace.
	Foods uncovered	Cover or seal all foods, especially liquids.
	Clogged drains	Open and clean drains.
	Defective defrost timer, heater, or thermostat	Check timer, heater, or thermostat.
Refrigerator makes noise.	Unit is not level.	Adjust unit.
	Rattling drain pan	Move pan so it doesn't touch sides.
	Hard or broken compressor mounts	Replace rubber mounts (see p. 41, under *Air Conditioners*).
	Obstructed fan blades	Check evaporator and compressor fans.
Refrigerator smells bad.	Clogged drains	Open and flush drains.
	Dirty drain pan	Clean and disinfect pan.
Water leaking underneath or inside unit.	Broken drain hose or drain pan	Replace broken parts.
	Clogged drains or full pan	Open drains.

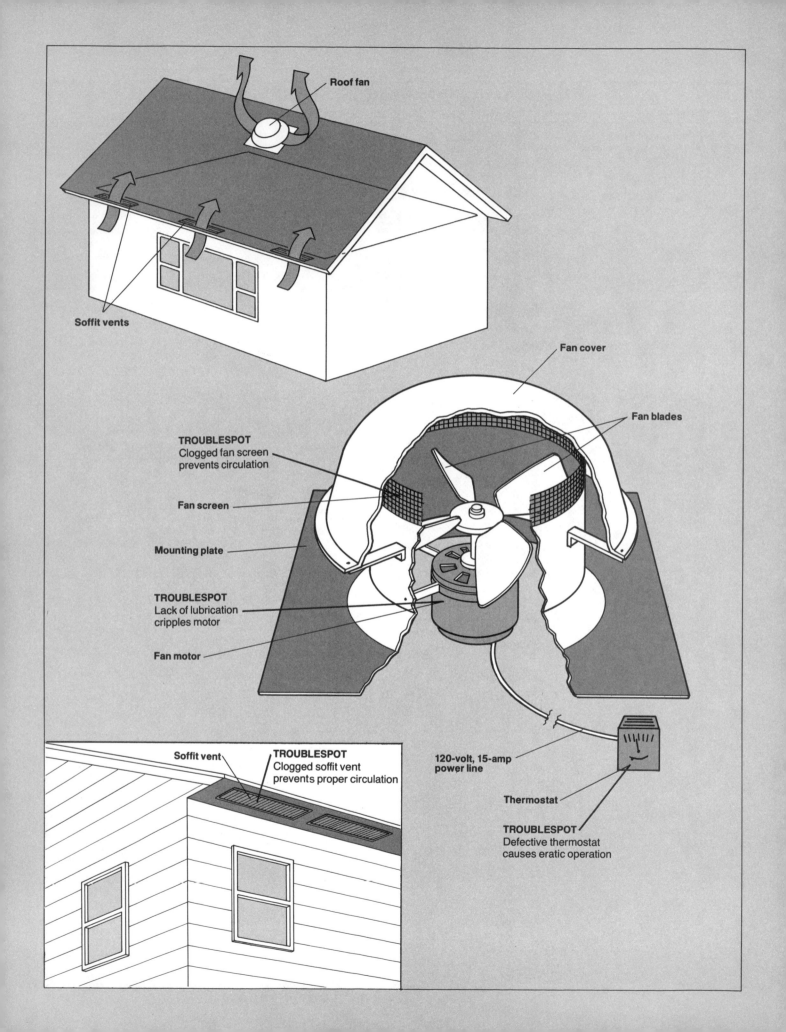

Roof fan

Soffit vents

Fan cover

Fan blades

TROUBLESPOT
Clogged fan screen
prevents circulation

Fan screen

Mounting plate

TROUBLESPOT
Lack of lubrication
cripples motor

Fan motor

Soffit vent

TROUBLESPOT
Clogged soffit vent
prevents proper circulation

120-volt, 15-amp
power line

Thermostat

TROUBLESPOT
Defective thermostat
causes eratic operation

Roof and Attic Fans

Roof fans

In these days of widespread refrigerated air conditioning, it's easy to forget that simply moving the air around you makes you more comfortable, no matter what the temperature. The secret is that moving air increases evaporation of perspiration, which makes you feel cooler.

So fans can reduce the need for air conditioning dramatically. In many situations, a properly installed fan can eliminate the need for air conditioners altogether. This saves roughly 90% of the energy costs of cooling.

Two ways to use fans for energy savings are described here. A fan installed in the roof (opposite) exhausts very hot air from the attic, thus lightening the burden on an air conditioner working downstairs. An attic fan, sometimes called a "whole-house" fan, ventilates the entire house (following pages), saving cooling costs at night and often during the day as well.

Roof fans cut home air conditioning costs by moving hot air out of the attic. During hot summer days the temperature in the attic can reach 130° F. or even higher, depending on where you live. Even with heavy insulation on the attic floor, heat is bound to radiate into the rooms below, making the air conditioner's work much harder. Lowering the attic temperature can reduce the load on the air conditioner by as much as 50%.

A roof fan is installed as close as practical to the highest and hottest point, the ridge line. A thermostat turns the fan on automatically whenever the temperature reaches a preset level, usually 100°F. Since they have to change only the air in the attic, roof fans need a capacity of only 1,000 cubic feet per minute. A 14- or 16-inch fan driven by a small motor—usually $\frac{1}{10}$ horsepower — can handle the job adequately. This size motor can be connected directly to the normal 15-amp house electrical circuit.

Since these fans exhaust directly through the roof, they must be enclosed by weatherproof housings.

Maintenance and repair

At the start of hot weather, clean the fan blades thoroughly and check that they turn freely. Make sure the screen is unobstructed. You may have to climb up on the roof to dislodge leaves or birds' nests. If the motor has oil ports, put a few drops of machine oil in each. Make sure the soffit vents are unobstructed, both outside and inside the attic. Listen occasionally on hot days to verify that the fan is operating. Since it's automatic, it's easily forgotten. If it fails to operate, you can check the thermostat as described at far right. If the motor seems at fault, remove the blades, take the motor out of its mounting, and test it (see Appliance Repair Basics: *How to Test a Universal Motor*). If defective take it to a repair shop or replace it. **CAUTION** Disconnect the fan before doing any maintenance.

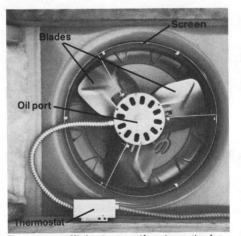

To ensure efficient operation, keep the fan blades and the screen clean; lubricate the motor annually if it has oil ports. Keep the attic area near the fan open for good air circulation.

To test the thermostat, turn the power off and attach VOM clips to the two leads from the thermostat to the motor. Turn the power on, and turn the thermostat control button all the way up and down. You should get a reading of 120 volts AC at the top of the thermostat's scale and no voltage at the bottom. If the thermostat fails this test, replace it. If it is OK, but the motor does not turn on, the problem is in the motor or the wiring from the thermostat to the motor. **CAUTION** This is a power-on test, so be very careful.

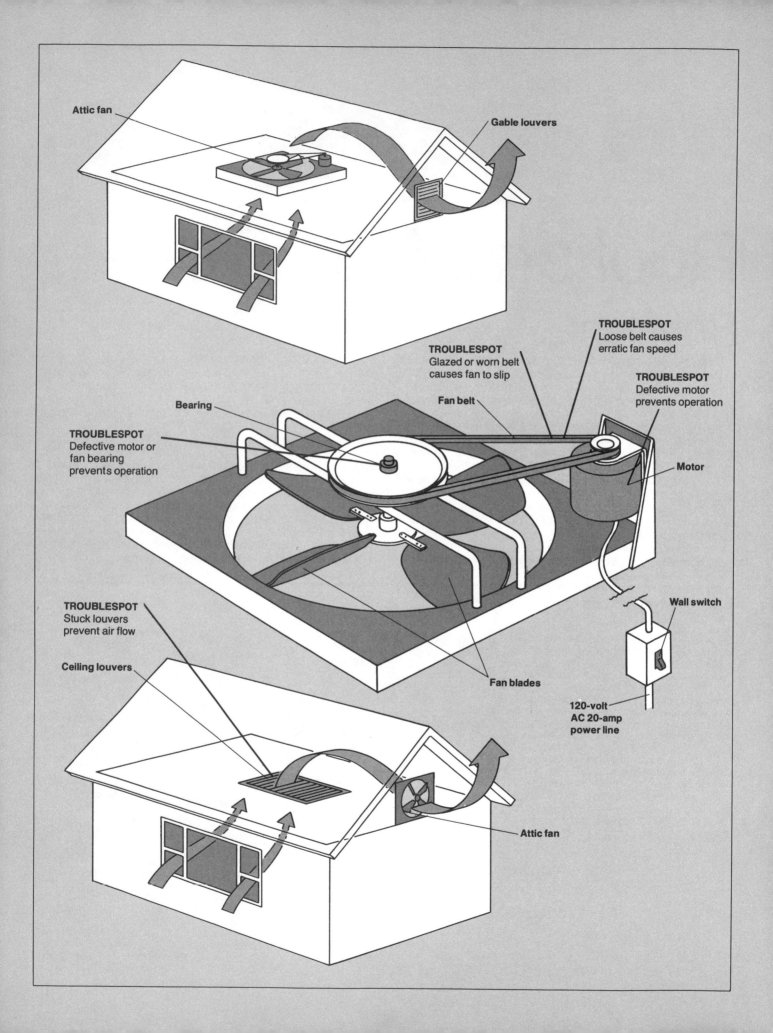

Attic fan

Gable louvers

TROUBLESPOT
Glazed or worn belt
causes fan to slip

TROUBLESPOT
Loose belt causes
erratic fan speed

TROUBLESPOT
Defective motor
prevents operation

Bearing

Fan belt

TROUBLESPOT
Defective motor or
fan bearing
prevents operation

Motor

TROUBLESPOT
Stuck louvers
prevent air flow

Ceiling louvers

Fan blades

Wall switch

**120-volt
AC 20-amp
power line**

Attic fan

ROOF AND ATTIC FANS
Attic fans

Attic fans cool the entire house by drawing air in at lower levels and exhausting it through the attic. This works effectively at night when cooler outdoor air can be drawn in through the windows to replace hot, stale indoor air. If the outdoor temperature is not too high, say, up to 80°F., cooling by attic fan can replace air conditioning altogether, at a considerable energy saving.

To be effective, an attic fan must move at least 5,000 cubic feet of air a minute through an average house. This requires a 24-inch fan, which needs a ⅓- or ½-horsepower motor to drive it. To guarantee an adequate electricity supply, an attic fan should be connected to its own individual 20-amp circuit.

In many installations the fan is mounted horizontally on the floor of the attic just above a set of louvers (opposite, top). Air is exhausted through gable louvers. Alternately, the fan can be mounted vertically in the gable itself just in front of the louvers (opposite, bottom). In this setup, another set of louvers is mounted in the attic floor, normally in a central hallway. In all these cases the louvers are normally spring-loaded; that is, when the fan is on, the airflow forces the louvers open; when the fan stops, the springs hold the louvers closed. If passive louvers are installed (those that are always open) you will want to seal them during the heating season to avoid heat loss.

Maintenance and adjustment

At the beginning of the cooling season, make sure the fan blades are clean and the louvers (both ceiling and gable, if you have two sets) are clean and move freely. Apply a drop of oil to each pivot point in the louvers. Oil the motor bearings (if there are oil ports) and the pulley bearings. Check the drive belt; replace it if its sides are glazed (shiny, smooth, and slippery), or if there are cracks or fraying. Check drive-belt tension and adjust as necessary (see right). Spin the blades; they should turn easily and quietly. If there is noise or resistance, you may have bearing problems; call a serviceman. **CAUTION** Never touch the belt while the fan is running.

To adjust drive-belt tension, turn the power off, loosen the motor-mounting bolts, and push the motor away from the fan shaft to take up the slack in the belt. Then tighten the bolts. The belt should deflect about ½ inch when pressed inward at its middle.

To remove a drive belt, turn the power off and press down on the belt near the motor pulley. Turn the blades slowly and the belt will slip off. To put a new belt on, slip one end around the fan pulley and press the other end into one side of the motor pulley. Turn the blades slowly while pressing the belt into the pulley, and it will slip on. NOTE: You will probably have to readjust the drive-belt tension.

Roof and Attic Fans Troubleshooting Chart		
WHAT'S WRONG	**REASONS WHY**	**WHAT TO DO**
Motor doesn't run.	No power	Check fuse box/circuit breaker.
	Faulty switch	Check switch; replace.
	Shaft bearings seized up	Lubricate or replace bearings.
	Defective motor	Take motor to repair shop or replace it.
Motor runs but no air circulates.	Broken belt	Replace belt with a duplicate.
	Louvers stuck shut	Lubricate louver pivot points.
Air circulates poorly.	Glazed belt	Replace belt with a duplicate.
	Loose drive belt	Adjust motor mount to tighten drive belt.
	Fan too small for the job	Buy a larger fan.
	Louvers partially closed or blocked	Lubricate louver pivot points; remove obstructions.

One family's investment in solar heating. The house shown here was designed to make both passive and active solar heating principles work for the occupants. The house faces south with generous areas of glass open to catch the sun. A greenhouse absorbs solar warmth at a high level of efficiency. At night or in warm weather, the greenhouse can be closed with insulating blinds. The house is especially well insulated from roof to basement. The interior of the house uses an open design, so that heat trapped by the greenhouse naturally circulates and rises through all the rooms. Most of the roof is a solar hot-air heat collector, which sends its heat through ducts to a storage pit in the basement. From there a small electric fan forces it throughout the house as needed. Just underneath the deck are two solar hot-water collector panels that collect heat to provide domestic hot water. These solar heating systems are described and illustrated on the following pages.

Solar Heating Systems

Someone has calculated that every three weeks the sun beams to earth as much energy as is locked up in all the known coal, oil, and gas reserves in the world. Surely this mind-boggling quantity of free energy could satisfy all our domestic heating needs many times over. That is, it could if the sun always shone on our house and if we had the technology at hand to capture it. But our industrialized society has been committed over the centuries to building self-contained, totally isolated miniclimates in homes and other buildings; we've tried to shut out all the surrounding weather and create our own. When fuels were cheap, perhaps it didn't matter. Today, however, attitudes are changing.

Not all Americans have tried to shut out the sun's free gift of heat. Centuries ago, the pueblo builders in the Southwest knew how to make the most of solar energy (see below). Not until the last ten years or so have many others begun to think seriously about building homes that take advantage of the sun's energy, and finding the best means to collect and store it. These new solar design concepts may bring about some radical changes in how our homes look, as the following pages show. On the other hand, many "solar-smart" techniques are not radical at all. If you orient your house toward the sun, you may save up to 30% of your heating bill. If you insulate your house effectively, you may save another 30%. Such "passive" solar heating techniques could save enormous amounts of fuel and slash heating bills, but old building habits are hard to change, and economic interests in conventional construction methods are deeply entrenched.

Some Americans have been going even further and building "active" solar heating systems. They're called active because they include the installation of special heat collecting and storing devices, as well as plumbing, pumps, fans, and controls to circulate the heat. Some people are adding solar water heaters to existing homes, especially in the sunbelt states. Others are designing their new homes to be solar efficient from the ground up, like the one shown on the opposite page, which uses solar heat to provide both hot water and space heating.

Solar technology is a new field, still in its expanding stages. Solar heating is not for everyone, and not for every part of the country. The information on the following pages gives some of the basic ideas and devices current in solar heating practice. If you're interested in adding solar heating, you should visit solar supply stores, talk to solar architects, read books on solar construction, and visit solar homes in your neighborhood. You'll find an endless variety of installations that are custom designed to fit individual families' needs and resources. Before you can answer the question "Is solar heating for me?" you need answers to technical and economic questions that only experts can supply.

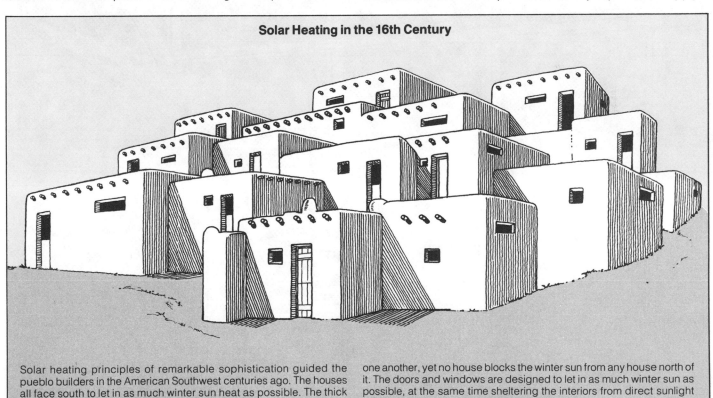

Solar Heating in the 16th Century

Solar heating principles of remarkable sophistication guided the pueblo builders in the American Southwest centuries ago. The houses all face south to let in as much winter sun heat as possible. The thick adobe walls absorb heat during the day and release it slowly during the cold nights. The houses are clustered together, providing shelter for one another, yet no house blocks the winter sun from any house north of it. The doors and windows are designed to let in as much winter sun as possible, at the same time sheltering the interiors from direct sunlight during the summer months.

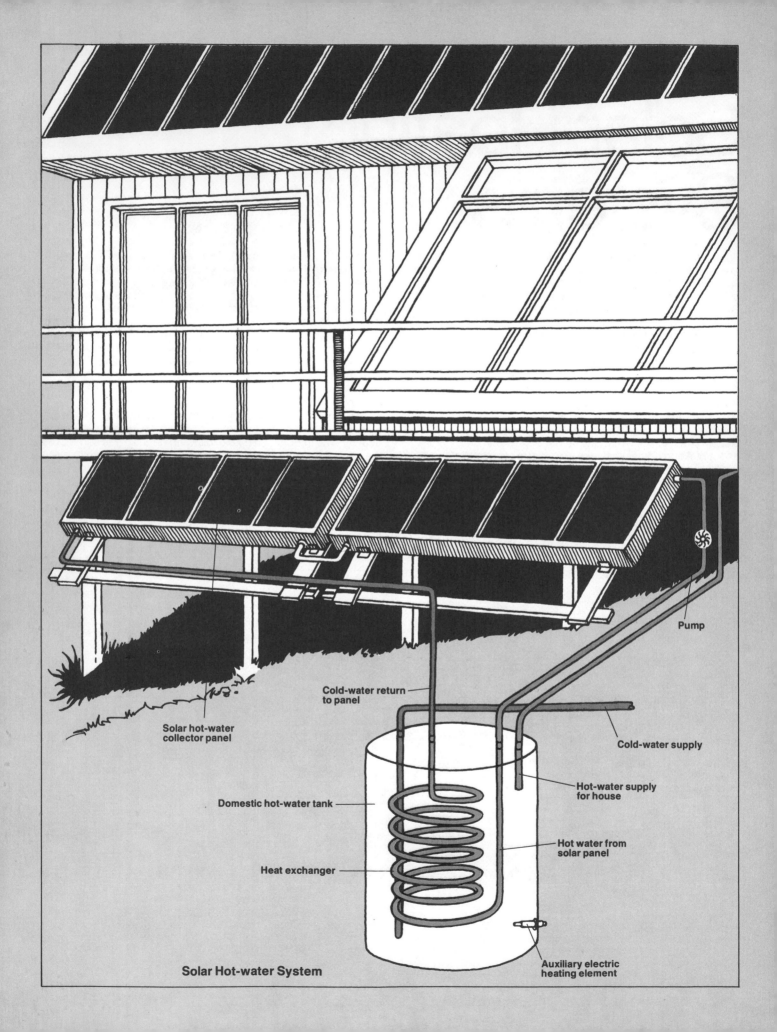

Cold-water return to panel

Solar hot-water collector panel

Pump

Cold-water supply

Hot-water supply for house

Domestic hot-water tank

Hot water from solar panel

Heat exchanger

Auxiliary electric heating element

Solar Hot-water System

Solar hot-water systems

The energy-efficient house shown on page 112 uses a solar hot-water system to heat water for domestic use. Two solar heat-collecting panels are mounted at the front of the deck, facing south. They are elevated so that the noon rays of the winter sun strike them at right angles, in order to raise the temperature inside the panels to the highest possible level. The water in the panels (the panels themselves are described below) absorbs the sun's heat and is pumped down into the hot-water storage tank in the basement. The hot water from the panels passes through a heat exchanger inside the tank, heating the domestic water that surrounds the exchanger. A thermostat controls the pump so that only hot water is drawn down from the panel to the tank.

Since the house is located in a region of winter freezing, the water in the panels contains antifreeze so that there is no danger of damage to panels or plumbing on cold nights. This also means that the panel water must be isolated in a closed loop that prevents any mixing of panel water with domestic water in the storage tank. (An alternate drain-down system is described at the bottom of the page.) Hot water is drawn out of the storage tank as needed for bathing and washing. An electric heating element in the tank provides auxiliary heating when the sun is hidden for long periods.

Hot-water collector panels

The sun's rays penetrate the glass cover of the collector panel and are trapped inside, creating a kind of greenhouse heating effect. Nearly 60% of the sun's heat is absorbed directly by the black absorber plate inside the panel. The plate can be aluminum, steel, copper, or plastic. Water running through the plate absorbs the heat and is pumped through the plumbing connections to the storage tank. In the parabolic collectors (below, right), the inside mirror surface focuses the sun's rays on the liquid-filled center tube. In some commercial applications, small motors drive banks of parabolic collectors so that they follow the sun across the sky for the most efficient heat collecting.

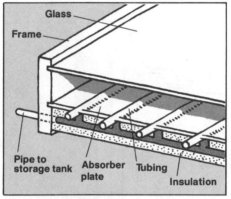

Water flowing through the tubes in the absorber plate absorbs the heat of the sun's rays that strike the plate.

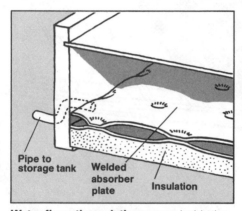

Water flows through the spaces inside the spot-welded absorber plate, picking up heat from the sun-warmed panel.

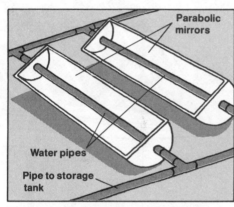

The mirror inside the curved collector focuses the sun's heat on the pipe in the center, raising the temperature of the water flowing through the pipe.

A drain-down water-heating system

In a drain-down solar water-heating system, the hot water from the collecting panels passes directly into the storage tank from which domestic hot water is drawn. The plumbing system for the panels is "open," i.e., not kept separate in a heat exchanger as in the system shown on the opposite page. This is a more efficient way of heating water for domestic use than the closed-loop system. In regions where there is danger of freezing, an automatic system drains the panels of water when the temperature falls near freezing.

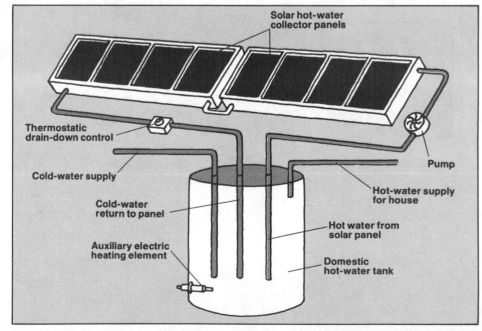

Solar Hot-air Heating System

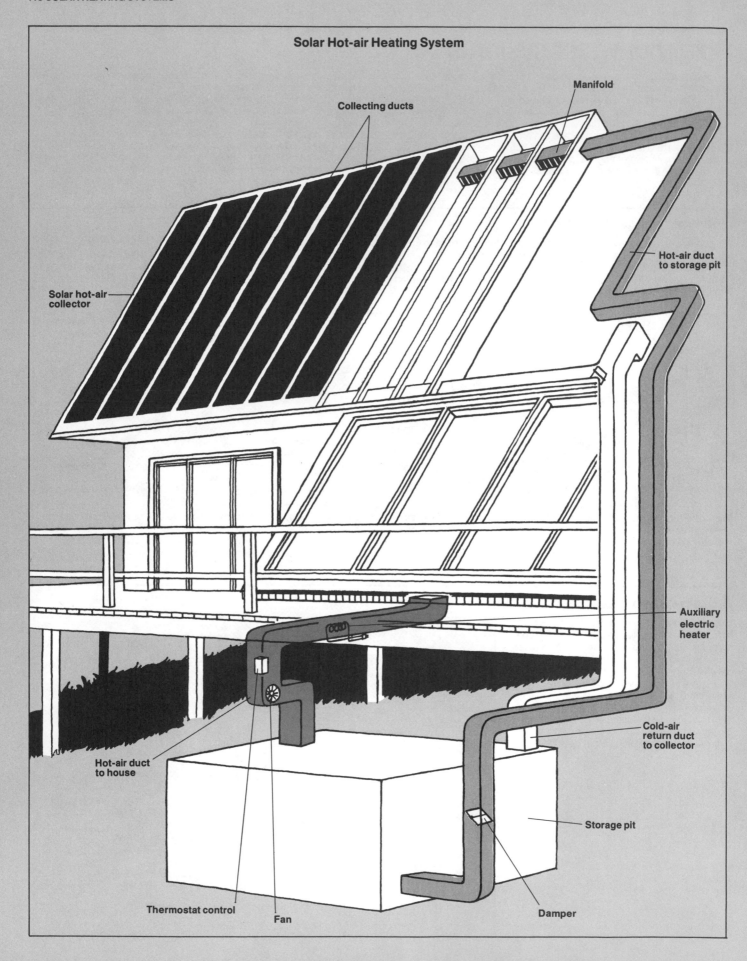

Collecting ducts

Manifold

Hot-air duct to storage pit

Solar hot-air collector

Auxiliary electric heater

Cold-air return duct to collector

Hot-air duct to house

Storage pit

Thermostat control

Fan

Damper

Solar hot-air heating system

The solar energy house on page 112 uses a solar hot-air system to satisfy space-heating requirements. Nearly the entire roof is covered with solar hot-air collecting ducts. The roof faces south and is elevated so that the rays of the winter sun strike the roof at right angles at noon; this raises the temperature inside the collecting ducts as high as possible. The hot air rises to the top of the collecting ducts and is drawn by fan down into the storage pit in the basement. The pit (described at the bottom of the page) holds the heat for distribution around the house when the thermostat calls for heat. Cold air from the house returns to the bottom of the collecting ducts on the roof to be reheated. Heat stored in the pit is withdrawn during the night hours as needed. An electric heater provides auxiliary heat during cloudy periods.

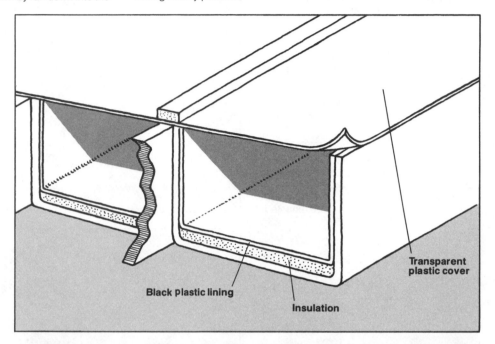

A single hot-air collecting duct can be about 1½ feet wide and 1 foot deep; the duct in this installation is about 18 feet tall. The duct is covered with a sheet of transparent plastic, which traps the sun's heat inside. The duct is lined with black plastic sheeting, which absorbs the heat. A layer of insulation on the bottom prevents heat loss. House air passing through the collecting duct is heated directly by the sun and by radiation from the surfaces of the duct.

Black plastic lining

Insulation

Transparent plastic cover

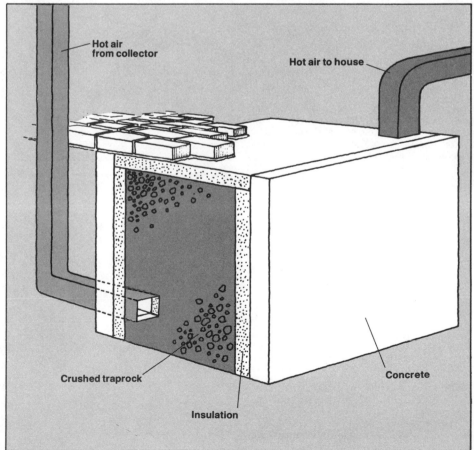

Hot air from collector

Hot air to house

The hot-air storage pit in the basement of the house is a massive concrete chamber with additional thick insulation on sides and top. In this installation, it occupies about 150 cubic feet. The pit is filled with traprock (the kind used as railroad ballast), which readily absorbs the heat from the air that is drawn down from the collecting ducts on the roof and forced through the pit by the fan. Even on a cold night there is normally enough heat trapped in the rock to keep the house comfortable.

Crushed traprock

Insulation

Concrete

How a solar heating system copes with weather changes

An active solar heating system is designed to collect solar heat when the sun is shining and store it for use at night or other times when the sun is hidden. The system also distributes this heat around the house and includes an auxiliary heating source that takes over when the solar heat-storage device is exhausted.

The solar hot-air system described on the previous pages automatically shifts from direct sun heat to stored heat to auxiliary heat, so that the demands of the home thermostat are constantly satisfied. These three phases of operation are described below.

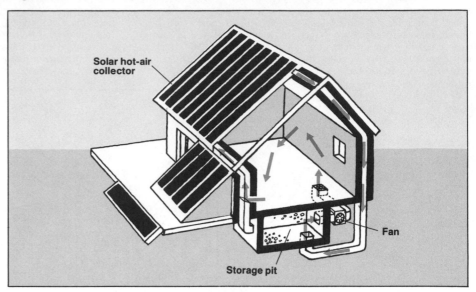

When the sun is shining, hot air from the collector flows into the storage pit. If the thermostat calls for heat, the fan draws hot air from storage and circulates it throughout the house. Cool air returns to the collector to be reheated.

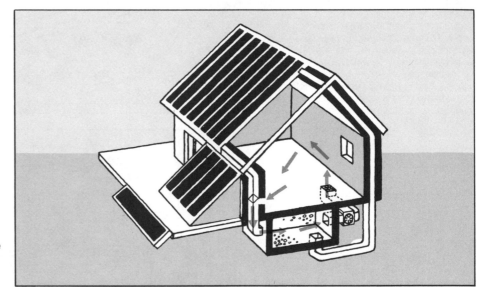

During the night, the air ducts to and from the collector are shut off, and hot air from the storage pit circulates around the house. During cold spells, a wood fire may be lit in a wood stove to supplement the solar heat.

When the sun is hidden for long spells, or during severe cold weather, both collector and storage pit are shut off. The auxiliary heater in the duct is turned on automatically to provide the necessary heat as demanded by the thermostat. A fire in a wood stove also adds warmth.

Making the most of your solar heating potential

Should you invest in solar heating? The answer to this question depends on many factors. Do you live in a region that gets sufficient sunshine to run a solar heating system efficiently? Is your house shaded by trees, buildings, or hills that could seriously cut the amount of sunlight reaching your collectors? What are your heating needs? How big is your family? Are you building a new house that can be solar-efficient from the ground up, or are you trying to adapt solar heating to an older, less efficient house? How much money are you willing to invest? Can you get financing in your locality for solar technology? What are the building requirements in your town? To answer these and many other questions you need the help of skilled solar consultants and solar architects. Some of the factors to be considered and some solar-efficient design concepts are described on this and the following pages.

As you ponder the various questions, don't forget to take a long view of costs. Initial costs for solar technology currently are higher than for conventional technology, but the cost of the fuel—the sun's heat—is and always will be zero.

Regions vary not only in the amount of sun they receive but also in the heating demands imposed by climate. Region A on the map at right has excellent sunshine, perhaps 70% or more of the possible sunshine. Region B has good sunshine, perhaps 50% to 60%. Region C has only fair sunshine, from 40% to 50%. The shaded area has a high heat demand during the heating season. Other areas have moderate or low heating demands. These are approximate areas and figures; you should get basic information from your local weather bureau to use as a starting point in calculating your solar heating potential.

You may live in a sunny region, but can the sun reach your house easily? Examine the microclimate surrounding your home. Is the sun blocked by trees, by other buildings, or by a hill? Any of these obstructions could prevent sufficient sun from reaching your solar heat collectors to make them economically justifiable. A tree can be cut down, but other permanent sun shades must be carefully considered in evaluating any possible solar heating investment.

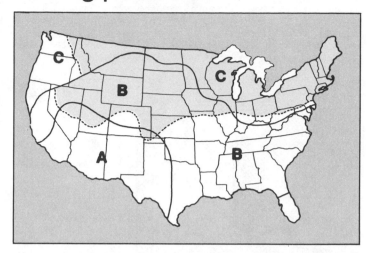

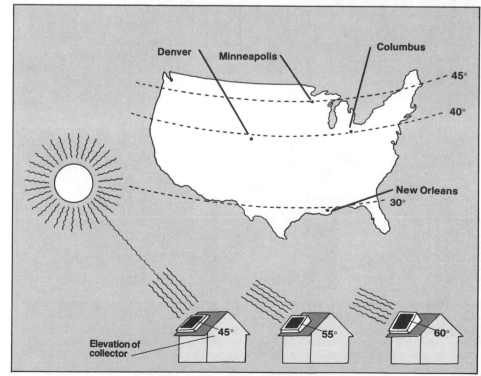

For highest heat collecting efficiency, solar collectors must face straight south, and must be elevated so that the rays of the winter sun strike them at right angles at noon. A rule of thumb says, add 15 degrees to your latitude to determine the proper elevation for a solar collector. As the map at right indicates, in a southern city like New Orleans, a collector should be at a 45-degree angle of elevation. In Denver or Columbus, Ohio, a 55-degree elevation would be about right. In Minneapolis, about 60 degrees.

Designs for passive solar heating

You can take advantage of the sun's free energy without installing any active collecting machinery at all. All the passive designs and devices on this page catch and conserve the sun's heat without plumbing, pumps, fans, drains, or special duct work. Adapted singly or in combination, these solar-oriented concepts will make new houses energy efficient. In any construction plans, remember to include adequate insulation of roof and walls to stop heat loss. Use thermopane or double glazing in all windows. Rebuilding an existing house along these lines may be too costly, but some remodeling for greater efficiency is usually possible, as described on the opposite page.

Build the house so it faces the sun. Let the long side and the windows face south to catch all the heat available during the heating season in your locality.

Provide overhangs or other shading devices to keep hot summer sun out of east, south, and west windows.

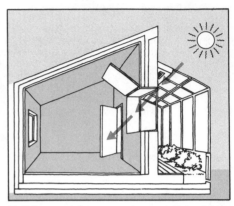

Build a greenhouse on the south side of the house; it will catch an enormous amount of the sun's heat during the day and radiate it into the house at night.

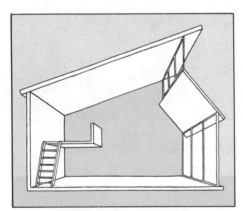

Design an open interior for your house, so that heat from the ground floor and greenhouse rises throughout the house, heating upstairs rooms.

Build a berm—an insulating bank of earth—around your house on the cool side to hold heat inside and block cold northern winds.

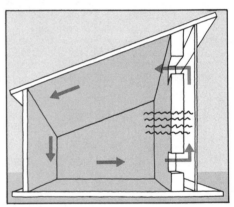

Build a Trombe wall—a massive stone or concrete heat-storage wall—on the south side of your house, to provide winter heating by convection during the day and by radiation at night.

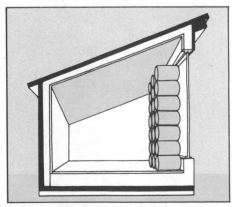

Set up a wall of water-filled steel drums or tubes to soak up the sun's heat during the day and to radiate it into the home during the night.

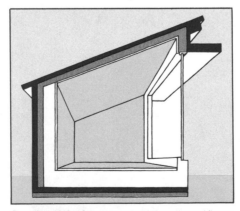

Surround the house with thick walls and floors of concrete, stone, masonry, or adobe to catch and store sun heat directly during the day and to radiate it throughout the house at night.

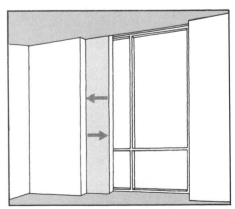

Cover windows with insulating panels or shades to keep heat in when the sun is not shining, or to block out the sun when it is too hot.

Adapting older homes for solar efficiency

Passive solar heaters

Rebuilding older homes to incorporate the passive solar heating devices described on the opposite page is often uneconomical. The house may not be oriented toward the south, there may be too much shade, or the house may lose too much heat through loose construction. There may simply be too little sun during the heating season. But many homes can profit by the addition of a greenhouse or a window-box collector to help meet space-heating requirements on sunny winter days.

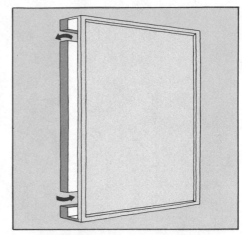

Build a greenhouse on the southern wall of the house if you get a lot of sun there. Provide doors or windows into the house so that heat can flow in during the day and night cold can be kept out.

Install window-box collectors on sunny eastern, southern, or western walls to absorb sun heat, which is carried into the house by convection or driven inside by a small fan.

Active solar collectors

Solar hot-water heat collectors can be added to any home that has a place to mount collectors at right angles to the sun, has a place to install a storage device, and, of course, gets enough sun to run the collecting system economically. In sunny southern states, solar heaters can supply all the domestic hot water needed. Even in northern states, they can fill most of the domestic hot water needs. Heating water for a swimming pool is a job well suited to a solar heater in most localities.

If the roof faces south, the solar collectors can be mounted at the right elevation on the roof and the storage tank installed directly below, in the basement.

If the roof is unsuitable for solar collectors, they can be mounted on a rack or shed oriented properly, with the storage tank installed inside or nearby.

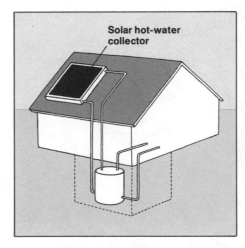

Solar hot-water collector

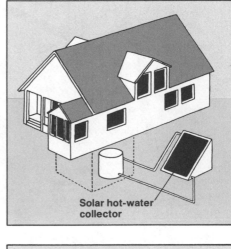

Solar hot-water collector

In some localities, solar hot-water collectors may be connected to hot-air space-heating systems to provide heating on sunny days. The same collectors may also be part of the domestic hot-water supply system.

Solar heaters for swimming pools can be mounted near the pool or on a nearby roof. An auxiliary heater for cloudy days is usually part of the system.

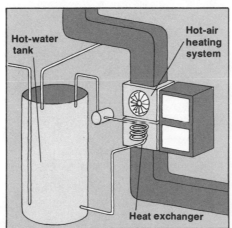

Hot-water tank

Hot-air heating system

Heat exchanger

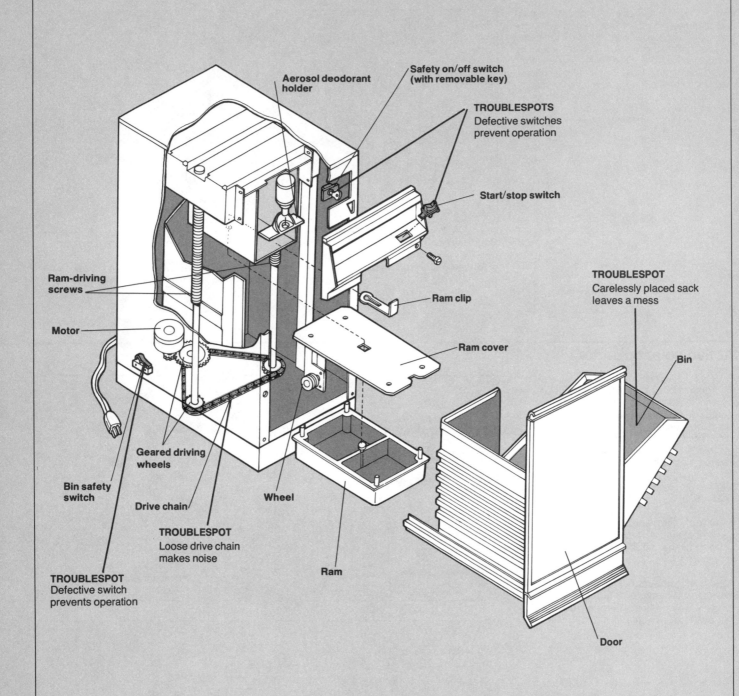

Aerosol deodorant holder

Safety on/off switch (with removable key)

TROUBLESPOTS
Defective switches prevent operation

Start/stop switch

Ram-driving screws

Ram clip

Motor

Ram cover

TROUBLESPOT
Carelessly placed sack leaves a mess

Bin

Geared driving wheels

Bin safety switch

Wheel

Drive chain

TROUBLESPOT
Loose drive chain makes noise

Ram

TROUBLESPOT
Defective switch prevents operation

Door

Trash Compactors

A trash compactor reduces unmanageable amounts of dry garbage and trash to neat, convenient packages by applying a surprising amount of brute force. For example, two full 20-gallon garbage bags subjected to 2,000 pounds pressure are compacted into one 9 x 17 x 18-inch package. The compacting ram that delivers this force is driven by reducing gears, which deliver great power, and by ram driving screws. Since such machinery can be dangerous, compactors have numerous fail-safe switches: the compactor will not operate if the door is open, if the unit is not level, if the safety lock is off, and so on. Some manufacturers build their units so you can't get access to the works. In such cases, all you can do is clean the unit regularly and follow the operating tips on the following page. For those who *can* get inside their compactors, directions for lubrication, adjusting the belts and gears, and checking switches are also given.

Basic maintenance

Install the trash sack so that it fits neatly into its bin, the top folded flat around the rim of the bin and the edges held firmly in the clips. A sloppily installed bag means a mess in the compactor. Clean the bin every month or so with warm water and detergent, and dry thoroughly to prevent odors and rust. If the bin does rust, sand and repaint it.

Lubricate the bin latch mechanism. Apply white grease (not oil) to all parts that turn or rub against one another. If a finger full of grease bothers you, use a cotton-tipped swab.

To lubricate inside, unplug the unit first. Lift the door and bin assembly off its track. Be careful, the door is heavy! In most units the door comes out easily in any position; in some units it must be pulled forward first.

Lubricate all the wheels on the door and inside the unit that supports the door. If the wheels run on ball bearings, use a few drops of light oil on each. If they are nylon wheels without ball bearings, squirt a little silicone lubricant onto each wheel shaft.

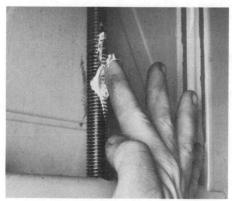

Apply white grease generously to the ram-driving screws, both at the base and along the threaded parts. Then put the door back in, close it securely, plug the unit in, and run the ram up and down for a cycle or two. Check that the grease is spread all over the threaded parts of the screws.

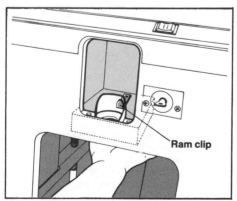

Ram clip

Take the ram out every month or so to clean it and its rubber cover pad with soap and water. Unplug the unit. To get the ram out, pull the clip that lies above the ram in the center of the unit. (It's directly behind the aerosol can holder in this model.) Support the ram with your other hand as it drops out of the clip.

Getting inside

Many trash compactors are designed to discourage owners from working on the inside mechanism. A unit carelessly repaired could become dangerous because of its great power. But the faceplates of most models can be removed to allow testing and replacement of switches.

To remove the faceplate, take the screws out and (in this model) knock the plate sharply upward with the heel of your hand to dislodge it. On other models, the plate may fall forward when all screws are removed.

Switch problems

Different models have different combinations of switches, but start/stop, safety on/off, the door latch switches, and the top-limit switch (stops the ram at the top of its run) appear on all models. If any of these switches fails a continuity test, take the defective switch to an appliance store and replace.

To test and replace the start/stop switch, first unplug the unit and take the door out (see preceding page). Before removing the switch, label it to identify the START and STOP positions so you can tell which is which when the switch is dangling outside the panel. Then remove the faceplate (see above).

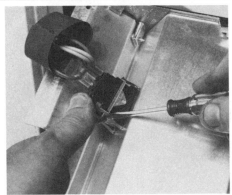

1 **To test the start/stop switch for continuity,** detach the switch from the faceplate. On this typical model, it is a rocker-type switch clipped to the faceplate. To release it, insert a screwdriver carefully under the clip, spread the clip, and angle the switch out.

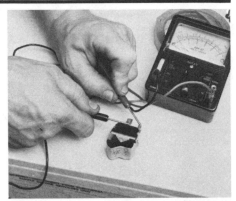

2 Before detaching any wires, label them to correspond to the switch terminals they connect to. There are usually helpful letters or numbers next to the terminals on the back of the switch. (The wires can always be put back right if you can read the schematic electrical diagram pasted somewhere on the unit, but careful labeling saves a lot of time.) Test the switch with a VOM (see Blue Pages: *Electrical testers*). START should show continuity; STOP should show no continuity. All the other switches on the unit can be tested in the same way.

Working on the drive mechanism

Repairing the motor drive assembly is impossible in many units because the manufacturer has deliberately sealed it up. But it is sometimes possible to get inside if you're willing to do a little more work. You can get inside the unit shown here, for example, through the bottom. First, unplug the unit. Take the door out (see preceding page), and lay the unit on its side. Remove the bottom panel screws and take the panel off.

Lubricate the sprocket (or pulley) wheels with white lubricant. Put a little on the plastic gears, too. Adjust the tension if the drive chain is loose and replace gears if the teeth are worn or missing. On most models, the permanently sealed motor cannot be reached without totally dismantling the unit. If you suspect a defective motor, call a repairman.

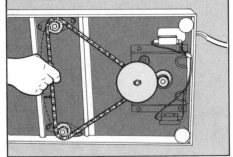

1 **Test the drive chain** (or drive belt) for proper tension by pushing it sideways. If there is more than ½ inch play, the chain is too loose. A loose chain can cause noisy, rough operation.

2 To tighten the drive chain (or drive belt), loosen the four motor mount bolts (the four *outer* bolts on this model) and move the motor mount until there is no more than ½ inch play in the chain. Tighten the bolts carefully. The motor bolts (the four *inner* bolts here) should also be kept tight.

Trash Compactors Troubleshooting Chart

WHAT'S WRONG	REASONS WHY	WHAT TO DO
Compactor doesn't go on.	No power at outlet	Check fuse box/circuit breaker.
	Defective cord	Test cord and replace.
	Safety lock is off.	Turn it on.
	Drawer not closed	Remove obstructions.
	Motor overloaded with ram down	Pull wall plug and wait 10 minutes for motor to cool. Check drive chain or drive belt; look for broken gears and worn ram screws.
	Defective switch	Check start/stop switch, safety switch, overload switch. Check your owner's manual for the switches on your unit.
	Loose electrical connection	Check all wires and connections.
Unit starts but blows fuse or trips circuit breaker.	Too many appliances on circuit	Run unit on its own circuit.
	Short circuit in cord or plug	Test plug and cord for continuity (see Blue Pages: *Electrical testers*).
	Short circuit in switch	Test switches for continuity.
	Short circuit in motor	Call repairman.
Motor runs but trash is not compacted.	Loose or broken drive chain (belt)	Check chain; adjust and replace.
	Loose gears or pulleys	Check; tighten and replace.
	Ram seized up	Ram screws need lubrication; if screws are stripped, replace them.
Unit is too noisy.	Drive chain (belt) too loose	Tighten chain.
	Unit needs lubrication	Lubricate.
	Loose parts	Tighten every bolt and screw in sight.
Unit smells bad.	Aerosol can (or other deodorant supply) empty	Put in a new can.
	Aerosol nozzle clogged	Ream out with thin wire.
Unit won't stop running.	Defective top-limit switch	Pull plug; check switch for continuity.
	Defective start/stop switch	Check and replace.
Unit makes a mess.	Bag not in proper position	Check bag and clips that hold it.
Drawer won't open.	Ram stalled part way down	Make sure unit is plugged in. Check that door is completely closed. Unplug, look for broken belt, chain or pulleys, or drive screws.
	Motor overloaded	(See above, "Compactor doesn't go on.")

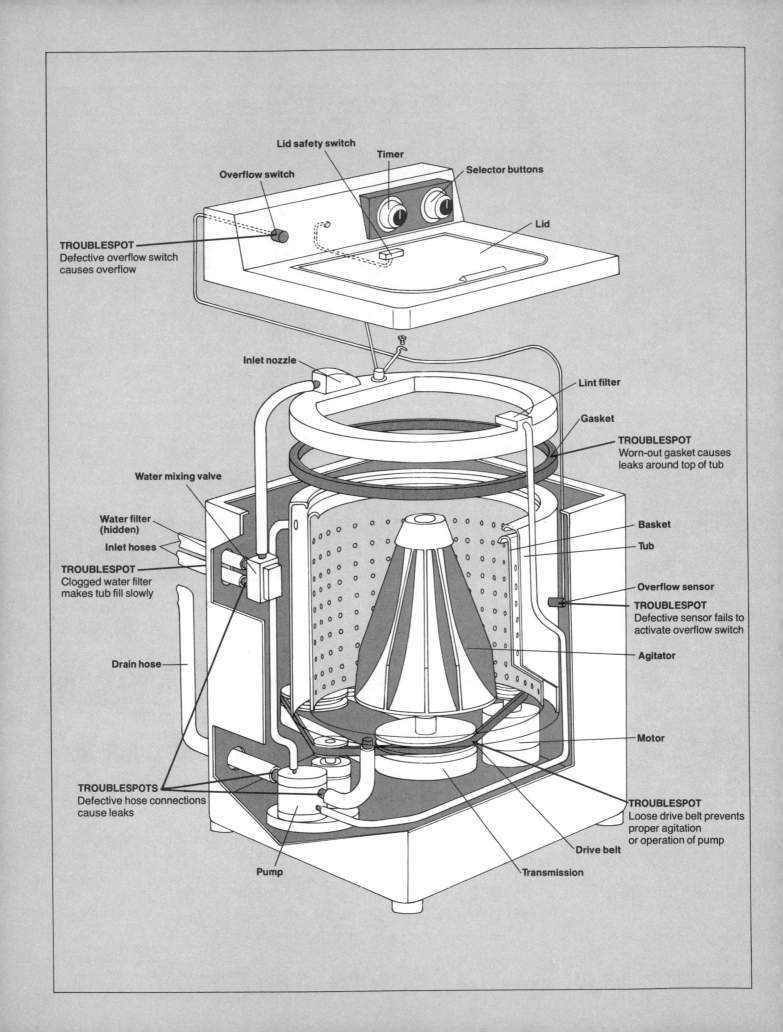

Overflow switch

Lid safety switch

Timer

Selector buttons

Lid

TROUBLESPOT
Defective overflow switch
causes overflow

Inlet nozzle

Lint filter

Gasket

TROUBLESPOT
Worn-out gasket causes
leaks around top of tub

Water mixing valve

**Water filter
(hidden)**

Inlet hoses

TROUBLESPOT
Clogged water filter
makes tub fill slowly

Basket

Tub

Overflow sensor

TROUBLESPOT
Defective sensor fails to
activate overflow switch

Agitator

Drain hose

Motor

TROUBLESPOTS
Defective hose connections
cause leaks

TROUBLESPOT
Loose drive belt prevents
proper agitation
or operation of pump

Drive belt

Pump

Transmission

Washing Machines

Washing machines are ruggedly built to withstand the violent back-and-forth motion of agitating a heavy load and the high-speed spinning that follows. Modern washing machines have a combination of valves, switches, and temperature sensors to give you options in water temperature and quantity, and in wash cycles. The timer controls all these operations. With all this convenience, little maintenance is required—just clean the lint and water filters regularly and check the drive belt occasionally.

The electrical problems that may occur involve a defective overflow switch (see next page), and faulty overload and lid safety switches. Standard continuity tests can be used to test the latter (see Blue Pages: *Electrical testers*). The solenoids in the mixing valves can be tested the same way you test those found on refrigerators (see page 105). The washing machine timer can be treated the same way as the dishwasher timer (see page 62).

Mechanical problems eventually do crop up. (1) A hose may spring a leak. Instructions for handling this situation are given on the next page. (2) The drive belt can break. On most models it is very difficult to replace a belt without complicated disassembly, and you had better call a repairman. On a few models, drive belt replacement is easy: when you tip the unit on its side and open up the bottom, the belt and its pulleys are all out in the open. (3) The pump wears out. Replacing the pump is a job for an experienced repairman. (4) The motor wears out. By this time the unit has come to the end of its useful life; rather than replace the motor, buy a new washing machine.

> **CAUTION** Electricity and water can be a lethal combination. Always pull the cord from the wall receptacle before making any tests or repairs inside the machine. Never work on an electrical appliance while standing on a wet floor. After completing repairs, check all electrical connections to make sure they're tight. Take special care that the grounding wires are correctly and tightly connected.

Easy maintenance

To clean the water filters (near right), close the water faucets or valves, pull the unit away from the wall, and disconnect the hoses. Have a pan handy to catch the runout. Take out the fine-mesh filters just inside the connections on the machine and the other end of the hoses, and clean them thoroughly. Do this every two months if you have a well and twice a year if you're on city water. When the machine is back in place, be sure the hoses are not kinked. ✂ If a hose must be bent to make a connection, install a right-angle hose.

To tighten a loose drive belt (far right), unplug the unit and pull it away from the wall to reach the motor mounting. There may be a panel to re-move. Loosen one motor mounting bolt, pull the motor against the belt, and tighten the bolt again. There should be no more than ½ inch play when you push against the belt. If you can rotate any pulley against the belt, it should be tight-ened. Examine the belt for signs of wear. A worn belt usually should be replaced by a repairman.

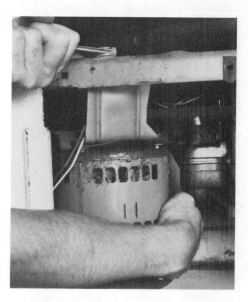

Getting inside from the top

To get the top panel off, first check to see whether your unit uses clips in front to hold the top, like the top-loading model shown here, or has screws at the back. If you can slip a credit card all around under the top except at two points all in front, you have clips. If you can see hinges at the back of the top, there will be screws.

To lift a clip-held top, pry the top up carefully but firmly at the side (not at the clips) with a screwdriver. ✂ Wrap the screwdriver end with tape or paper to prevent damage to the finish. When the top pops off the clip, lift it up.

If your unit has screws at the back of the top, remove them, pull the top forward, and then lift it up at the front.

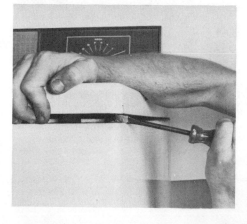

🔌	**TIPS FOR ENERGY EFFICIENCY**

Wash when you have a full load, but don't overload.

Don't use too much soap.

If you have a "gentle wash" cycle, switch to "fast spin" for drying; it saves drying time.

Use the cold water cycle whenever possible; hot water is expensive.

🔌	**TIPS FOR EFFICIENT OPERATION**

Make sure the unit sits level and doesn't wobble and that the load is evenly distributed in the basket.

Make sure the hot water is at least 140°F.

Check the lint filter regularly; keep it clean.

Always turn the water supply faucets or valves off after washing; if a water mixing valve fails, it could cause a flood.

Water leaks

If you discover water leaking out of your washing machine while it's filling, STOP! Don't touch the machine. First turn off the electricity. Then examine the unit. If the water is running over the top of the tub, the overflow switch has failed. See the instructions at the bottom of this page. If the tub is not overflowing, then the water inlet hoses or valves at the back of the unit may be defective. If the unit leaks after filling, then an inside hose or hose connection has failed, the gasket is worn out (see below), or the pump has sprung a leak (call a repairman). You'll have to open the top, peer in at the back or lay the unit on its side to check all these possibilities. When you must empty the tub or disconnect a hose, remember that there's always some water left in the hoses and pump even after the tub is empty. Have a pan ready to catch the runout, unless the unit is near a floor drain.

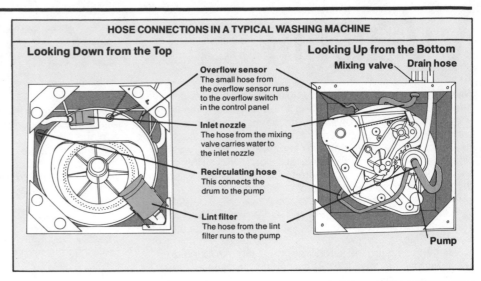

HOSE CONNECTIONS IN A TYPICAL WASHING MACHINE

Looking Down from the Top

Looking Up from the Bottom

Mixing valve   Drain hose

Overflow sensor
The small hose from the overflow sensor runs to the overflow switch in the control panel

Inlet nozzle
The hose from the mixing valve carries water to the inlet nozzle

Recirculating hose
This connects the drum to the pump

Lint filter
The hose from the lint filter runs to the pump

Pump

Replacing hoses and gaskets

Replace any hose that leaks from a crack or puncture. If the leak seems to be at the connection, try moving the clamp to a slightly different position on the hose. Be sure the clamp grips both hose and pipe end. The best tool to use is hose-clamp pliers, because it's made for the job. If you use regular pliers, watch your fingers! This tool easily slips off the springy clamp. To replace a worn-out gasket, just lift it off the tub rim and slip a duplicate on. (On some models you'll have to remove the splash guard that sits just above the gasket.)

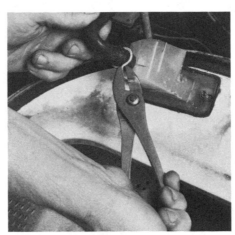

To remove a defective hose or to adjust a hose clamp, use hose-clamp pliers to squeeze the clamp open.

In place of the common pinch clamps, you can also use screw-type clamps. They are more easily adapted to different-sized connections.

Testing and replacing an overflow switch

When the water in the tub rises above the level of the overflow sensor, it creates air pressure in the air tube that connects the sensor with the overflow switch in the control panel. This pressure turns the switch off and stops the water flow.

If the tub overfills, the problem may be a defect in the tubing, in the switch, or in the sensor. First, turn off the power. Make sure the air tube is securely in place at both the switch and the sensor. If it slips off too easily, clip ½ inch off the end of the hose and press it on firmly. Test the switch mechanically by detaching the tube at the sensor and blowing through the tube into the switch. You should hear a click as the switch is activated to turn off. If you do not hear a click, test for continuity across the two terminals that are closed under normal circumstances (see Blue Pages: *Electrical testers*). Check your wiring diagram to identify the terminals. There should be no continuity while you are blowing into the tube. If the switch itself is OK, check the sensor in the tub. Attach the tube at the sensor and detach it from the switch. Fill the tub with water and blow through the hose into the sensor. You should feel solid pressure.

1 **To test the overflow switch,** first label the wires or the terminals by color or number. Then remove the push-on connectors carefully.

2 Blow through the air hose into the overflow switch; there should be no continuity between the normally closed terminals.

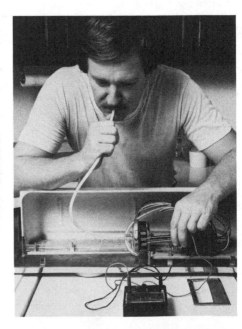

Washing Machines Troubleshooting Chart

WHAT'S WRONG	REASONS WHY	WHAT TO DO
Washing machine doesn't run at all.	No power at outlet	Check fuse box/circuit breaker.
	Safety switch tripped	Make sure lid is closed; distribute clothes evenly in basket.
Machine doesn't fill with water.	Filters clogged	Check inlet hose filters and clean.
	Hoses kinked	Straighten water supply hoses.
	Timer not set	Turn timer slightly; push buttons firmly.
Water doesn't shut off.	Overflow switch hose disconnected	Replace hose.
	Defective overflow switch	Check and replace switch.
	Defective timer	Replace timer or call repairman.
	Defective mixing valve	Replace valve.
Tub fills but motor doesn't run.	Lid safety switch tripped	Make sure lid is closed; test switch.
	Tub overloaded	Reduce load; wait 15 minutes for motor to reset.
	Motor defective	Call repairman. (You may hear humming sound.)
	Defective timer	Replace timer.
Motor runs but machine doesn't agitate or spin.	Drive belt loose or broken	Tighten or replace belt.
	Defective gears or transmission	Call repairman.
Machine vibrates or walks across floor.	Machine or load not level	Adjust feet or distribute load evenly.
Machine leaks.	Loose hose connections	Check and tighten connections.
	Defective hoses	Replace hoses.
	Defective gasket	Check gasket and replace.
	Defective mixing valve	Check valve; replace if cracked.
	Defective pump	Call repairman.
	Defective overflow switch or sensor	Check and replace.
Machine doesn't drain.	Drain hose kinked	Straighten hose.
	Drain hose too high	Hose should empty no more than 4 feet above floor.
	Defective timer	Replace timer or call repairman.
	Drain pump jammed	Call repairman.
Water isn't hot enough.	Water heater set too low	Set water heater thermostat at 140°-160°F.
	Water supply hoses misconnected	Reverse the hoses.
	Defective mixing valve	Replace valve.
	Defective timer	Replace timer or call repairman.

Electric Water Heater

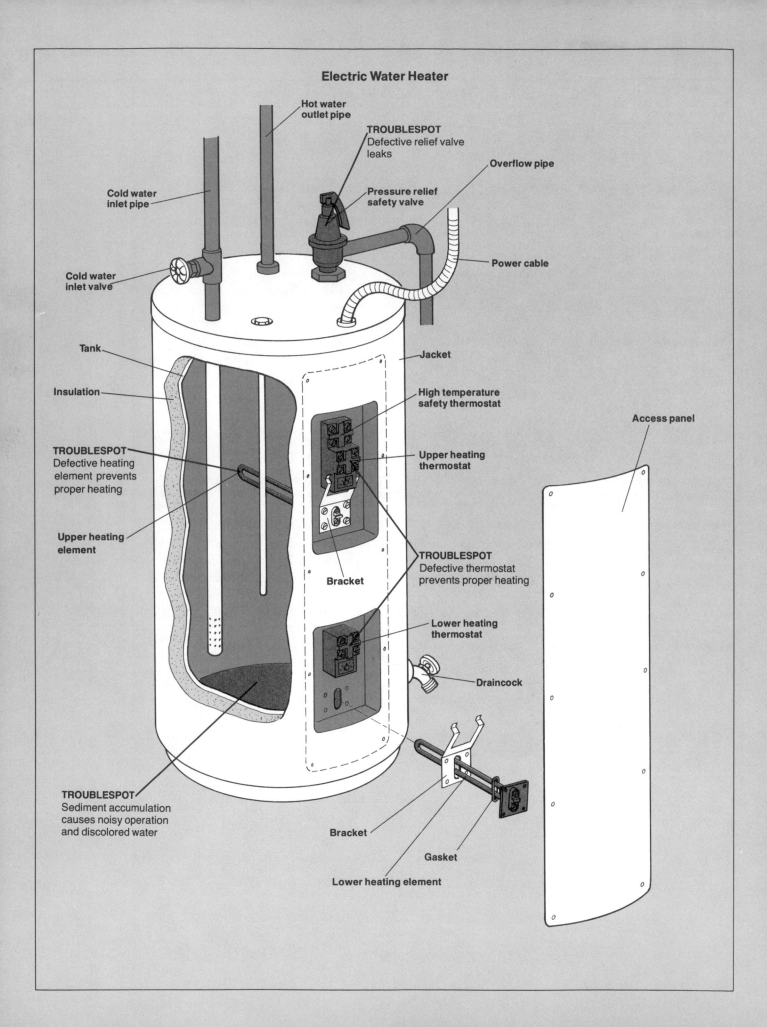

Hot water outlet pipe

TROUBLESPOT
Defective relief valve leaks

Overflow pipe

Cold water inlet pipe

Pressure relief safety valve

Power cable

Cold water inlet valve

Tank

Jacket

Insulation

High temperature safety thermostat

TROUBLESPOT
Defective heating element prevents proper heating

Upper heating thermostat

Upper heating element

Access panel

TROUBLESPOT
Defective thermostat prevents proper heating

Bracket

Lower heating thermostat

Draincock

TROUBLESPOT
Sediment accumulation causes noisy operation and discolored water

Bracket

Gasket

Lower heating element

Water Heaters

Electric

In most homes water heaters are the forgotten appliances. These simple, long-lived devices carry on their job of providing hot water automatically without anyone paying them any attention, sometimes for five or ten years at a stretch. In fact, most complaints about water heaters have nothing to do with any mechanical failure, but rather with the user's misunderstanding about how much hot water there is in the tank and how long it takes the heater to replenish the supply. For example, if you have a 40-gallon tank, there will be about 30 gallons of really hot water at the top of the tank ready to be drawn out. This is about the amount it takes for a good bath. And if your unit requires another forty-five minutes or an hour to heat another 30 gallons (its "recovery rate"), you can see how you can easily run out of hot water. If this happens often in your home, perhaps you need a larger tank, or a heater with a faster recovery rate. The capacity and recovery rate are shown on the nameplate of the heater.

Eventually, any hot water tank will wear out and begin to leak because of rust and corrosion inside. When this happens, get a new water heater. There isn't any practical way to repair a leaky tank. Make sure, though, that the puddle under the heater is not from a leaking safety valve (see page 133) or water pipe connection. Besides replacing a failed safety valve, you can also test and replace defective thermostats and heating elements in an electric water heater. Instructions are given on the following pages. And be sure to take the following paragraph to heart.

CAUTION Water and electricity are a lethal combination, especially the 240 volts that power most electric water heaters. Always turn off the power at the fuse box/circuit breaker before starting any tests or repairs. Always drain the tank before replacing elements or thermostats. Never go into a flooded basement if electrical appliances are on. Never touch an operating appliance while standing in water or on a damp floor.

TIPS FOR ENERGY EFFICIENCY

If the water heater is intended to supply only one bath or shower, set both thermostats at 130°F. If the heater supplies two baths or dishwasher, too, set both thermostats at 140°F. For every increase of 10° above 140°F. the cost goes up 3%.

Locate the heater near the points of use if possible.

Use the smallest pipe to carry hot water; this lowers both heat loss and the amount of hot water trapped in the pipe.

Insulate the hot water pipe from the heater to the points of use.

A quick shower uses much less hot water than a bath. For a long soak, however, a bath is more economical. Test your own consumption: the next time you take a bath, put a piece of tape at the high water mark (when you're not lying in the tub). Then the next time you shower, leave the plug in and see if the water rises to the tape mark.

Draining the tank

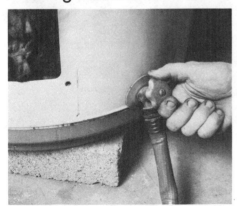

Try draining the tank to remove sludge and rust scale if your hot water runs cloudy or rusty, or if your heater makes rumbling noises. Turn off the power at the fuse box/circuit breaker, close the cold water inlet valve, and open the draincock at the bottom of the tank. (If the tank is not near a floor drain, connect a hose to the draincock; the end of the hose must be lower than the draincock.) Then, open a hot water faucet upstairs to let air into the heater. When the tank is empty, close the draincock and let in a little cold water for a final flush. Drain. Close the draincock, leaving the upstairs hot water faucet open. Open the cold water supply valve. When water runs out of the upstairs faucet, close the tap. You can now turn the power back on.

Getting inside

To gain access to thermostats or heating elements, turn off the power at the fuse box/circuit breaker and remove the access panel by taking out the screws that hold it to the jacket. You will find insulation covering the thermostats and elements; push it to the side, or take it out if it's a separate piece. When closing up the heater, always replace the insulation just as you found it before you put the access panel back.

Adjusting the thermostats

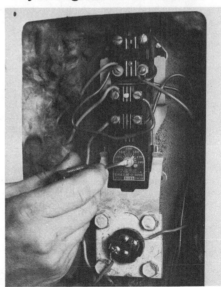

To set the water heater's thermostats, turn the small pointer at the bottom of the thermostat to the desired temperature. Some pointers can be turned by hand; others require a small screwdriver. If you want your hot water to come out about 140°F., set both thermostats at 140°F.

Checking thermostats and heating elements

If the thermostats are correctly set, the fuse box/circuit breaker is OK, and there's still no hot or only lukewarm water, make the following tests to locate the difficulty. (Turn the power off!) (1) Test the heating elements. (If your heater suddenly takes a lot longer to heat water, it may mean that one of the elements has failed.) (2) Test the heating thermostats. (3) Test the safety thermostat at the top of the upper thermostat. (4) Test the power coming into the unit.

CAUTION The last test is a power on test. If you haven't found the trouble through the first three tests and don't want to make this test, call an electrician.

To replace a defective heating element, see the instructions given on the opposite page.

To replace a defective thermostat, be sure the power is off. Label the wires connected to the defective part and disconnect them. Lift the bracket and remove the thermostat. Install an exact duplicate. Replace the insulation and the access panel before turning the power on.

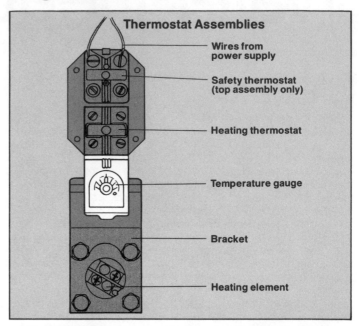

Thermostat Assemblies

- Wires from power supply
- Safety thermostat (top assembly only)
- Heating thermostat
- Temperature gauge
- Bracket
- Heating element

To test either heating element, turn the power off, and disconnect one wire leading to the element. Attach VOM clips to the two external element terminals to test resistance. With the VOM set at RX1, you should read about 10 ohms. A much higher reading or no reading means a defective element. To replace it, see the opposite page.

To test either heating thermostat, turn the power off and disconnect one of the two wires from its terminal on the left side of the thermostat or from the heating element. Make a continuity test between the two left terminals (see Blue Pages: *Electrical testers*). If the water in the tank is cold, there should be continuity at any temperature setting of the thermostat. If the water is hot, the thermostat should click at some point as you turn the temperature-setting shaft higher. At that point the continuity should drop to zero. Test the two terminals on the right side in the same manner. Put the other thermostat through the same procedure. If either thermostat fails either test, replace it.

To test the safety thermostat, turn the power off and remove the wires from one of the two terminals on the left side of the thermostat. Test for continuity between the terminals (see Blue Pages: *Electrical testers*); there should be continuity. Test the two terminals on the right in the same manner. If the thermostat fails either test, replace it with a duplicate.

To test the power reaching the heater, turn the power off and attach VOM clips to the two topmost terminals on the safety thermostat. Set the meter to read at least 250 volts AC. Then turn the power on. **CAUTION** Do not touch any part of the heater or the clips. You should read within 10% of the required voltage indicated on the identification plate of the heater (120 or 240 volts). If you don't, turn the power off, remove the VOM clips, and call the power company.

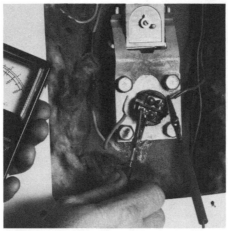

Testing a heating element

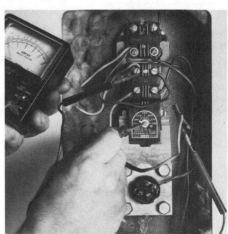

Testing a heating thermostat

Testing the safety thermostat

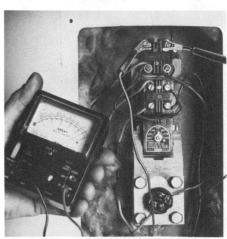

Testing the power reaching the heater

Replacing a heating element

If either heating element fails the tests described opposite, here's how to replace it. First, turn the power off and drain the tank (page 131). Then remove the two wires connecting the element to its thermostat: using a socket wrench, loosen the four bolts holding the element in place. The bolts and the bracket come off (there may also be a gasket). Then pull the bad element out of the tank. Before installing the new element, ream out the hole and clean all scale away. Dry the surfaces of the hole and apply a coat of gasket cement to the mounting surfaces on element and tank. Put the new element (and gasket) and bracket back in place; put the bolts in and screw them in *tight*. Replace the insulation and access panel before turning the power on.

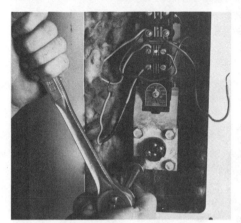

Loosen the bolts with a socket wrench.

Pull the defective element out of the tank.

Coat the mounting surface of the new element with gasket cement before installing it.

Checking the safety valve

If the safety valve starts steaming or dripping, turn the power off at once. Your thermostat may be defective, causing overheating, or the safety valve itself may be defective. Take the temperature of the hot water upstairs by putting a candy or meat thermometer into a pan of running hot water. If the water is near normal—140°F.—the thermostat is OK, and the safety valve is defective. It must be replaced as described here. If you have a well, check the water pressure; high pressure may have blown the safety valve. Call the plumber.

If the hot water temperature is well above your thermostat setting, the thermostat is defective and must be replaced. See page 132 for directions.

NOTE: Never "test" the safety valve by lifting the metal lever to let it blow off. The valve seldom will reseat itself correctly.

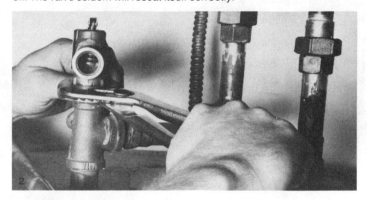

1 **To replace a defective safety valve,** first turn off the power and the cold water supply. Open a hot water faucet upstairs and partially drain the tank to relieve the pressure (see page 131). Then unscrew the overflow pipe (if your valve has one) with a wrench.

2 After the pressure has been relieved, unscrew the safety valve from the pipe on top of the heater with a wrench.

3 Before screwing on the new safety valve, wrap two turns of Teflon thread-seal tape clockwise around the threads of the valve. Install the valve, attach the overflow pipe, and open the cold water inlet valve. When water runs out of the faucet upstairs, close the tap. You can now turn the power back on.

Electric Water Heaters Troubleshooting Chart

WHAT'S WRONG	REASONS WHY	WHAT TO DO
No hot water	No power at heater	Check fuse box/circuit breaker.
		If heater repeatedly blows fuses, call electrician.
	Safety thermostat has cut out	Push reset button (if you have one).
		Test heating thermostats and elements.
	Defective heating thermostats	Test thermostats and replace.
	Defective heating elements	Test elements and replace them.
	Rust, scale, or sediment accumulation in tank or pipes	Drain and flush out tank and pipes.
Not enough hot water	Thermostat set wrong	Reset thermostat to higher temperature.
	Tank too small	Install larger heater.
	Heat lost in pipes	Locate heater near point of use if possible; insulate hot water pipes.
	Defective heating element	Test and replace element.
	Leaking hot water faucets	Repair or replace faucets.
Water is too hot.	Thermostat set wrong	Reset thermostat to lower temperature.
	Not enough insulation around thermostats	Pack insulation tightly around thermostats.
	Defective elements	Test and replace elements.
	Defective thermostats	Test and replace thermostats.
Heater leaks water.	Defective gasket or seal on heating element	Check and replace.
	Defective safety valve	Check and replace valve.
	Tank rusted through	Buy a new heater.
	Leaky plumbing connection	Call a plumber if not covered in this article.
Heater is noisy.	Rust, scale, or sediment accumulation in tank	Drain and flush out tank.
	Scale-encrusted elements	Remove elements, soak in vinegar, scrape off scale.
Hot water is rusty or discolored.	Rust or sediment accumulation in tank	Drain tank.
	Scale-encrusted elements	(See under "Heater is noisy," above.)
	Corroded water pipes	Call a plumber to replace pipes.

Gas Water Heater

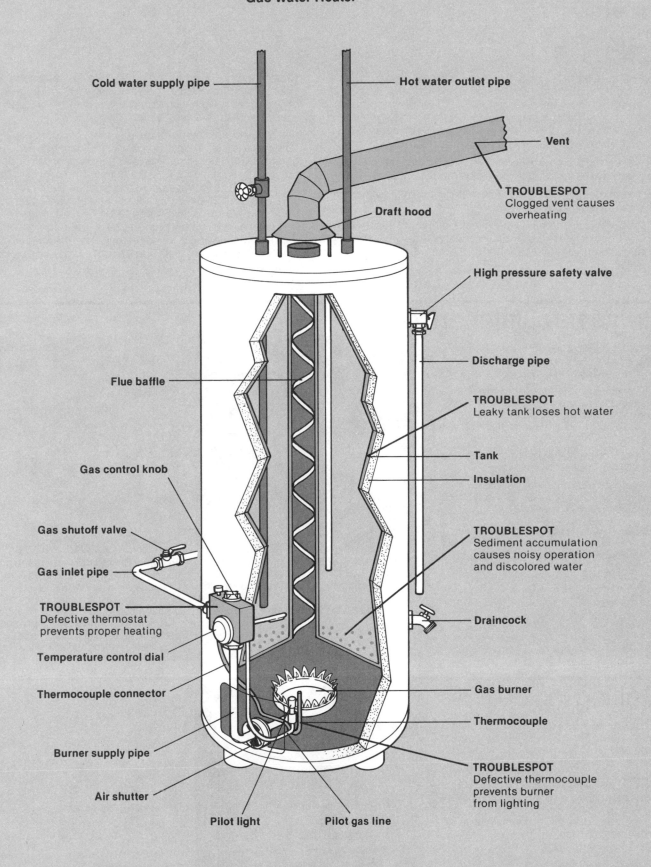

Cold water supply pipe

Hot water outlet pipe

Vent

TROUBLESPOT
Clogged vent causes overheating

Draft hood

High pressure safety valve

Discharge pipe

TROUBLESPOT
Leaky tank loses hot water

Flue baffle

Tank

Insulation

Gas control knob

TROUBLESPOT
Sediment accumulation causes noisy operation and discolored water

Gas shutoff valve

Gas inlet pipe

TROUBLESPOT
Defective thermostat prevents proper heating

Temperature control dial

Draincock

Thermocouple connector

Gas burner

Thermocouple

Burner supply pipe

TROUBLESPOT
Defective thermocouple prevents burner from lighting

Air shutter

Pilot light

Pilot gas line

WATER HEATERS

Gas

Gas water heaters are efficient, long-lasting appliances that require a minimum of attention from the user. Care must be taken, however, to install the heater correctly. You should allow 3 feet of open space all around the heater for proper ventilation and fire safety. The vent pipe must rise at least ¼ inch for every foot it travels horizontally. Observe these precautions:

1. If you find soot around the vent or the top of the tank, call the gas company. Don't try to make any adjustments.

2. If the burner flame burns yellow, call the gas company. Don't attempt any adjustments.

3. Gas heaters are adjusted for either LP or natural gas. If you want to change from one to the other, you must call the gas company to regulate the heater or install another model.

4. If you need to drain the tank to remove sediment, or if you are shutting the house up for the winter, turn the gas control knob off. Then follow the procedure given on page 130 for draining the tank of an electric heater. Don't turn the gas back on or light the pilot light until the tank is full of water.

Any repair or adjustment of the gas lines, gas controls, or the burner is a job for the gas company. You can, however, replace a defective thermocouple. This is a heat-sensing safety device that prevents gas from flowing to the burner if the pilot light has gone out. Instructions for replacing a thermocouple are given on page 137. You can also replace a defective safety valve. See directions in *Electric Water Heaters,* page 133.

Read the introductory paragraphs on page 130 for other pertinent information about water heaters. The *Tips for energy efficiency* for electric units apply equally to gas units (see box, page 130).

Regular maintenance

1. Every six months, inspect the exhaust vent to make sure it's unobstructed. The vent pipe should rise at least ¼ inch per foot.

2. Every six months remove the covers of the burner unit and inspect for dust and dirt. See directions below. Be sure the air shutter openings are unobstructed. Use a small, soft brush to clean them.

3. To adjust the temperature of the hot water, turn the control dial to the desired setting.

4. To relight the pilot light, carefully follow the directions printed on your heater. See also the directions on the next page.

CAUTION If you smell gas, ventilate the room thoroughly before lighting a flame. Never "test" for a leak with a lighted match. Call the gas company.

To check the vent, remove the draft hood while the heater is on. You should feel a strong flow of hot air. If you do not, check the vent pipe and the chimney to see if they are obstructed. If there is still no draft, call the gas company.

To adjust the temperature of the hot water, set the control dial at the desired level. This typical model shows WARM, NORMAL and HOT, instead of specific temperatures. WARM is probably about 120°F., NORMAL about 140°F., HOT about 160°F. Test the temperature with a candy or meat thermometer in a pan of hot running water upstairs, and adjust the dial.

Getting inside

To clean the air shutter openings or check the thermocouple, remove the covers that protect the burner unit. On this model, both the outer and inner covers simply lift out.

CAUTION Be careful not to bend or kink any tubing, especially the soft copper kind. If a tube gets bent, call the gas company to fix it. Don't attempt to adjust the air shutter; that's a job for the gas company, too.

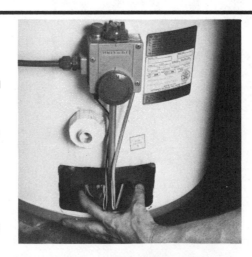

To get inside the bottom of the heater, lift off the protective covers.

Problems inside the heater

You can relight the pilot light or replace a defective thermocouple in a gas heater. Instructions for these two jobs are given here. All other repairs to the gas mechanism of the heater should be left to the gas company. Don't attempt to adjust the air shutters or the burner; an improper adjustment can cause an explosion. If you replace the thermocouple, test the pilot gas line for leaks, using soapy water.

To relight the pilot light, follow the directions for your heater; they normally appear on the control unit. On this model, you press a button while touching a flame to the pilot. Use a twist of lighted paper about 6 to 8 inches long, so you don't have to cram your hand inside.

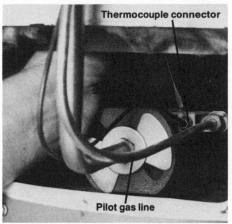

Thermocouple connector

Pilot gas line

1 **If the burner won't start,** but the pilot light can be lit, then the thermocouple may have failed. Turn the gas control knob off. Use a small screwdriver to remove the screw that holds the pilot and thermocouple mounting bracket inside the heater.

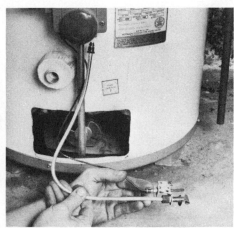

2 Pull the mounting bracket out of the heater. You may have to disconnect the pilot gas line with a wrench. Then pull the thermocouple out of the bracket and disconnect it from the control unit. Take it to your appliance dealer to get an exact duplicate to install.

Gas Water Heaters Troubleshooting Chart

WHAT'S WRONG	REASONS WHY	WHAT TO DO
No hot water	Pilot light out	Relight pilot.
	Pilot won't stay lit.	Make sure gas controls are fully on.
		Check the thermocouple; it must be firmly connected to the gas control unit and positioned near the pilot flame.
	Burner clogged	Call the gas company.
	Defective thermocouple	Replace thermocouple.
	No gas	Call the gas company.
Not enough hot water	Thermostat not properly set	Reset thermostat higher.
	Defective thermostat	Call the gas company.
	Exposed hot water pipes	Insulate hot water pipes.
	Tank too small	Install larger unit.
	Burner clogged	Call gas company.
	Sediment in tank	Drain tank; shut off gas first.
	Leaky hot water faucets	Repair or replace faucets.
Operation is noisy.	Scale and sediment in tank	Drain tank; shut off gas first.
Water is too hot.	Thermostat not properly set	Reset thermostat lower.
	Defective thermostat	Call gas company.
	Blocked vent	Check vent and clear.
Water leaks from heater.	Draincock leaking	Close tightly or replace.
	Safety valve leaking	Check water temperature; too-high temperature may indicate faulty thermostat.
		Replace safety valve if defective.
	Hole in tank	Buy a new water heater.
	Leaky plumbing connection	Call a plumber if not covered in this article.

Basic Appliance Tools

A small selection of the right tools will make a tremendous difference in the speed, ease, and professional results of your appliance repairs and maintenance. The tools shown on these pages are a basic selection that will serve most appliance repair requirements.

Always buy quality tools; a cheap tool is no bargain. A poorly-made tool can let you down when you need it most, and can damage expensive appliances. Look for drop-forged tools rather than cast-iron ones—a drop-forged hammer will outlast a cast-iron one, and will not chip so easily. Look for strong handles and precise machining; a screwdriver with a flimsy handle and an ill-fitting blade may break off or strip screws.

Quality tools deserve quality maintenance. Clean tools thoroughly every time you use them. To prevent metal parts from rusting, wipe them with a cloth impregnated with a few drops of light oil. Protect sharp cutting edges by taking care not to bang them against other tools. Follow the manufacturer's instructions for maintaining power tools.

The insides of most appliances are somewhat delicate, so it is important to use tools of the right size. For example, an oversized screwdriver can slip off a screw as you twist, and damage or scratch the appliance's surface. Also, many appliances have rough or sharp edges inside. If you use too large a wrench to turn a nut and the wrench slips, you can get a nasty cut or scratch.

A volt-ohm meter (VOM) is used to test continuity and measure resistance (from 1 ohm to infinity), voltage (from 1/10 volt to 1,000 volts AC or DC), and current (only in the milliamp range).

A VOM's test leads and jacks are color-coded—the black lead is inserted in the black jack and the red lead in the red jack. When the metal probes or clips at the ends of the leads touch the items being tested, the meter indicates continuity or other circuit measurements. Many VOMs have insulated clips that are safer to use when making power-on tests.

A jumper lead is used to complete a circuit between two points that are normally not connected (such as the two prongs on an ordinary plug) when a test for continuity is being conducted.

A voltage tester is an insulated device consisting of a neon lamp and two probes. It indicates the presence or absence of voltage but does not measure the amount. When the probes touch the item being tested, the neon lamp lights if there is voltage; no voltage, no light.

A continuity tester merely indicates the presence or absence of continuity—whether or not a circuit is open. There are many types of continuity tester. The tester shown here is an electrician's flashlight with two clips. The jack plugs into the back of the flashlight and the flashlight switch is set at ON. The light goes on only if the tested circuit has continuity (or if the two probes touch each other). Without the tester leads, the flashlight works like an ordinary flashlight. Note the alligator clips at the ends of the probes.

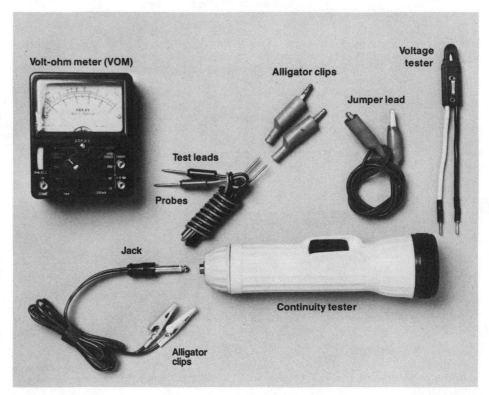

Volt-ohm meter (VOM)

Alligator clips

Voltage tester

Jumper lead

Test leads

Probes

Jack

Alligator clips

Continuity tester

Round-nose pliers are used to make loops in wires to be wrapped around screw terminals.

Flat-nose pliers are handy for removing small nuts or retrieving parts from shallow and easy-to-reach locations.

Diagonal cutters are used to cut wires and to cut off damaged or excess wire after a splice or a new connection is made.

Needle-nose, or long-nose, pliers are useful for getting into deeply recessed or other hard-to-reach places.

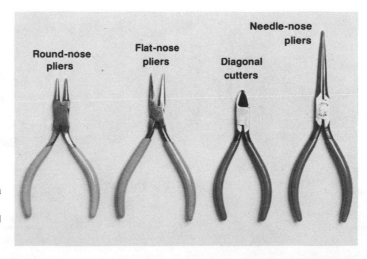

Round-nose pliers

Flat-nose pliers

Diagonal cutters

Needle-nose pliers

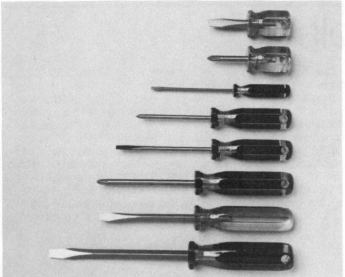

Screwdrivers are probably the most useful tools for appliance work. Shown here at the top are a flat-blade and a Phillips screwdriver, both with stubby shanks. They are called stubbies, and are used when space is too cramped for a driver with a longer shank. The next four screwdrivers (two flat-blade and two Phillips) have medium-length shanks and blades of increasing size; these are for larger screws. The bottom two screwdrivers have larger blades for very large screws (the bottom one has a thicker shank, for greater strength). The shank of a high-quality screwdriver is embedded deep in the handle, so that handle and shank cannot easily become loosened. Rubber-cushioned handles help prevent calluses and painful blisters.

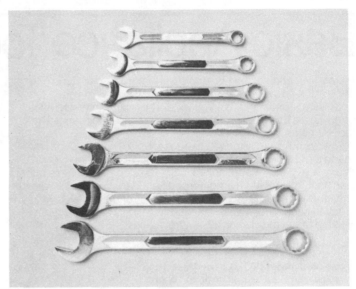

Open-end wrenches, available in various sizes, are used to tighten or remove nuts and bolts. High-quality open-end wrenches are made of chrome vanadium steel machined to fine tolerances so that their openings provide a good fit around a nut. The openings on the wrenches are offset—set at an angle to the handle—to provide flexibility in tight spaces.

The box wrench at the opposite end of the tool can loosen nuts that are particularly tight. It surrounds the nut, providing turning force on all sides. Finely machined wrenches have a better fit, lessening chances that the wrench may slip—which could damage the appliance or injure your hand.

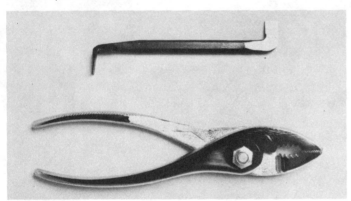

An offset screwdriver (top) is used to reach such inaccessible screws as those under the overhanging part of an appliance.

Ordinary pliers (bottom) have jaws that adjust to two positions. The jaws have a flat surface and a curved, serrated surface, for gripping both flat and curved objects.

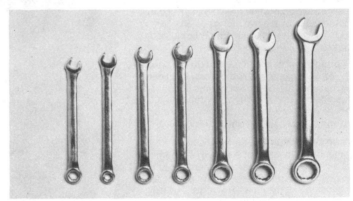

Ignition wrenches are similar to open-end wrenches but smaller and lighter in construction; they are used on small nuts and bolts and in tight areas, where hexagonal nuts are often located. The box end can be used for very tight nuts or bolts.

Jeweler's screwdriver sets (right), for use on tiny screws, contain both Phillips and flat-blade screwdrivers, usually in five different sizes. The detachable shafts are interchangeable, fitting into one handle.

Allen wrenches (far right) are used on screws with recessed hexagonal heads. In effect, they are L-shaped keys, with hexagonal shafts, that fit into a recessed screw and also provide leverage. A basic set comprises eight sizes.

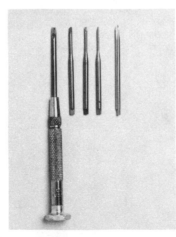

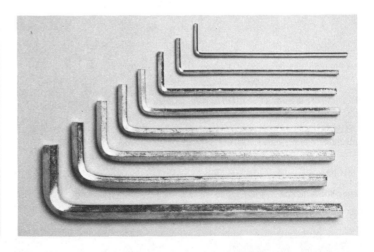

A socket wrench fits down over a nut or bolt to tighten, loosen or adjust it, exerting force on all sides, much like a box wrench (see page 140). The set of sockets (middle) fits nuts and bolts of different sizes, but each one has a ¼-inch drive socket in its bottom end. To work, sockets are attached to a nut driver with a ¼-inch drive (bottom), or to a ratchet handle with a ¼-inch drive (top). The ratchet can be set to turn the nut or bolt in one direction, and slip on the return swing. Working with a ratchet handle is often the fastest and easiest way to use socket wrenches. Other sockets and tools are shown at the top of the opposite page.

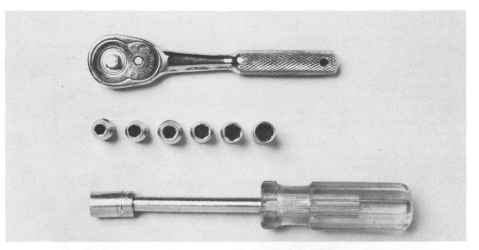

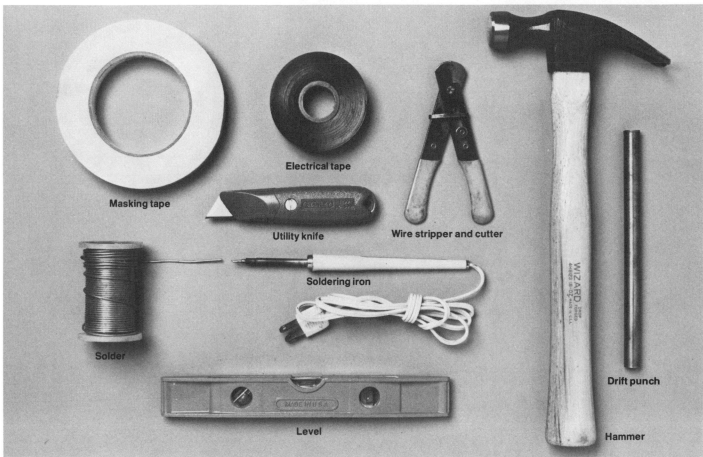

Masking tape

Electrical tape

Utility knife

Wire stripper and cutter

Solder

Soldering iron

Drift punch

Level

Hammer

Anyone repairing appliances at home should have on hand, in addition to the tools discussed, a number of ordinary basic tools and materials.

Masking tape is best for holding things in place and for labeling wire leads.

Electrical tape is used for taping wires together and insulating them, and for repairing cords.

Wire strippers and cutters are invaluable; they can be used for many sizes and types of wire, such as stranded or braided. An adjustable screw sets the blade opening so that a large number of identical wires can be cut or stripped rapidly. Most strippers have a spring that pops the cutter's handles open after each cut.

Hammers belong in every household. A high-quality claw hammer (shown here) with a solid handle (hickory, fiberglass, or tubular steel) and a drop-forged head is the best choice.

A drift punch is a brass rod used to separate or remove jammed steel components, such as the flywheel from the motor shaft of a garbage disposer. Since brass is softer than steel, the rod gives when it is hammered against the steel part and the latter is not damaged. (Often, a block of wood can be used for this purpose instead.)

A utility knife with a sharp blade has a number of uses in do-it-yourself repair. A knife with a retractable blade is safe and also keeps its edge when stored with other tools.

A soldering iron and solder are necessary for many electrical repairs. Shown here is a pencil-type soldering iron with an electrically heated tip, and a roll of electrical solder. Use only electrical rosin-core solder—not plumber's acid-core solder, which is corrosive on electrical connections.

A level comes in handy when, for example, you are installing an air conditioner. It is important that the unit tilt properly, so the water runs out the window rather than into the room. The level registers the tilt of the appliance instantly.

A set of sockets with a ⅜-inch drive (bottom right) is available to fit nuts and bolts from ¼-inch to 1 inch in diameter. The size increases in increments of 1/16 inch. Like the smaller sockets on the opposite page, these can be used with a nut driver (opposite, third from the top) or a ratchet handle, shown opposite without a socket, and middle, right with a socket attached. To reach recessed nuts or bolts, sockets can also be use with an extension (top) that is attached at right angles to the ratchet handle. The extension fits over the driver on the handle, while the socket fits over the small end of the extension. Socket sets can also be driven by breaker bars, T-bars, torque wrenches and impact wrenches.

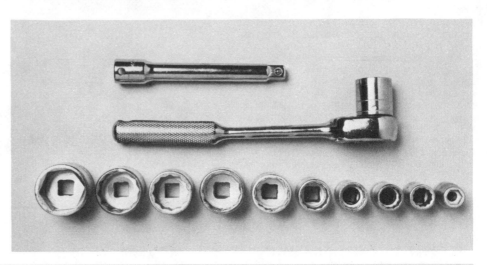

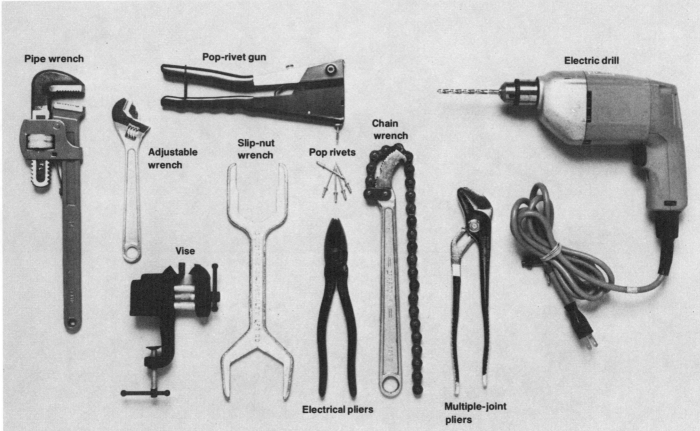

Pipe wrench

Pop-rivet gun

Electric drill

Adjustable wrench

Slip-nut wrench

Pop rivets

Chain wrench

Vise

Electrical pliers

Multiple-joint pliers

A pipe wrench is for fairly large jobs where considerable force must be applied to loosen and remove a fastener. (The wrench's toothed jaws can damage bright or soft metal.)

An adjustable wrench is an open-end wrench with smooth jaws. It is used for small jobs and is extremely useful and adaptable for appliance repair.

The pop-rivet gun and pop rivets are used where rivets must be replaced. Pop-riveting is much simpler than solid riveting and can be done when only one side of the work is accessible.

An electric drill is versatile. Bits are specialized for use on many materials such as wood, masonry, and metal, and they are available in a wide range of sizes. A power drill is necessary for drilling out rivets that hold defective appliance components. Power drills also have accessories for polishing, sanding, and grinding.

Multiple-joint pliers are for larger nuts and bolts. The number of span adjustments varies from tool to tool; five adjustments should be enough for

home repairs. Handles also vary in length. The longer the handle, the better the leverage; a 10-inch handle is usually adequate for home use.

The chain wrench and its companion, the strap wrench (not shown), are used when jobs are too large for an adjustable wrench. The chain (for hard surfaces) or the strap (for soft surfaces) is tightened around the piece to be removed, and the handle provides the leverage to turn the piece.

Electrical pliers have insulated handles that protect you from shock. They have a built-in diagonal cutter for wire cutting, and the jaws in front are flat for gripping flat surfaces. They are ideal for twisting wires together.

A slip-nut wrench is used to remove large nuts, like those on garbage disposers and plumbing traps.

The vise is useful for holding an appliance or component steady when you need both hands free—for example, when removing the spring-loaded leads from a switch or the brushes from an electric motor. A good vise should have jaws about 4 inches wide that open to at least 4 to 6 inches. The one shown here clamps onto any table or workbench.

Index